ACCT 203

STUDY GUIDE TO ACCOMPANY
SURVEY OF **ACCOUNTING**

SCHOOL OF MANAGEMENT
George Mason University

Taken from:

Study Guide: Chapters 1-13 to accompany *Accounting*, Sixth Edition
by Ann DeCapite

Study Guide: Chapters 12-26 to accompany *Accounting*, Sixth Edition
by Ann DeCapite

PEARSON
Custom
Publishing

PEARSON
Prentice
Hall

Taken from:

Study Guide: Chapters 1-13 to accompany *Accounting,* Sixth Edition
by Ann DeCapite
Copyright © 2005 by Pearson Education, Inc.
Punlished by Prentice-Hall, Inc.
Upper Saddle River, New Jersey 07458

Study Guide: Chapters 12-26 to accompany *Accounting,* Sixth Edition
by Ann DeCapite
Copyright © 2005 by Pearson Education, Inc.
Punlished by Prentice-Hall, Inc.

This special edition published in cooperation with Pearson Custom Publishing.

All trademarks, service marks, registered trademarks, and registered service marks are the property of their respective owners and are used herein for identification purposes only.

The information, illustrations, and/or software contained in this book, and regarding the above-mentioned programs, are provided "As Is," without warranty of any kind, express or implied, including without limitation any warranty concerning the accuracy, adequacy, or completeness of such information. Neither the publisher, the authors, nor the copyright holders shall be responsible for any claims attributable to errors, omissions, or other inaccuracies contained in this book. Nor shall they be liable for direct, indirect, special, incidental, or consequential damages arising out of the use of such information or material.

Printed in the United States of America

10 9 8 7 6 5 4 3 2 1

ISBN 0-536-98503-0

2005160390

CS

Please visit our web site at *www.pearsoncustom.com*

PEARSON CUSTOM PUBLISHING
75 Arlington Street, Suite 300, Boston, MA 02116
A Pearson Education Company

Contents

Chapter 1—Accounting and the Business Environment

CHAPTER OVERVIEW

Chapter One introduces you to accounting. Some of the topics covered in this chapter are the types of business organization, the basic accounting equation, analyzing business transactions, and preparing financial statements. Like many disciplines, accounting has its own vocabulary. An understanding of accounting terminology and the other topics covered in this chapter will give you a good foundation towards mastering the topics in upcoming chapters. The learning objectives for this chapter are to

1. Use an accounting vocabulary
2. Apply accounting concepts and principles
3. Use the accounting equation.
4. Analyze business transactions.
5. Prepare the financial statements.
6. Evaluate business performance.

CHAPTER REVIEW

Objective 1 - Use accounting vocabulary.

Accounting is the information system that measures business activities, processes that information into reports, and communicates the results to decision makers.

The users of accounting information are:

- **Individuals** use accounting information to make decisions about whether to purchase or rent (lease) a home or vehicle and to manage their bank accounts.
- **Business managers** use accounting information to set goals for their businesses and to evaluate progress toward achieving those goals.
- **Investors** use accounting information to evaluate the prospect of future returns on their investments.
- **Creditors** use accounting information to evaluate a borrower's ability to make the scheduled payments to repay the loan.
- **Government regulatory agencies, taxing authorities, and nonprofit organizations** also use accounting information.

The users of accounting information are further categorized into external users and internal users. This distinction relates to the two fields of accounting:

1.) **Financial accounting** focuses on providing financial information for individuals *outside* (external to) the business or organization.
2.) **Managerial accounting** focuses on providing financial and other business information for individuals *within* (internal to) a business or organization.

> Helpful hint: Review Exhibit 1-2 to review the relationship between financial and managerial accounting.

The Financial Accounting Standards Board (FASB), the Securities and Exchange Commission (SEC), the American Institute of Certified Public Accountants (AICPA) and the Institute of Management Accountants (IMA) are four groups that influence the practice of accounting in the United States. **Generally Accepted Accounting Principles** (GAAP) are the rules governing accounting. In addition, accountants are expected to maintain high ethical standards. Similarly, many corporations also have standards of ethical conduct to which they expect their employees to adhere.

> Helpful hint: Review Exhibit 1-3 in your text to review the key accounting organizations.

The three forms of business organization are:

1. **Proprietorship** - a business owned by one person who has *unlimited* liability for the debts of the business
2. **Partnership** - a business owned by two or more individuals who all share *unlimited* liability for the debts of the business
3. **Corporation** - a business owned by many owners called stockholders (or shareholders) whose liability for business debts is *limited* to the amount the stockholders invested in the corporation.

In the United States, proprietorships are the largest form of business numerically, whereas corporations are the dominant form in terms of total assets, income, and number of employees.

> Helpful hint: Review Exhibit 1-4 in your textbook for the comparison of the three forms of business organization.

Objective 2 - Apply accounting concepts and principles.

As previously mentioned, the rules governing accounting practice are called Generally Accepted Accounting Principles (GAAP). GAAP includes five important concepts and principles:

1.) **The entity concept:** The financial records of a business entity should be separate from the personal financial records of the owner. For example, if a business owner borrows money to remodel her home, the loan is a personal debt, not a debt of the business.

2.) **The reliability (or objectivity) principle:** Accountants should attempt to provide reliable, accurate records and financial statements. All data that the accountant uses should be verifiable by an independent observer. Ideally, accounting records should be determined by objective evidence. For example, the most objective and reliable measure of the value of supplies is the price paid for the supplies. The objective evidence documenting the price is the invoice from the supplier.

3.) **The cost principle:** Assets and services should be recorded at their actual (historical) cost. For example, if a business pays $25,000 for land, then $25,000 is the price actually paid for the land or the "cost" and the amount recorded in the accounting records, even if an independent appraiser estimates that the land is worth $34,000.

4.) The going-concern concept: Assumes that the entity is expected to remain in operation for the foreseeable future. This assumption provides accountants with the guidelines on how to record the value of the entity's assets in the accounting records. If an entity is assumed to be a going concern, then the relevant measure of the entity's assets is the historical cost, as established by the cost principle. However, if the entity were going out of business, meaning it is no longer expected to be a going concern, then, the relevant measure of its assets would be market value.

5.) The stable-monetary-unit concept: Assumes that the purchasing power of the dollar is relatively stable. Therefore, the effects of inflation are ignored in accounting, which allows accountants to add and subtract dollar amounts as though each dollar had the same purchasing power as any other dollar at any other time.

Objective 3 - Use the accounting equation.

The **accounting equation** is expressed as:

Economic resources = Creditor's claims to economic resources + Owner's claims to economic resources

Total claims to economic resources

Or,

ASSETS = LIABILITIES + OWNER'S EQUITY

Assets are a firm's resources that are expected to provide future benefits. You can also think of assets as the things that the business owns. **Liabilities** are claims by outsiders (creditors) to those resources. If a business purchases a piece of land and borrows money from the bank for the purchase, then the bank, the creditor, has claim to the land until the loan is repaid. The land would be an asset of the business because it is a resource of the business, and the amount of money borrowed to purchase the land would be a liability until the loan is repaid. Claims by insiders (owners) are called **owner's equity** or capital. If a creditor does not have claim to the assets of the business, then the owner does. The accounting equation must always reflect what the business has, assets, and who has claim to those assets, either creditors or the owner(s).

Some of the most common examples of assets are cash, accounts receivable, notes receivable, supplies, land, and buildings.

- A business acquires cash from capital investments made by the owner, from borrowing money, and when the business makes sales to customers and collects from those customers either at the time the sale occurs or sometime in the future.
- Accounts receivable and notes receivable both arise when a business makes sales to customers on credit, meaning the cash payment from the customer is expected sometime in the future. Accounts receivable result from general trade credit where the customer promises a future payment of all amounts owed to the business.
- Notes receivable are similar to accounts receivable in that they both represent a promise of future payment for sales; however, they are different in that notes receivable are evidenced by a written promissory note whereas accounts receivable are not.
- Supplies represent things that will be used up in the normal course of doing business, such as office supplies, restaurant supplies, and medical supplies to name a few.
- Land represents unimproved real property.
- Buildings are structures that may be located on the land.

3

Liabilities represent claims on assets by outsiders (creditors) or things that the business owes to others. A business can owe cash, inventory or services to other businesses or its customers. The most common examples of liabilities are accounts payable and notes payable, which arise when the business makes purchases on credit.

- An account payable results from general trade credit where the business promises to pay all amounts owed to its supplier.
- Notes payable are similar to accounts payable in that they both represent a promise of future payment for purchases; however, they are different in that notes payable are evidenced by a written promissory note whereas accounts payable are not.
- Other liabilities will be introduced and explained in future chapters.

Owner's equity represents claims on assets by insiders (owners). Owner's equity is also referred to as the net assets (or residual equity) of the business and reflects, in total, what is left of the assets after subtracting the liabilities. The accounting equation can be rewritten to reflect this relationship:

$$ASSETS - LIABILITIES = OWNER'S\ EQUITY$$

There are only four things that will affect a change in owner's equity:

- Owner's investments of assets into the business (increase owner's equity)
- Owner's withdrawal of assets from the business (decrease owner's equity)
- Revenues generated by delivering goods or providing services to customers (increase owner's equity). Revenues result when the business does what it is in the business of doing. For, example an attorney will generate service revenue from providing legal services because that is what an attorney is in the business of doing. Gay Gillen eTravel will generate service revenue when the business provides travel services to its customers because that is that is what a travel agent is in the business of doing. Amazon.com will generate sales revenue when it sells products to its customers because that is what Amazon.com is in the business of doing. As these examples indicate, the nature of revenue may differ according to each different type of business; however, revenue is always generated when a business does what it is in business to do.
- Expenses result from using assets or increasing liabilities to deliver goods or provide services to customers (decrease owner's equity). Expenses are those costs incurred to support the generation of revenues. Examples of expenses include rent, utilities, and employees' salaries.

> Helpful hint: Review Exhibit 1-6 in the textbook to review the transactions that increase or decrease owner's equity.

The owner's investment or withdrawal of assets represents transactions that occur between the business and insiders or the owners of the business. The generation of revenues and the incurrence of expenses represent transactions that occur between the business and outsiders or the business's customers, suppliers, or creditors. Profitability results from the transactions that occur between the business and those entities outside of the business. If the business is profitable, then owner's equity increases when the revenues are greater than the expenses of the business.

Objective 4 - Analyze business transactions.

Every transaction will have, at minimum, a dual effect on the accounting equation, meaning that each transaction has at least two parts. Recording the two (or more) components of each transaction maintains the equality of the accounting equation or we might say that the accounting equation always remains "in balance". Study carefully the eleven business transactions analyzed in the text, and reinforce your understanding by following the demonstration problem and explanations in this chapter of the Study Guide. Pay particular attention to how each transaction affects the accounting equation. Take notice of the duality of each of the transactions. You should also pay attention to how each time a transaction is determined to have an effect on owner's equity; the type of owner's equity transaction is noted. Next, study how the summary of the transactions is reflected on the Balance Sheet. The balance sheet reports the assets, liabilities, and owner's equity of the business at any given moment in time. You should observe that the balance sheet is very similar to the accounting equation, except that only the ending balances in each of the accounts are shown on the balance sheet. You must have a thorough knowledge of how transactions affect the accounting equation and how they are reflected on the balance sheet in order to proceed further in this course.

Objective 5 - Prepare the financial statements.

Accountants summarize the results of business activity in four primary financial statements:

1.) The **income statement** presents a summary of the firm's revenues and expenses for some period of time, such as a month, quarter or year, and reports **net income** if total revenues exceed total expenses. A **net loss** occurs if total expenses are greater than total revenues. The information used to prepare the income statement comes from the Owner's Equity column of the accounting equation. Notice that only those transactions that represent revenues and expenses should appear on the income statement. Remember that revenue and expense transactions result from transactions that occur between the business and its customers and vendors. Owner's investments and withdrawals are do not appear on the income statement because they represent transactions that occur between the business and the owner(s).

2.) The **statement of owner's equity** presents a summary of changes in owner's equity during the same period of time as the income statement. As we have mentioned before, owner's equity increases with owner's investments and net income, and decreases with owner's withdrawals and net losses. The net income or net loss information will carry forward from the income statement and the owner's investment and withdrawal information will come from the Owner's Equity column of the accounting equation.

3.) The **balance sheet** reports all assets, liabilities, and owner's equity, as of a specific date. The date shown on the balance sheet will be the same date as the last day of the period for which activities are summarized in the income statement and the statement of owner's equity. The information that appears on the balance sheet will come from the ending account balances for each asset and liability account off of the accounting equation, and the ending balance in owner's equity from the statement of owner's equity.

4.) The **statement of cash flows** shows the cash inflows and outflows, organized into three areas—operating activities, investing activities, and financing activities. The statement of cash flows is prepared from the "Cash" column of the accounting equation with each item of cash classified according to whether it resulted from an operating, investing or financing activity. This financial statement is covered in detail in Chapter 17.

> Helpful hint: See how the data provided in Exhibit 1-7 correlates with the financial statements in Exhibit 1-8.

Objective 6 - Evaluate business performance.

All financial statements begin with three line headings, as follows:

Name of Business
Name of Financial Statement
Date or time period covered

The income statement is prepared first, listing the revenues and expenses for the period. The result is either net income (when revenues are greater than expenses) or net loss (when revenues are less than expenses). This result is carried forward to the next statement, the statement of owner's equity.

The statement of owner's equity is prepared after the income statement. It details the amounts and sources of changes in capital during the period, as follows:

Beginning Capital Balance
+ Owner's Investment
+ Net Income (or – Net Loss)
- Owner's Withdrawals
_____
Ending Capital Balance

Ending capital is carried forward to the next financial statement, the balance sheet.

The balance sheet is a formal listing of the accounting equation as of the last day in the financial period. The individual assets are added together to equal total assets. The liabilities are totaled and added to ending capital.

The statement of cash flows reports cash flows (receipts and payments) for the same period covered by the other financial statements, and groups these into three types of business activities—operating, investing, and financing. The amount of net cash increase (or decrease) will, when added to the beginning cash balance, agree with the ending cash balance reported on the balance sheet.

Study Tip: The statement order is important to remember.
1. Income Statement
2. Statement of Owner's Equity
3. Balance Sheet
4. Statement of Cash Flows
Helpful hint: Review Exhibit 1-8 in the text.

TEST YOURSELF

All the self-testing materials in this chapter focus on information and procedures that your instructor is likely to test in quizzes and examinations.

I. Matching   *Match each numbered term with its lettered definition.*

C	1.	AICPA		N	9.	IMA
G	2.	Assets		K	10.	Partnership
E	3.	Corporation		B	11.	Proprietorship
M	4.	Expenses		J	12.	Revenues
F	5.	FASB		L	13.	SEC
H	6.	GAAP		O	14.	Statement of Cash Flows
A	7.	Income Statement		D	15.	Statement of Owner's Equity
I	8.	Liabilities		P	16.	Balance Sheet

A. A summary of revenues and expenses for a period.
B. A business owned by one person.
C. A professional organization of Certified Public Accountants.
D. A financial statement summarizing changes in capital.
E. A legal entity, owned by stockholders, which conducts its business in its own name.
F. The body that formulates GAAP.
G. Resources expected to provide future benefit.
H. The "rules" of accounting.
I. Claims on assets by outsiders.
J. Inflows of assets from the sale of a product or service.
K. A business co-owned by two or more individuals.
L. A federal agency with the legal power to set and enforce accounting and auditing standards.
M. Costs incurred to generate revenue.
N. A professional organization of management accountants.
O. Details the net change in cash from one period to the next.
P. Lists an entity's assets, liabilities, and owner's equity as of a specific date.

II. Multiple Choice *Circle the best answer.*

1. An example of a liability is:

   A. Fees earned
   B. Supplies

   C. Note payable
   D. Investments by the owner

2. When cash is paid on an account payable:

   A. total assets increase.
   B. total assets decrease.

   C. total assets are unchanged.
   D. Cannot be determined

3. A receivable is recorded when a business makes:

   A. sales on account.
   B. purchases on account.

   C. sales for cash.
   D. purchases for cash.

4. When cash is received on an accounts receivable:

   A. total assets increase.
   B. total assets decrease.

   C. total assets are unchanged.
   D. Cannot be determined

5. An investment of equipment by the owner will result in:

   A. an increase in both assets and liabilities
   B. an increase in both liabilities and owner's equity

   C. an increase in both assets and owner's equity
   D. no change in assets or owner's equity

6. An investment of cash by the owner will result in:

   A. an increase in both assets and liabilities.
   B. an increase in both liabilities and owner's equity.

   C. an increase in both assets and owner's equity.
   D. no change in assets or owner's equity.

7. If the date on a financial statement is June 30, 20X5, then the financial statement must be:

   A. the income statement.
   B. the statement of owner's equity.

   C. the balance sheet.
   D. the statement of cash flows.

8. On March 17, 20X5, ShopJLo.com sold 700 swimsuits on account for $78 each. How would this transaction affect the accounting equation?

   A. An increase in both assets and liabilities, $54,600
   B. An increase in both assets and owner's equity, $54,600

   C. An increase in both assets and owner's equity, $70,000
   D. No change in assets or owner's equity

9. On April 10, 20X5, ShopJLo.com collected $30,000 on account from the previous sale on March 17. What is the effect on the accounting equation?

A. An increase in cash and a decrease in accounts receivable, $30,000

B. A decrease in cash and an increase in JLo, Capital, $30,000

C. An increase in both cash and JLo, Capital, $30,000

D. No change in assets or owner's equity

10. If the financial statement is dated For the Month Ended June 30, 20X5, then the financial statement must be:

A. the income statement.

B. the statement of owner's equity.

C. the statement of cash flows.

D. All of the above

11. Net income equals:

A. Assets - Liabilities

B. Liabilities + Owner's equity

C. Revenues + Expenses

D. Revenues – Expenses

12. If total assets equal three times the liabilities, and owner's equity is $90,000, what are total assets?

$$3x = x + 90$$
$$2x = 90$$
$$x = 45$$

A. $45,000

B. $90,000

C. $135,000

D. $80,000

13. On January 1, 20X5, David Designs had assets of $265,000 and owner's equity of $130,000. During the year, assets decreased by $75,000 and owner's equity increased by $24,000. What were the liabilities on December 31, 20X5?

A. $36,000

B. $135,000

C. $99,000

D. $154,000

14. If the beginning balance in owner's equity was $300, the ending balance is $544, net income for the month was $325, and there were no investments by the owner, how much did the owner withdraw during the month?

A. $72

B. $119

C. $369

D. $81

15. For the month ended June 30, 20X5, if revenues were $57, 500, and the expenses for the period were $67,250, owner's investments were $10,000 and owner's withdrawals were $27,500, was the business profitable for the month of June?

A. Yes, it generated $9,750 in net income

B. No, it generated a $9,750 net loss

C. Yes, it generated $19,750 in net income

D. No, it generated a $27,250 net loss

9

III. Completion *Complete each of the following statements.*

1. The four primary financial statements are: 1) _Income statement_
   2) _Balance sheet_ , 3) _Owners Eq_
   and 4) _Cash flows_ .

2. Keeping accounting records for a business separate from the owner's personal accounting records follows the _GAAP_ concept.

3. Revenues are _money gained by services_ .

4. _Expenses_ are the costs incurred in operating a business.

5. Outsider claims against assets are called _liabilities_ and insider claims are called _accounts_ .

6. What is the accounting equation?
   Assets = L + Eq .

7. When a firm purchases assets, they are recorded at _____ .

8. _____ is the clerical recording of the data used in an accounting system.

9. What is the three-line heading with which all financial statements begin?

   _____
   _____
   _____

10. Assuming the purchasing power of the dollar remains relatively stable over time underlies the _____ concept.

IV. Daily Exercises

1. For each of the following questions, indicate the financial statement where the answer can be found:

Question	Financial Statement
a. Where did all the money go?	_____
b. How much is the business worth?	_____
c. How much does the business owe?	_____
d. Is the business profitable?	_____
e. Is my investment in the business more or less than last period?	_____

2. At the beginning of the year, a business purchased a building for $100,000, paying $35,000 cash and signing a promissory note for $65,000. By the end of the first year, the amount due on the note had been reduced to $60,000, and real estate values had increased by 20% in the area. At what amount should the building be listed on the balance sheet? Which decision guideline supports your answer?

3. At the end of its first month of operations, a business had total revenues of $7,300, cash receipts from customers of $6,500, total expenses of $5,500, and an owner's withdrawal of $1,800. Was the business profitable during its first month of operations?

4. Refer to question #3 above. Assuming the owner made no additional investments during the month, did the value of the business increase or decrease during the period? Explain your answer.

V. Exercises

1. Ashley Granger operates a small tax preparation business. During the first month of operations the following events occurred:

   A. Ashley invested $20,000 to start the business.
   B. She paid rent of $675.
   C. She purchased $5,000 of computer equipment on account.
   D. She purchased $475 of supplies for cash.
   E. She performed tax services on account, $2,750.
   F. She paid $1,000 on the computer equipment purchased in C.
   G. She received $425 from a customer on account.
   H. She sold supplies (which cost $40) to a friend for $40.

   Prepare an analysis of transactions showing the effects of each event on the accounting equation. (Helpful hint: You may want to refer to Exhibit 1-7 in your text.)

| | | | ASSETS | | | = | LIABILITIES | + | OWNER'S EQUITY |
	Cash +	Accounts Receivable +	Supplies +	Computer Equipment	=	Accounts Payable	+	Granger, Capital
A.								
B.								
C.								
D.								
E.								
F.								
G.								
H.								

2. Presented below are the balances in the assets, liabilities, revenues, and expenses for Clarence's Clunker Repair and Body Shop on June 30, 20X7.

Accounts Payable	$ 250
Accounts Receivable	200
Cash	120
Clarence, Capital	?
Equipment	160
Service Revenues	220
Supplies	70

Prepare a balance sheet for Clarence's Clunker Repair and Body Shop for June 30, 20X7.

Clarence's Clunker Repair and Body Shop
Balance Sheet
June 30, 20X7

Assets:		Liabilities:	
Cash		Accounts Payable	
Accounts Receivable	_____	Total Liabilities	_____
Supplies	_____	Owner's Equity:	_____
Equipment	_____	Clarence, Capital	
	_____	Total Liabilities	_____
Total Assets		and Owner's Equity	
	_____		_____

3. The following are the balances in the accounts of Paul's Delivery Service on August 31, 20X6.

Accounts Receivable	$ 220
Accounts Payable	260
Equipment	2,980
Notes Receivable	130
Salaries Payable	240
Salaries Expense	500
Service Revenue	3,210
Supplies	180
Supplies Expense	280
Telephone Expense	270
Paul, Capital	1,160
Truck Rental Expense	500

Prepare an income statement for Paul's Delivery Service for the month of August, 20X6.

Paul's Delivery Service
Income Statement
For the Month Ended August 31, 20X6

Service revenue		$_____
Expenses:		
Salaries	$_____	
Truck Rental	_____	
Supplies	_____	
Telephone	_____	_____
Net income		$_____

VI. Beyond the Numbers

Can a profitable business (one where revenues consistently exceed expenses) become insolvent (unable to pay their bills)? Conversely, can an unprofitable business remain solvent?

_____

_____

_____

_____

VII. Demonstration Problems
Demonstration Problem #1

Nick Russell, CMA (Certified Management Accountant) opened a consulting practice in Midtown, USA. Solely, Russell owns the business, which is named Russell Consulting. During the month of May, 20X8 (the first month of operation), the following transactions occurred:

5/1   Russell invested $25,000 of personal funds to start the business and deposited the funds in a checking account in the name of the business.

5/1   An office was located and rent of $1,250 was paid for the first month.

5/3   Office equipment was purchased for cash at a cost of $2,100.

5/5   A computer and a laser printer to be used in the business were purchased on account for $3,200.

5/8   Office supplies costing $200 were purchased on account.

5/10   Services of $1,500 were provided on account to a client.

5/15   Russell provided consulting services, $2,300 during the first half of the month. The fees for these services were collected from clients at the time the service was provided. Russell made one deposit in the business checking account.

5/16   Cash of $1,300 was collected for the services rendered on 5/10.

5/18   Paid for the office supplies purchased on 5/8.

5/21   Russell withdrew $3,000 from the business for personal use.

5/31   Consulting services, $4,100, were performed during the second half of the month. The fees for these services were collected from clients at the time the service was performed. Russell made one deposit in the business checking account.

Required:

1. Prepare an analysis of transactions of Russell's Consulting. Use Exhibit 1-7 and the Summary Problem in Chapter 1 of the text as a guide and the format below for your answers.

2. Prepare the income statement, the statement of owner's equity, and balance sheet of the business after recording the May transactions. Include proper headings. Use Exhibit 1-8 as a guide for completing the financial statements.

Requirement 1 (Analysis of transactions)

	ASSETS			=	LIABILITIES	+	OWNER'S EQUITY
Cash +	Accounts Receivable +	Supplies +	Equipment	=	Accounts Payable	+	Capital

Requirement 2 (Income Statement, Statement of Owner's Equity, and Balance Sheet)

Income Statement

Statement of Owner's Equity

Balance Sheet

Demonstration Problem #2

Mildred Mann Amis is an artist living in the Outer Banks of North Carolina. Her business is called Mann Made Designs. From the following information, prepare an Income Statement, Statement of Owner's Equity, and Balance Sheet for Mann Made Designs for the month of May, 20X9.

Accounts Payable	$	700
Accounts Receivable		1,800
Advertising Expense		500
Building		55,000
Cash		8,200
Commissions Earned		12,000
Equipment		6,600
Interest Expense		200
Interest Receivable		100
Mildred Amis, Capital 5/1/20X9		59,325
Mildred Amis, Withdrawals		2,000
Notes Payable		14,000
Notes Receivable		1,000
Salaries Expense		1,750
Salaries Payable		250
Supplies		2,325
Supplies Expense		2,900
Utilities Expense		100
Vehicle		3,800

Income Statement

Statement of Owner's Equity

Balance Sheet

SOLUTIONS

I. Matching

1. C	5. F	9. N	13. L
2. G	6. H	10. K	14. O
3. E	7. A	11. B	15. D
4. M	8. I	12. J	16. P

II. Multiple Choice

1.   C   Of the choices given, only "Notes Payable" meets the definition of a liability. Fees Earned is revenue, supplies are assets, and investments by the owner are increases in equity.

2.   B   When cash is paid an account payable: cash is decreased and accounts payable is decreased. This results in a decrease in total assets and a decrease in total liabilities

3.   A   Only sales on account cause a receivable to be recorded. Purchases on account cause a payable to be recorded, sales for cash and purchases for cash do not affect receivables.

4.   C   When cash is received on an account receivable, two assets are affected: cash is increased and accounts receivable is decreased. Since the increase in cash is equal to the decrease in accounts receivable, total assets are unchanged.

5.   C   The owner's investment of equipment in the business causes an increase in the assets of the business. Since the owner has a claim to those assets he or she invested in the business, there is also an increase in owner's equity.

6.   C   The owner's investment of cash in the business causes the same result as if he or she had invested any other asset into the business. Therefore, the investment of cash causes an increase in the assets of the business. Since the owner has a claim to those assets he or she invested in the business, there is also an increase in owner's equity.

7.   C   The balance sheet lists all the assets, liabilities, and owner's equity as of a specific date. The income statement, statement of owner's equity, and statement of cash flows cover a specific time period.

8.   B   The sale of swimsuits would result in an increase in assets, specifically the accounts receivable account, for $54,600 (700 swimsuits x $78 each) and an increase in owner's equity resulting from the generation of revenue.

9.   A   The collection of $30,000 on the account affects two asset accounts: cash is increased and accounts receivable is decreased. Since the increase in cash is equal to the decrease in accounts receivable, total assets are unchanged. There is no effect on owner's equity because the sale (revenue) was recorded on March 17 at the time the sale was made.

10.   D   The income statement, statement of owner's equity, and statement of cash flows all cover a specific period of time. The balance sheet lists all the assets, liabilities, and owner's equity as of a specific date.

11.   D   Revenues minus expenses equal net income. Assets minus liabilities equals owner's equity. Liabilities plus owner's equity equals assets. Revenues plus expenses has no meaning.

12.   C   Let "L" stand for liabilities. Given that total assets equals 3L and that owner's equity equals $90,000, then according to the accounting equation:

$3L = L + \$90,000$

Subtract L from both sides of the equation.

$2L = \$90,000$, therefore $L = \$45,000$

Total Assets = 3L or 3 x $45,000 = $135,000

To double check your work, plug the amounts into the accounting equation:

Assets   = Liabilities + Owner's Equity
$135,000 = $45,000 + $90,000

> **Study Tip**: Memorizing and understanding the basic accounting equation is important and will be helpful in future chapters.

13.   A

Assets	=	Liabilities	+	Owner's Equity	
$265,000	=	$135,000	+	$130,000	Jan. 1
-75,000				+24,000	
$190,000	=	$36,000	+	$154,000	Dec. 31

14.   D

Beginning balance in owner's equity	$300
+ Net income	325
Subtotal	625
- Withdrawals	81
Ending balance in owner's equity	$544

> **Study Tip**: There is an important concept in this problem that you can use over and over throughout your accounting course. In general terms the concept can be stated:
> Beginning balance + Additions - Reductions = Ending balance.

15.   B   Profitability is determined by evaluating revenues and expenses.

Revenues – Expenses = Net Income (Loss)

$57,500 – $67,250 = (9,750). Therefore, the business was not profitable for the month of June.

III. Completion

1. Income Statement, Statement of Owner's Equity, Balance Sheet, and Statement of Cash Flows
2. entity (The most basic concept in accounting is that each entity has sharp boundaries between it and every other entity.)
3. amounts earned by delivering goods and providing services to customers
4. expenses
5. liabilities, owner's equity
6. Assets = Liabilities + Owner's equity
7. cost
8. Bookkeeping
9. Name of business, name of financial statement, date or time period covered
10. Stable Monetary Unit

IV. Daily Exercises

1.
    a. The statement of cash flows lists the cash inflows and outflows (i.e., receipts and payments) for the period and would, therefore, answer the question.
    b. The balance sheet indicates the financial position of the business on any particular date. The net worth of the business would be equal to the owner's equity.
    c. The balance sheet includes a list of all liabilities (amounts owed to creditors) on any particular date.
    d. Profitability is determined by comparing revenues with expenses and is reported on the income statement.
    e. The statement of owner's equity starts with beginning capital and calculates ending capital by adding net income and additional investment for the period then deducting any owner withdrawals.

2. The building should be listed on the balance sheet at $100,000. This amount is supported by the cost principle, which states that assets and services should be recorded in the accounting records (the books) at the actual price paid for the asset or service.

3. Yes. A business is profitable when revenues exceed expenses (net income) and is not profitable when expenses exceed revenues (net loss). Therefore, net income was $1,800 ($7,300-$5,500). Cash receipts from customers and owner's withdrawals are irrelevant with respect to determining profitability.

4. The value of the business to the owner did not change during the period. Net income of $1,800 was offset by the $1,800 the owner withdrew during the period. Therefore, beginning capital and ending capital were the same amount. The change in owner's equity shows the change in the value of the business. The value of the business is equal to owner's equity.

V. Exercises

1.

	Cash	+	Accounts Receivable	+	Supplies	+	Computer Equipment	=	Accounts Payable	+	Granger, Capital
A.	$20,000							=			$20,000
B.	(675)							=			(675)
	$ 19,325							=			$19,325
C.							$5,000	=	$5,000		
	$ 19,325					+	$5,000	=	$5,000	+	$19,325
D.	(475)			+	$ 475			=			
	$ 18,850			+	$ 475	+	$5,000	=	$5,000	+	$19,325
E.			$2,750					=			$ 2,750
	$ 18,850	+	$2,750	+	$ 475	+	$5,000	=	$5,000	+	$22,075
F.	(1,000)							=	(1,000)		
	$ 17,850	+	$2,750	+	$ 475	+	$5,000	=	$4,000	+	$22,075
G.	425		(425)					=			
	$ 18,275	+	$ 2,325	+	$ 475	+	$5,000	=	$4,000	+	$22,075
H.	40				(40)			=			
	$ 18,315	+	$ 2,325	+	$ 435	+	$5,000	=	$4,000	+	$22,075

2.

Clarence's' Clunker Repair and Body Shop
Balance Sheet
June 30, 20X7

Assets:			Liabilities:		
Cash	$	120	Accounts Payable	$	250
Accounts Receivable		200	Total Liabilities		250
Supplies		70	Owner's Equity:		
Equipment		160	Clarence, Capital		300
			Total Liabilities		
Total Assets	$	550	and Stockholders' Equity	$	550

3.

Paul's Delivery Service
Income Statement
For the Month Ended August 31, 20X6

Service revenue			$3,210
Expenses:			
Salaries	$	500	
Truck Rental		500	
Supplies		280	
Telephone		270	1,550
Net income			$1,660

VI. Beyond the Numbers

The answer to both questions is yes. How is this possible? Profitability is presented on the Income Statement and occurs when revenues exceed expenses. Solvency is analyzed by examining the Balance Sheet and comparing assets (specifically cash and receivables) with liabilities. A business is solvent when there are sufficient assets on hand to pay the debt as the debt becomes due. Remember, however, there is a third financial statement—the Statement of Owner's Equity—which links the Income Statement to the Balance Sheet. A profitable business will become insolvent if, over time, the owner withdraws cash in excess of net income. In addition, if the company invests heavily in long-term assets or inventory, solvency will decrease even if the company is profitable. Conversely, an unprofitable business can remain solvent over time if the owner is able to contribute personal assets in excess of the net losses.

VII. Demonstration Problems

Demonstration Problem #1 Solved and Explained

Requirement 1 (Analysis of transactions)

5/1   Russell's investment of $25,000 increased his equity in the business by the same amount. Thus:

Assets	=	Liabilities	+	Owner's Equity
Cash				Russell, Capital
+25,000		no change		+25,000

5/1   Monthly rent of $1,250 was paid, so Cash decreased by $1,250. In return for the rent payment, Russell's business received the right to use the office space. However, since Russell owns no part of the office, his right to use the office cannot be considered an asset. By a process of elimination you can evaluate that since Russell has paid $1,250 cash but has not received an asset in return, nor paid a liability, his equity in the business has decreased by $1,250 attributable to rent expense. Russell must have an office from which he can conduct his business, therefore, the payment of rent can be considered a cost incurred to generate revenue or an expense.

Assets	=	Liabilities	+	Owner's Equity
Cash				Russell, Capital
-1,250		no change		-1,250

5/3 $2,100 was paid for office equipment. In exchange for cash, Russell's business received ownership of the office equipment. When a business owns a resource to be used in the business, that resource is an asset. Since the $2,100 cash was exchanged for $2,100 worth of assets, owner's equity was not affected. Remember: When cash is exchanged for an asset, owner's equity is unaffected.

Assets		=	Liabilities	+	Owner's Equity
Cash	Office Equipment				
-2,100	+2,100		no change		no change

22

5/5   A computer and laser printer were purchased for $3,200 on account. Russell's business now owns some additional equipment, which we already established as an asset on 5/3. The words "on account" indicated that payment was not made at the time he purchased this equipment, but rather promised sometime in the future. The promise of payment represents money that is owed and is a debt or liability. By promising the computer sales company $3,200, Russell has added $3,200 to his company's liabilities. Up to this point Russell had no liabilities.

Assets	=	Liabilities	+	Owner's Equity
Computer +3,200		Accounts Payable +3,200		no change

5/8   Office supplies costing $200 were purchased on account. As indicated in the 5/5 transaction, when a business incurs a debt in exchange for an asset, the business has added the asset and it has also added a related liability.

Assets	=	Liabilities	+	Owner's Equity
Supplies +200		Accounts Payable +200		no change

5/10   Consulting services of $1,500 were provided on account to a client. The words "on account" indicate that the customer did not pay for the services at the time the services were rendered. Therefore, the client has promised to pay for the services rendered sometime in the future. This promise represents an asset to the business, or an account receivable. A business earns revenue when it performs a service, whether it receives cash immediately or expects to collect the cash later. Revenue transactions cause the business to grow, as shown by the increase in total assets and equities. Note that both the assets and the owner's equity in the business have increased.

Assets	=	Liabilities	+	Owner's Equity
Accounts Receivable +1,500				Russell, Capital +1,500

5/15   Fees totaling $2,300 were earned and collected. When services are rendered and cash is collected, the asset cash increases by the amount collected and the owner's equity also increases due to the earning of revenue. We determine that revenue has been earned because the services were rendered.

Assets	=	Liabilities	+	Owner's Equity
Cash +2,300		no change		Russell, Capital +2,300

5/16   Collected $1,300 cash on the account receivable created on 5/10. The asset Cash is increased and the asset Accounts Receivable is decreased by the same amount. Note that revenue is unaffected by the actual receipt of the cash since the firm already recorded the revenue when it was earned on 5/10.

Assets		=	Liabilities	+	Owner's Equity
Cash	Accounts Receivable				
+1,300	-1,300		no change		no change

5/18   Paid for the supplies purchased on 5/8. The payment of cash on account does not affect the asset Office Supplies because the payment does not increase or decrease the amount of supplies available to the business. The effect on the accounting equation is a decrease in the asset Cash and a decrease in the liability Accounts Payable. The business has simply paid for an amount that it owed to the business from which it purchased the office supplies.

Assets	=	Liabilities	+	Owner's Equity
Cash		Accounts Payable		
-200		-200		no change

5/21   The owner withdrew $3,000 for personal use. The withdrawal of cash decreases the asset Cash and reduces the owner's equity in the business. Note that the withdrawal does not represent a business expense.

Assets	=	Liabilities	+	Owner's Equity
Cash				Russell, Capital
-3,000		no change		-3,000

5/31   Fees totaling $4,100 were earned and collected. When services are rendered and immediately collected, the asset Cash increases by the amount received, and the owner's equity increases as well attributable to the earning of revenue.

Assets	=	Liabilities	+	Owner's Equity
Cash				Russell, Capital
+4,100				+4,100

RUSSELL CONSULTING

	ASSETS				=	LIABILITIES + OWNER'S EQUITY		
	Cash +	Office Supplies +	Accounts Receivable +	Equipment	=	Accounts Payable +	Russell, Capital	Type of owner's equity transaction
5/1	+25,000						+25,000	Owner investment
5/1	-1,250						-1,250	Rent expense
5/3	-2,100			+2,100				
5/5				+3,200		+3,200		
5/8		+200				+200		
5/10			+1,500				+1,500	Service revenue
5/15	+2,300						+2,300	Service revenue
5/16	+1,300		-1,300					
5/18	-200					-200		
5/21	-3,000						-3,000	Owner withdrawal
5/31	+4,100						+4,100	Service revenue
	$26,150	$200	$200	$5,300		$3,200	$28,650	
	$31,850					$31,850		

Requirement 2 (Income Statement, Statement of Owner's Equity, and Balance Sheet)

Russell Consulting
Income Statement
For the Month Ended May 31, 20X8

Service Income	$7,900
Less: Expenses	
Rent	1,250
Net Income	$6,650

Russell Consulting
Statement of Owner's Equity
For the Month Ended May 31, 20X8

Russell, Capital 5/1/X8		$0
Add: Capital Investment	$25,000	
Net Income	6,650	
Less: Withdrawals	(3,000)	28,650
Russell, Capital 5/31/X8		$28,650

Russell Consulting
Balance Sheet
May 31, 20X8

ASSETS		LIABILITIES	
Cash	$26,150	Accounts Payable	$ 3,200
Accounts Receivable	200		
Office Supplies	200		
Equipment	5,300	**OWNER'S EQUITY**	
		Russell, Capital 5/31/X8	28,650
Total Assets	$31,850	Total Liabilities & Owner's Equity	$31,850

Demonstration Problem #2 Solved

Mann Made Designs
Income Statement
For the Month Ended May 31, 20X9

Commissions Earned		$12,000
Less: Expenses		
Advertising	$500	
Interest	200	
Salaries	1750	
Supplies	2900	
Utilities	100	
Total Expenses		5,450
Net Income		$ 6,550

Mann Made Designs.
Statement of Owner's Equity
For the Month Ended May 31, 20X9

Mildred Amis, Capital 5/1/X9		$59,325
Add: Net Income	$6,550	
Less: Withdrawals	2,000	4,550
Mildred Amis, Capital 5/31/X9		$63,875

Mann Made Designs
Balance Sheet
May 31, 20X9

ASSETS		**LIABILITIES**	
Cash	$ 8,200	Accounts Payable	$ 700
Accounts Receivable	1,800	Notes Payable	14,000
Notes Receivable	1,000	Salaries Payable	250
Interest Receivable	100	Total Liabilities	$14,950
Supplies	2,325		
Equipment	6,600		
Vehicle	3,800	**OWNER'S EQUITY**	
Building	55,000	Mildred Amis, Capital 5/31/X9	63,875
Total Assets	$78,825	Total Liabilities and Owner's Equity	$78,825

Chapter 2—Recording Business Transactions

CHAPTER OVERVIEW

Chapter Two uses the foundation established in the previous chapter and expands the discussion of recording business transactions. A thorough understanding of this process is vital to your success in mastering topics in future chapters. The learning objectives for this chapter are to

1. Use accounting terms
2. Apply the rules of debit and credit.
3. Record transactions in the journal.
4. Post from the journal to the ledger.
5. Prepare and use a trial balance.
6. Analyze transactions without a journal.

CHAPTER REVIEW

Objective 1 - Use accounting terms

The terms used in accounting sometimes have meanings that differ from ordinary usage. You must learn the accounting meaning of terms now. Some key terms you must learn are:

- **Account:** The basic summary device used to record all the changes that occur in a particular asset, liability, or owner's equity during a period.

- **Ledger:** The record holding all of the individual accounts used by a business. The list of accounts that appear in the ledger are referred to as the **chart of accounts**. Each account is assigned a unique number (this account number is used as a reference in the posting process). The order of the accounts and the corresponding account numbers in this list parallels the accounting equation. In other words, assets are listed first, followed by liability accounts, and lastly, owner's equity. Owner's equity is subdivided into capital, withdrawals, revenue and expense accounts. The numbers are assigned in ascending order so assets are assigned the lowest numbers while expenses carry the highest numbers.

- **Journal:** The chronological record of an entity's business transactions. In practice, when a business transaction occurs, the transaction will first be recorded in the journal. So, you can think of the journal as the first place a business transaction will appear in the accounting records. Transactions are recorded in the journal chronologically, or in the order in which the transactions occurred.

- **Trial Balance:** A list of all the accounts with their balances. The trial balance is prepared from the ledger and the accounts are listed in the order in which the accounts appear in the ledger.

- **Assets:** Economic resources that will benefit the business in the future. When we talk about assets, we are referring to the category, or classification of accounts. Within each category or classification, there are specific account titles that are used that are representative of the nature of each type of asset. Examples of asset accounts are Cash, Notes Receivable, Accounts Receivable, Prepaid Expenses, Land, Buildings, Equipment, Furniture, and Fixtures.

- **Liabilities:** Obligations that the business owes to an entity in the future. Remember that liabilities represent creditor's claims to the assets of the business. The term "liabilities" represents the category of accounts that summarizes the total debt of the business. Within the liabilities category, there are specific liability accounts. Examples of liability accounts include Notes Payable, Accounts Payable, Taxes Payable, Interest Payable, and Salary Payable to name a few. Notice the word "payable" implies that cash will be paid in the future. So, whenever you see an account title that includes the word "payable" you will know that it is a liability account. A business can have obligations where it owes something other than cash. A business can owe a service or a product, too. We will address these other obligations in future chapters.

- **Owner's equity:** The claim that the owner has on the assets of the business. Owner's equity represents the value of the business and can also be referred to as the net worth of the business. Owner's equity is the category that houses the individual owner's equity accounts. The individual owner's equity accounts are:
    - **Capital:** The specific account that reflects the owner's claims to the business assets.
    - **Withdrawals:** The assets that the owner removes for personal use
    - **Revenues:** The account classification that represents the increases in owner's equity created by delivering goods or services to customers or clients. Examples of specific revenue accounts are Service Revenue, Sales Revenue, and Interest Revenue.
    - **Expenses:** The account classification that represents decreases in owner's equity resulting from the using up of assets or the creation of a liability in the normal course of doing business. Remember that expenses are created to support the generation of revenues. Examples of specific expense accounts are Rent Expense, Salary Expense, Utilities Expense and Interest Expense.

- **Double-entry accounting:** The accounting system that records the dual effects of every business transaction. Every transaction affects at least two accounts.
    - **T-accounts:** In accounting education, the T-account is an abbreviated version of the general ledger used as an illustrative tool used to show the dual effects of a transaction in specific accounts. In practice, you would ask to see the ledger. You would never ask to see the T-accounts.
    - **Debit (Dr):** The left side of the T-account.
    - **Credit (Cr):** The right side of the T-account.

Helpful Hint: Debit means left and credit means right. That's all! In order to learn the accounting use for the words debit and credit, you must depart from your personal knowledge of debits and credits as they relate to your bank account.

Objective 2 - Apply the rules of debit and credit.

To learn the rules of debit and credit, you need to start with the basic accounting equation. You know that the accounting equation must always be in balance. This rule will carry forward as you learn about the rules of debit and credit. The account category (assets, liabilities, or owner's equity) governs how increases and decreases are recorded in each individual account. The rules of debit and credit refer to the side of the T-account on which an increase or decrease is recorded. It is easiest to first focus on the side of the account on which increases are recorded. According to the rules of debit and credit, when a business transaction results in an increase in assets, the increase is recorded on the left side of the T-account or the debit side. In accounting language, we would simply say to "debit the account" when we mean to increase the account balance of an asset. When a business transaction results in an increase in liabilities or owner's equity the increase is recorded on the right side of the T-account or the credit side. In accounting language, we would say to "credit the account" when we mean to increase the balance of a liability account or to increase owner's equity.

$$Assets = Liabilities + Owner's\ Equity$$

Notice that when we say that assets equal liabilities plus owner's equity, we are really saying that the left side must always equal the right side of the equation. Or, using accounting language, we could simply say that the debits must equal the credits.

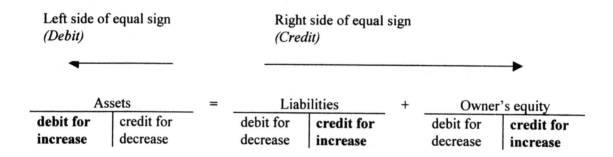

Once you understand which side of the T-accounts increases are recorded, it stands to reason that decreases would be recorded on the opposite side. Thus, to decrease an asset account, you would "credit" the account, and to decrease the liabilities and owner's equity, you would "debit" the account.

> **Study Tip:** Refer to the basic accounting equation to understand the debit/credit rules. Increases in items on the *left side* of the equation are placed on the *left side* (debit) of the account. Increases in the items on the *right side* of the equation are placed on the *right side* (credit) of the account.

Take some time to make sure that you understand the basic rules of debit and credit as they apply to the accounting equation illustrated above. Once you are comfortable with the accounting equation, then we need to look a little more closely at Owner's Equity.

Remember that Owner's Equity has four components:

1. **Owner's investments** that increase overall owner's equity and are always recorded in the Capital account.
2. **Owner's withdrawals** that decrease overall owner's equity and are always recorded in the Withdrawals account.
3. **Revenues** that increase overall owner's equity and are always recorded in a specific revenue account such as Service Revenue.
4. **Expenses** that decrease overall owner's equity and are always recorded in the specific expense accounts such as Advertising Expense and Utilities Expense.

To apply the rules of debit and credit to owner's equity, you must first understand the difference between these four components and the effect of each (increase or decrease) on owner's equity. Now review the following illustration:

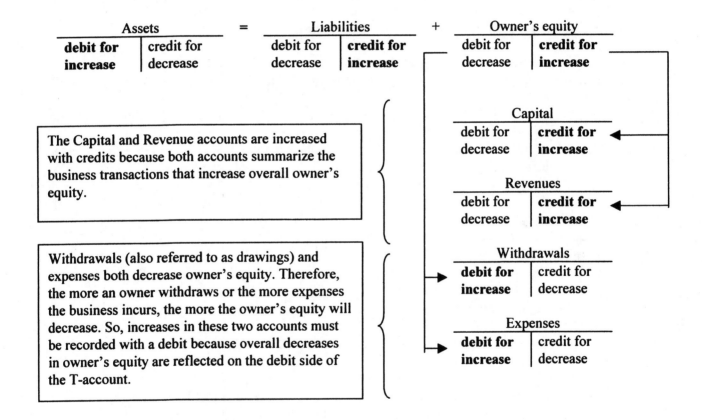

The Capital and Revenue accounts are increased with credits because both accounts summarize the business transactions that increase overall owner's equity.

Withdrawals (also referred to as drawings) and expenses both decrease owner's equity. Therefore, the more an owner withdraws or the more expenses the business incurs, the more the owner's equity will decrease. So, increases in these two accounts must be recorded with a debit because overall decreases in owner's equity are reflected on the debit side of the T-account.

Helpful Hint: You can use a pneumonic to learn the rules of debit and credit: **DEAD CLRC** or

Debit to increase:	Credit to increase:
Expenses	**Liabilities**
Assets	**Revenues**
Drawings (withdrawals)	**Capital**

The term **normal balance** refers to the type of balance (debit or credit) the account usually carries. The normal balance for any account is always the side of the account where increases are recorded. Therefore, the normal balances are:

Account	Normal Balance
Assets	debit
Liabilities	credit
Capital	credit
Withdrawals	debit
Revenues	credit
Expenses	debit

> Helpful Hint: See Exhibit 2-13 for a summary of the rules of debit and credit and the normal balance of accounts.

Objective 3 - Record transactions in the journal.

Remember, the journal is a chronological record of a business's transactions. It is the first place where a transaction is recorded. To record a transaction in the journal, follow these three steps:

1. Specify each account affected and determine whether it is an asset, a liability, or an owner's equity account.
2. Determine whether each account balance is increased or decreased, and then use the rules of debit and credit to determine whether to "debit" or "credit" the account. (Note: The rules of double-entry accounting also require that every journal entry will consist of at least one debit and at least one credit. A journal entry that affects more than two accounts is referred to as a compound entry.)
3. Record the transaction in the journal:
   - Enter the date of the transaction
   - Record the debit first
   - Record the credit second
   - Last record a brief explanation of the transaction.

To illustrate, suppose that Bob Bush, borrows $10,000 from the bank to expand the business. What is the journal entry for this transaction?

1. The accounts affected are Cash (an Asset) and Notes Payable (a Liability).
2. Both accounts will increase by $10,000. Debit Cash for $10,000 to increase Cash, and Credit Notes Payable for $10,000 to increase Notes Payable.
3. Record the journal entry:

Date	Accounts	Debit	Credit
Jan. 10	Cash	10,000	
	Notes Payable		10,000
	Bank loan for business expansion.		

(Notice that the debit appears on the left and the credit is indented below the debit to the right, which is consistent with the definitions of debit and credit that you have learned.)

As you become more proficient with journal entries, you will be able to "read" the entries and work your way backwards to describe the transaction. For example, when you see the debit to cash, you will know that cash was increased meaning the business received some cash; and, the credit to notes payable indicates that an account titled note payable was increased meaning that the business now owes some money. If the business receives cash from increasing a liability, then you know the original transaction has to be that the business borrowed some money.

Study Tip: If you determine that one of the accounts affected is Cash, first determine whether Cash increases or decreases. This allows you to use a process of elimination to determine the debit or credit for the other account affected by the transaction. Using the example above, if you determine that the account Cash has increased, and you know that the increase has to be recorded with a debit, then you can conclude that the other account you have identified, Notes Payable, will have to be the credit, since every transaction must have at least one debit and at least one credit.

Examples of some typical journal entries are:

Accounts	Debit	Credit
Cash	25,000	
Smith, Capital		25,000
Owner invests money into the business.		
Prepaid Insurance	3,000	
Cash		3,000
Purchased a three-year insurance policy.		
Supplies	1,500	
Accounts Payable		1,500
Purchased supplies on account.		
Accounts Payable	1,500	
Cash		1,500
Paid amount owed for supplies.		
Accounts Receivable	2,200	
Service Revenue		2,200
Billed clients for services rendered.		
Cash	1,400	
Accounts Receivable		1,400
Received payments from clients previously billed.		
Salary Expense	2,800	
Cash		2,800
Paid salaries.		
Withdrawals	2,000	
Cash		2,000
Owner withdraws cash for personal use.		

Objective 4 - Post from the journal to the ledger.

Posting means to copy the amounts from the journal to the appropriate accounts in the ledger. The journal entry for the bank loan in the previous example would be posted this way:

Cash		Notes Payable	
10,000			10,000

Posting updates the ledger by transferring all of the transactions that affect a specific account from the journal to each respective account. Posting to the ledger and calculating an account balance is the only way that you can determine the balance in any account. You cannot look at the journal and determine the account balance for Cash. This can only be determined by going to the ledger and reviewing the Cash account.

> Helpful Hint: Review Exhibit 2-9 in your text for a detailed illustration of journalizing and posting. Remember we are using the T-account as an abbreviated version of the ledger.

Objective 5 - Prepare and use a trial balance.

The **trial balance** is taken from the ledger and represents a listing of all accounts with their balances. The accounts are listed in the order in which they appear in the ledger. The trial balance tests whether the total debits equal the total credits. If total debits do not equal the total credits, an error has been made. Review Exhibit 2-8 in your text for an example of a trial balance.

Keep in mind that the trial balance is an internal document used by the business to make sure that the debits and credits are equal. The trial balance is NOT the same thing as the balance sheet. The balance sheet is a financial statement that is prepared to present to external users.

> **Study Tip**: Spend some time reading and thinking about the decision guidelines in your text. These should help you place the recording process in the proper context.

Objective 7 - Analyze transactions without a journal.

In general, the ledger is more useful than the journal in providing an overall model of a business. Therefore, when time is of the essence, decision-makers frequently skip the journal and go directly to the ledger in order to compress transaction analysis, journalizing, and posting into a single step.

TEST YOURSELF

All the self-testing materials in this chapter focus on information and procedures that your instructor is likely to test in quizzes and examinations.

I. Matching   *Match each numbered term with its lettered definition.*

A 1. Account
L 2. Capital
C 3. Chart of accounts
N 4. Compound entry
I 5. Credit
D 6. Debit
O 7. Double-entry system
J 8. Journal

H 9. Ledger
K 10. Normal balance
F 11. Posting
E 12. Post reference
G 13. Trial balance
M 14. Withdrawals
B 15. Revenues

A. Detailed record of changes in a particular asset, liability, or owner's equity during a period of time.
B. Increases in owner's equity that result from delivering goods or services to customers or clients.
C. A way of cross-referencing amounts between the journal and ledger.
D. Left side of an account.
E. List of all the accounts in the ledger and their account numbers.
F. Copying information from the journal to the ledger.
G. A list of all the accounts with their balances which tests whether total debits equals total credits.
H. The book of accounts.
I. Right side of an account.
J. Provides a chronological record of an entity's transactions.
K. The type of balance an account usually carries.
L. The account that shows the owner's claim to the business's assets.
M. The account that summarizes the removal of cash by the owner.
N. When more than two accounts are affected by a transaction.
O. Recording the dual effects of transactions.

II. Multiple Choice   *Circle the best answer.*

1. An attorney performs services for which he receives cash. The correct entry for this transaction is:

   A. Service Revenue
         Accounts Payable
   B. Service Revenue
         Cash

   C. Accounts Receivable
         Service Revenue
   D. Cash
         Service Revenue

2. An accountant debited Insurance Expense $1,500 and credited Cash $1,500 in error. The correct entry should have been to debit Prepaid Insurance for $1,500 and credit Cash for $1,500. As a result of this error:

   A. assets are overstated by $1,500.
   B. expenses are understated by $1,500.
   C. the trial balance will not balance.
   D. expenses are overstated by $1,500.

35

3. Accounts Receivable had total debits for the month of $3,500 and total credits for the month of $2,700. The beginning balance in Accounts Receivable was $3,200. What was the net change in Accounts Receivable?

A. A decrease of $800
B. An increase of $4,000

C. An increase of $800
D. A decrease of $4,000

4. Accounts Payable had a balance of $4,000 on April 1. During April, $2,750 of equipment was purchased on account. The April 30 balance was a credit of $3,850. How much were payments on Accounts Payable during April? 4000 + 2750 - 3850

A. $ 6,750
B. $ 7,850

C. $ 2,900
D. $ 6,600

5. Income statement accounts are:

A. assets and liabilities.
B. revenues and withdrawals.

C. revenues and expenses.
D. assets and withdrawals.

6. The posting reference in the ledger tells:

A. the page of the ledger on which the account is found.
B. the explanation of the transaction.

C. whether it is a debit or a credit entry.

D. the page of the journal where the original entry can be found.

7. The list of accounts and their account numbers is called the:

A. chart of accounts.
B. trial balance.

C. ledger.
D. accountants reference.

8. The revenue earned by lending money is called:

A. advertising expense.
B. loan revenue.

C. interest revenue.
D. prepaid expense.

9. When the owner of a business withdraws cash, the journal entry should include a:

A. debit to Accounts Payable.
B. credit to Capital.

C. debit to Cash.
D. debit to Withdrawals.

10. When cash was received on account in payment for services previously rendered, the accountant recorded the transaction by debiting Cash and crediting Service Revenue. As a result there was:

A. an overstatement of Cash and Service Revenue.
B. an understatement of assets and overstatement of revenues .
C. an overstatement of assets and an overstatement of revenues.
D. no over- or understatement of any accounts. This is the correct entry.

III. Completion *Complete each of the following statements.*

1. Put the following in proper sequence by numbering them from 1 to 3.

   __2__ a. Post to ledger
   __3__ b. Trial balance
   __1__ c. Journal entry

2. Indicate whether the following accounts would be increased or decreased with a debit.

	Increase	Decrease
a. Land	X	
b. Capital		X
c. Prepaid Insurance	X	
d. Interest Payable		X
e. Service Revenue		X
f. Rent Expense	X	
g. Interest Revenue		X
h. Accounts Payable		X
i. Withdrawals	X	
j. Advertising Expense	X	

3. Indicate the normal balance for each of the following.

	Debit	Credit
a. Notes Receivable	X	
b. Accounts Payable		X
c. Prepaid Advertising	X	
d. Building	X	
e. Capital		X
f. Accounts Receivable	X	
g. Rent Expense	X	
h. Interest Revenue		X
i. Land	X	
j. Withdrawals	X	

IV. Daily Exercises

1. Classify each of the following accounts as asset, liability, capital, withdrawals, revenue, or expense.

Account	Classification
a. Salaries Payable	_____
b. Supplies	_____
c. Fees Receivable	_____
d. Computer Equipment	_____
e. Fees Earned	_____
f. Insurance Expense	_____
g. James Brown, Capital	_____
h. Sales Revenue	_____
i. Notes Payable	_____
j. James Brown, Withdrawals	_____

2. Review the list of accounts in #1 above and indicate the normal balance of each account.

a. _____		f. _____	
b. _____		g. _____	
c. _____		h. _____	
d. _____		i. _____	
e. _____		j. _____	

2. Prepare a trial balance from the following list of accounts and balances. List the accounts in their proper order. All accounts reflect normal balances.

Accounts Payable	$ 830
Accounts Receivable	1,050
Capital	2,700
Cash	1,350
Fees Earned	3,700
Furniture and Fixtures	4,500
Insurance Expense	500
Notes Payable	1,700
Rent Expense	950
Supplies	380
Withdrawals	200

Accounts	Debit	Credit

V. Exercises

1. Walker Smith opened a financial planning firm on June, 20X6. During the first month of operations, the following transactions occurred:

    6/1   Walker invested $7,500 cash in the business.
    6/2   Purchased used office equipment for $3,000. He made an $800 cash down payment and gave the seller a note payable due in 90 days.
    6/3   Paid $500 for a month's rent.
    6/15 Walker provided financial planning services, $6,000 during the first fifteen days of the month. The fees for these services were collected from clients at the time the services were provided. Walker made one deposit in the business checking account.
    6/17 Withdrew $1,275 to pay the rent on his apartment.
    6/19 Purchased $250 of supplies on account.
    6/19 Paid the phone bill for the month, $130.
    6/21 Received the utility bill for July, $225. The utility bill is not due until next month.
    6/25 Paid his secretary a salary of $1,350.
    6/28 Paid for the supplies purchased on 6/19.
    6/30 Performed $10,500 in services for the last half of June. Clients paid for $4,000 of these services at the time the services were performed.

    Prepare the journal entries for each of these transactions, omitting the explanations. Use the following accounts: Cash; Accounts Receivable; Supplies; Equipment; Accounts Payable; Notes Payable; Walker Smith, Capital; Walker Smith, Withdrawals; Service Revenue; Rent Expense; Salary Expense; Telephone Expense; Utilities Expense.

Date	Accounts	PR	Debit	Credit

2. The following are normal balances for the accounts of Kevin's Landscaping & Lawn Service on August 31, 20X7.

Accounts Payable	$ 375
Accounts Receivable	5,370
Advertising Expense	700
Equipment	7,500
Cash	10,000
Gasoline Expense	1,200
Interest Payable	85
Lawn Care Supplies	875
Rent Expense	425
Prepaid Insurance	250
Salary Expense	3,125
Notes Payable	1,500
Kevin, Capital	?
Service Revenue	5,500
Kevin, Withdrawals	1,500

a. Prepare a trial balance based on the account balances above. List the accounts in their proper order and calculate the correct balance for the Kevin, Capital account.

Accounts	Debit	Credit

b. How much net income (loss) did Kevin's Landscaping & Lawn Service generate for the month of August? _____

3. Tommy's Totally Taxi Service had the following trial balance on October 31, 20X7:

Accounts	Debit	Credit
Cash	$ 36,000	
Accounts Receivable	18,000	
Notes Receivable	6,000	
Supplies	700	
Vehicles	40,000	
Accounts Payable		$ 1,400
Tommy, Capital		68,100
Service Revenue		34,000
Salary Expense		7,000
Insurance Expense		1,500
	$100,700	$ 106,000

The following errors caused the trial balance not to balance:

a. Tommy recorded a $1,500 note payable as a note receivable.
b. He posted a $3,000 credit to Accounts Payable as $300.
c. He recorded Prepaid Insurance of $1,500 as Insurance Expense.
d. He recorded a cash revenue transaction by debiting Cash for $3,000 and crediting Accounts Receivable for $3,000.

Prepare a corrected trial balance as of October 31, 20X7:

Tommy's Totally Taxi Service
Trial Balance
October 31, 20X7

Accounts	Debit	Credit

VI. Beyond the Numbers

The following errors occurred in posting transactions from the journal to the ledger.

1. A payment of $170 for advertising was posted as a $170 debit to Advertising Expense and a $710 credit to Cash.
2. The receipt of $300 from a customer on account was posted as a $300 debit to Cash and a $300 credit to Fees Earned.
3. The purchase of Supplies on account for $140 was posted twice as a debit to Supplies and once as a credit to Accounts Payable.
4. The payment of $220 to a creditor on account was posted as a credit to Accounts Payable for $220 and a credit to Cash for $220.

For each of these errors, determine the following:
   A. Is the trial balance out of balance, yes or no?
   B. If you answer "yes" to A., by what amount will the debits and credits be out of balance?
   C. Which column total, debit or credit, is larger as a result of the error?
   D. Which column total, debit or credit, reflects the correct total?

Error	Out of balance?	Column difference	Larger column amount	Correct column total
1.				
2.				
3.				
4.				

VII. Demonstration Problems

Demonstration Problem #1

Joe's Adventures Unlimited rents canoes to customers who want to spend a day canoeing down the Bluewater River. Joe Davidson established the business in 20X6.

During the month of May, the business performed the following transactions:

a. Joe Davidson borrowed $125,000 from a local bank signing a note payable in the name of the business.
b. A small parcel of land was acquired for $30,000 cash.
c. Canoe trips were provided for customers. Cash totaling $6,000 was received for these trips at the time the rentals were provided.
d. Supplies costing $1,800 were purchased on account.
e. Joe contracted with one of the local youth groups and canoe trips were provided for this group on account. The total amount of revenue earned on account, $4,500.
f. The following expenses were paid in cash:
    Salary Expense, $3,000
    Rent Expense, $1,700
    Advertising Expense, $650
    Interest Expense, $350
    Record these expenses using one compound entry.
g. Joe Davidson withdrew $2,800 for personal use.
h. Paid $3,800 owed on account.
i. Received $2,750 cash on account for services previously rendered.

Required:

1. Using the T-account format, open the following ledger accounts for Joe's Adventure's Unlimited with the beginning account balances as indicated.

ASSETS
Cash, $10,000
Accounts receivable, no balance
Supplies, no balance
Equipment, $26,000
Land, no balance
LIABILITIES
Accounts Payable, $7,000
Notes Payable, no balance

OWNER'S EQUITY
Joe Davidson, Capital, $29,000
Joe Davidson, Withdrawals, no balance

REVENUE
Rental Revenue, no balance

<u>EXPENSES</u>
Salary Expense, no balance
Rent Expense, no balance
Interest Expense, no balance
Advertising Expense, no balance

2. Journalize the transactions using the format illustrated in Exhibit 2-4 on page 45. Key each journal entry by its transaction letter. Omit explanations.
3. Post to the T-accounts on the next two pages. Key all amounts by letter and compute a balance for each account.
4. Prepare the trial balance as of May 31, 20X6 using the format illustrated in Exhibit 2-8 on page 49.

Requirements 1 and 3: (Open ledger accounts and post journal entries)

ASSETS

LIABILITIES

OWNER'S EQUITY

REVENUE

EXPENSES

Requirement 2 (Journal entries)

Date	Accounts and Explanation	PR	Debit	Credit

Requirement 4 (Trial balance)

Accounts	Debits	Credits

Demonstration Problem #2

Using the information from the Trial Balance in Demonstration Problem # 1, prepare an Income Statement, Statement of Owner's Equity, and Balance Sheet. Use proper headings.

Income Statement

Statement of Owner's Equity

Balance Sheet

SOLUTIONS

I. Matching

1. A	4. N	7. O	10. K	13. G
2. L	5. I	8. J	11. F	14. M
3. E	6. D	9. H	12. C	15. B

II. Multiple Choice

1. D   The receipt of cash for the performance of services causes an increase in assets and an increase in owner's equity. This increase in owner's equity from providing services is called revenue. Cash is increased with a debit and revenue is increased with a credit.

2. D   The recorded entry incorrectly increased expenses by $1,500. Accordingly, expenses are overstated. Since the entry should have debited the Prepaid Insurance account, and did not, assets are *understated.* To correct this error, Insurance Expense should be credited (or decreased) by $1,500 and Prepaid Insurance should be debited (or increased) by $1,500.

3. C   The $3,500 of debits to Accounts Receivable increased the balance, while the $2,700 of credits to Accounts Receivable decreased the balance. The net effect of the debits and the credits is $3,500 - $2,700 = $800 increase.

4. C   The following equation is used to solve this problem:

    Beginning balance
+ Increase (new purchases on account)
<u>- Decrease (payments on account)</u>
<u>= Ending balance</u>

Rearranged to solve for the payments on account, the equation is:
Payments = beginning balance + new accounts - ending balance
Payments = $4,000 + 2,750 - $3,850 = $2,900

5. C   Only "Revenues and Expenses" appear on the income statement and are referred to as "income statement accounts". The other three responses include at least one account that would appear on the balance sheet account.

6. D   The posting reference provides a "trail" through the accounting records for future reference. The post reference appears in the ledger and "refers" back to the location in the journal from which the entry was posted.

7. A   A list of accounts and account numbers is called a chart of accounts.

8. C   An entity may have as many revenue accounts as it has sources of revenue. Each account title should be descriptive of the source of the revenue. Since the revenue earned from lending money is "interest," interest revenue is the appropriate account title, just as the revenue earned from providing services to customers is called "service revenue".

9. D   Withdrawals of cash from a business by the owner decreases the cash account balance and

increases the balance in the withdrawals account. To decrease the cash balance it is necessary to credit the cash account; to increase the withdrawals account balance it is necessary to debit the withdrawals account. (Remember that the debit to the Withdrawals account has the affect of decreasing overall Owner's Equity.)

10. C The journal entry incorrectly credited (increased) the service revenue account balance. The correct entry should have been to credit (decrease) accounts receivable. As a result, assets (accounts receivable) are overstated and revenue (service revenue) is overstated.

III. Completion

1. a. 2; b. 3; c. 1. Journal entries are recorded first and then are posted to the ledger. The trial balance is prepared from ledger balances.

2. Increase: a; c; f; i; j
   Decrease: b; d; e; g; h

Debits increase accounts with a normal debit balance and decrease accounts with a normal credit balance. Assets, expenses and withdrawals have normal debit balances, while liabilities, capital, and revenue have normal credit balances.

3. A. debit   F. debit
   B. credit   G. debit
   C. debit   H. credit
   D. debit   I. debit
   E. credit   J. debit

Assets, expenses, and withdrawals have normal debit balances. Liabilities, capital, and revenue have normal credit balances.

IV. Daily Exercises

1. a. liability   g. capital
   b. asset   h. revenue
   c. asset   i. liabilities
   d. asset   j. withdrawals
   e. revenue
   f. expense

2. a. credit   g. credit
   b. debit   h. credit
   c. debit   i. credit
   d. debit   j. debit
   e. credit
   f. debit

3.

	Debit	Credit
Cash	$1,350	
Accounts Receivable	1,050	
Supplies	380	
Furniture and Fixtures	4,500	
Accounts Payable		$ 830
Notes Payable		1,700
Capital		2,700
Withdrawals	200	
Fees Earned		3,700
Rent Expense	950	
Insurance Expense	500	
Total	$8,930	$8,930

V. Exercises
1.

Date	Accounts	PR	Debit	Credit
6/1	Cash		7,500	
	Walker Smith, Capital			7,500
6/2	Equipment		3,000	
	Cash			800
	Notes Payable			2,200
6/3	Rent Expense		500	
	Cash			500
6/15	Cash		6,000	
	Service Revenue			6,000
6/17	Walker Smith, Withdrawals		1,275	
	Cash			1,275
6/19	Supplies		250	
	Accounts Payable			250
	Telephone Expense		130	
	Cash			130
6/21	Utility Expense		225	
	Accounts Payable			225
6/25	Salary Expense		1,350	
	Cash			1,350

			Debit	Credit
6/28	Accounts Payable		250	
	Cash			250
6/31	Cash		4,000	
	Accounts Receivable		6,500	
	Service Revenue			10,500

2. a.

Kevin's Landscaping & Lawn Service
Trial Balance
August 31, 20X7

	Debit	Credit
Cash	$ 10,000	
Accounts Receivable	5,370	
Lawn Care Supplies	875	
Prepaid Insurance	250	
Equipment	7,500	
Accounts Payable		$ 375
Interest Payable		85
Notes Payable		1,500
Kevin, Capital		23,485
Kevin, Withdrawals	1,500	
Service Revenue		5,500
Salary expense	3,125	
Gasoline Expense	1,200	
Advertising Expense	700	
Rent Expense	425	
Total	$30,945	30,945

b. Net income = Revenues – Expenses or
$5,500-3,125-1,200-700-425 = $50

3.

Tommy's Totally Taxi Service
Trial Balance
October 31, 20X7

	Debit	Credit
Cash	$ 36,000	
Accounts Receivable	21,000	
Notes Receivable	4,500	
Prepaid Insurance	1,500	
Supplies	700	
Vehicles	40,000	
Accounts Payable		$ 4,100
Notes Payable		1,500
Tommy, Capital		68,100
Service Revenue		37,000
Salary Expense	7,000	
Insurance Expense	0	
Total	$110,700	$110,700

VI. Beyond the Numbers

Error	Out of balance?	Column total difference	Larger column total	Correct column total
1.	yes	$540	credit	credit
2.	no			
3.	yes	$140	debit	credit
4.	yes	$440	credit	debit

VII. Demonstration Problems

Demonstration Problem #1 Solved and Explained

Requirement 1 (Open ledger accounts)

ASSETS

Cash		Accounts Receivable	
Bal. 10,000			

Supplies		Equipment	
		Bal. 26,000	

Land	

LIABILITIES

Accounts Payable		Notes Payable	
	Bal. 7,000		

OWNER'S EQUITY

Joe Davidson, Capital		Joe Davidson, Withdrawals	
	Bal. 29,000		

REVENUE

Rental Revenue	

EXPENSES

Salary Expense		Rent Expense	

Interest Expense		Advertising Expense	

Requirement 2 (Journal entries)

Date	Accounts and Explanation		Debit	Credit
a.	Cash		125,000	
	Notes Payable			125,000
	Borrowed cash and signed note payable.			
b.	Land		30,000	
	Cash			30,000
	Purchased land for future office location.			
c.	Cash		6,000	
	Rental Revenue			6,000
	Revenue earned and collected.			
d.	Supplies		1,800	
	Accounts Payable			1,800
	Purchased supplies on account.			
e.	Account Receivable		4,500	
	Rental Revenue			4,500
	Performed services on account.			
f.	Salary Expense		3,000	
	Rent Expense		1,700	
	Advertising Expense		650	
	Interest Expense		350	
	Cash			5,700
	Paid cash expenses.			
g.	Joe Davidson, Withdrawals		2,800	
	Cash			2,800
	Owner withdrawal for personal use.			
h.	Accounts Payable		3,800	
	Cash			3,800
	Paid on account			
i.	Cash		2,750	
	Accounts Receivable.			2,750
	Received on account.			

Requirement 3 (Posting)

ASSETS

Cash		
Bal. 10,000		
(a) 125,000	(b)	30,000
(c) 6,000	(f)	5,700
(i) 2,750	(g)	2,800
	(h)	3,800
Bal. 101,450		

Accounts Receivable	
(e) 4,500	(i) 2,750
Bal. 1,750	

Supplies	
(d) 1,800	
Bal. 1,800	

Equipment	
Bal. 26,000	
Bal. 26,000	

Land	
(b) 30,000	
Bal. 30,000	

LIABILITIES

Accounts Payable		
	Bal.	7,000
(h) 3,800	(d)	1,800
	Bal.	5,000

Notes Payable	
	(a) 125,000
	Bal. 125,000

OWNER'S EQUITY

Joe Davidson, Capital	
	Bal. 29,000
	Bal. 29,000

Joe Davidson, Withdrawals	
(g) 2,800	
Bal. 2,800	

REVENUE

Rental Revenue	
	(c) 6,000
	(e) 4,500
	Bal. 10,500

EXPENSES

Salary Expense	
(f) 3,000	
Bal. 3,000	

Rent Expense	
(f) 1,700	
Bal. 1,700	

Interest Expense	
(f) 350	
Bal. 350	

Advertising Expense	
(f) 650	
Bal. 650	

Requirement 4 (Trial Balance)

Accounts	Debits	Credits
Cash	$ 101,450	
Accounts Receivable	1,750	
Supplies	1,800	
Equipment	26,000	
Land	30,000	
Accounts Payable		$ 5,000
Notes Payable		125,000
Joe Davidson, Capital		29,000
Joe Davidson, Withdrawals	2,800	
Rental revenue		10,500
Salary expense	3,000	
Rent expense	1,700	
Interest expense	350	
Advertising expense	650	
Total	$169,500	$169,500

Total debits = total credits. The accounts appear to be in balance. If the trial balance did not balance, we would look for an error in recording or posting.

Demonstration Problem #2 Solved

Joe's Adventures Unlimited
Income Statement
For the Month Ended May 31, 20X6

Revenues:		
Rental Revenues		$10,500
Expenses:		
Salary Expense	$3,000	
Rent Expense	1,700	
Interest Expense	350	
Advertising Expense	650	
Total Expenses		5,700
Net Income		$4,800

Joe's Adventures Unlimited
Statement of Owner's Equity
For the Month Ended May 31, 20X6

Joe Davidson, Capital 5/1/X6	$29,000
Add: Net Income	4,800
	33,800
Less: Withdrawals	2,800
Joe Davidson, Capital 5/31/X6	$31,000

Joe's Adventures Unlimited
Balance Sheet
May 31, 20X6

ASSETS		LIABILITIES	
Cash	$ 101,450	Accounts Payable	$ 5,000
Accounts Receivable	1,750	Notes Payable	125,000
Supplies	1,800	Total Liabilities	130,000
Equipment	26,000		
Land	30,000	OWNER'S EQUITY	
		Joe Davidson, Capital	31,000
		Total Liabilities and	
Total Assets	$161,000	Owner's Equity	$161,000

Chapter 3—The Adjusting Process

CHAPTER OVERVIEW

Chapter Three extends the discussion begun in Chapter Two concerning the recording of business transactions using debit and credit analysis. Therefore you should feel comfortable with the debit and credit rules when you begin this chapter. The learning objectives for Chapter 3 are to:

1. Distinguish accrual accounting from cash-basis accounting.
2. Apply the revenue and matching principles.
3. Make adjusting entries.
4. Prepare an adjusted trial balance.
5. Prepare the financial statements from the adjusted trial balance.

Appendix to Chapter 3: Alternative Treatment of Prepaid Expenses and Unearned Revenues

CHAPTER REVIEW

Objective 1 - Distinguish accrual accounting from cash-basis accounting.

There are two methods used to do accounting:

- **Cash-basis accounting**: A business records revenues only when cash is received and expenses only when cash is paid.
- **Accrual accounting:** A business records revenues as they are earned and expenses as they are incurred. This means that with respect to the recognition of revenue under accrual accounting, the exchange of cash is irrelevant. Revenues are considered earned when services have been performed or merchandise is sold because the provider of the services or merchandise has a legal right to receive payment. Expenses are considered incurred when something has been used such as merchandise, services, or assets.

GAAP requires that businesses use accrual accounting so that financial statements will not be misleading. Financial statements would understate revenue if they did not include all revenues earned during the accounting period and would understate expenses if they did not include all expenses incurred during the accounting period.

Accountants prepare financial statements at specific intervals called accounting periods. The basic interval is a year, and nearly all businesses prepare annual financial statements. Usually, however, businesses need financial statements more frequently, at quarterly or monthly intervals. Statements prepared at intervals other than the one-year interval are called **interim statements**.

Whether financial statements are prepared on an annual basis or on an interim basis, they are prepared at the end of each accounting period. The cutoff date is the last day of the time interval for which financial statements are prepared. All transactions that occur up to the cutoff date should be included in the accounts. Thus, if financial statements are prepared for January, all transactions occurring on or before January 31 should be recorded.

Objective 2 - Apply the revenue and matching principles.

The **revenue principle** guides the accountant on 1) when to record revenue and 2) the amount of revenue to record. Revenue is recorded when it is earned; that is, when a business has delivered goods to the customer or provided a service to the customer. The amount of revenue to record is generally the cash value of the goods delivered or the services performed. When revenue is recorded, we would say that we are recognizing the revenue. This accounting language means that the revenue will appear on the income statement for the current accounting period.

The **matching principle** guides the accountant on when to record or recognize expenses. The objectives of the matching principle are 1) to identify the expenses that have been incurred in an accounting period; 2) to determine the amount of the expenses and 3) to match them against revenues earned during the same period. There is a natural relationship between revenues and some types of expenses. For example, if a business pays its salespeople commissions based on amounts sold, there is a direct relationship between sales revenue and commission expense. Other expenses, such as rent and utilities, do not have such an obvious relationship with revenues. However, we recognize that a business must pay the rent and the utility bill to operate the business. So, we typically assign these types of expenses to the accounting period (a month, quarter or year) in which the rent or utilities were used. When expenses are recognized, it means that they will appear on the income statement of the current accounting period, and subtracted from revenues to determine net income.

The **time-period concept** interacts with the revenue and the matching principles. It states that accounting information must be reported at regular intervals, which we refer to as accounting periods, and that income must be measured accurately each period.

Objective 3 - Make adjusting entries.

In order to accurately measure all of the revenues that have been earned and all of the expenses that have been incurred, accountants must make adjusting entries at the end of each accounting period. The purpose of adjusting entries is to obtain an accurate measure of the net income (loss) for the accounting period by bringing certain asset, liability, revenue, and expense accounts up to date prior to the preparation of financial statements. Adjusting entries also enable accountants to properly record the effect of transactions that span more than one accounting period. End-of-period processing begins with the preparation of a trial balance (from Chapter 2), which is sometimes referred to as an unadjusted trial balance. There are two broad categories of adjusting entries: deferrals and accruals. **Deferrals** can refer to deferred expenses or deferred revenues. In either case, with deferrals, the cash transaction occurs first, and the recognition of the expense or revenue is deferred to a later time when it is determined that the expense has been incurred or the revenue has been earned. **Accruals** can refer to accrued expenses or accrued revenues. In either case, with an accrual, the recognition of the expense or revenue occurs first when it is determined that the expense has been incurred and the revenue has been earned, and the cash transaction occurs later.

Adjusting entries fall into five categories:

1) **Prepaid expenses (prepaid assets)** refer to deferred expenses that are paid in advance. It is important to understand that at the time prepaid expenses are acquired, they are first recorded as assets because the future benefits are expected to extend beyond the present accounting period, and they become expenses later when they are used or have expired, thus, the term prepaid expenses.

For example, if on December 31 the business pays three months rent in advance in the amount of $3,000 ($1,000 per month for January, February, and March), then on December 31 the business will record Prepaid Rent (asset) of $3,000. None of the $3,000 payment is an expense for the month of December because the payment benefits future periods, specifically January, February, and March of the following year. At the end of each subsequent month, Rent Expense of $1,000 will be recorded as one-third of the Prepaid Rent expires.

Date	Accounts	Debit	Credit
Dec 31	Prepaid Rent	3,000	
	Cash		3,000
	Paid three months rent in advance		
Jan. 31	Rent Expense	1,000	
	Prepaid Rent		1,000
	To adjust for expired rent		
Feb. 28	Rent Expense	1,000	
	Prepaid Rent		1,000
	To adjust for expired rent		
Mar. 31	Rent Expense	1,000	
	Prepaid Rent		1,000
	To adjust for expired rent		

Prepaid Rent

12/31	3,000	Adj. 1/31	1,000
Bal.1/31	2,000	Adj. 2/28	1,000
Bal.2/28	1,000	Adj. 3/31	1,000
Bal. 3/31	0		

Balance Sheet

Rent Expense

Adj. 1/31	1,000	
Adj. 2/28	1,000	
Adj. 3/31	1,000	

Income Statement

Keep in mind, the amount of the adjusting entry for prepaid expenses represents the amount of expense recognized on the income statement and will always reflect the portion of the prepaid asset that has expired or has been used up. Thus, the accountant takes a portion of the cost of the asset and shifts it off of the balance sheet and onto the income statement as expense because the asset no longer has future benefit because it has expired or has been used. Other examples of prepaid expenses are supplies, prepaid insurance, and sometimes advertising fees may be paid for in advance. The adjusting entry for a prepaid expense always credits (decreases) the asset account and debits (increases) an expense account.

2) **Depreciation** is another deferred expense that results from the decline in usefulness over time related to long-lived, or plant assets. Plant assets are distinguished from other prepaid items due to the fact that plant assets are useful for longer periods of time. Examples of plant assets include buildings, office equipment, and office furniture. Compare these to the prepaid expenses described above such as supplies, rent, insurance and advertising which are usually used up or expire within one year. Buildings, office equipment and office furniture usually remain useful to a business for several years. Land is the only plant asset that does not depreciate because land does not decline in usefulness over time.

In an accounting context, depreciation does not refer to the decline in market value of an asset, but rather the decline in usefulness to the business. When making the adjusting entry for depreciation, the accountant systematically allocates a portion of the asset's cost as an expense over the asset's estimated useful life. In essence, the accountant is shifting a portion of the cost of the asset off of the balance sheet and onto the income statement as depreciation expense.

How we record depreciation is also different from the way in which we account for other prepaid expenses because the reduction in the usefulness of plant assets is not reflected in the specific plant asset account. The portion of the cost of the asset that is recognized as depreciation is recorded in a contra account called Accumulated Depreciation. Using the Accumulated Depreciation account allows the accountant to record the reduction in usefulness of the asset without changing the historical cost of the asset. A **contra accounts** has two unique characteristics:

1.) It always has a companion account.
2.) The normal balance of a contra account is opposite from the normal balance of its companion account.

For accumulated depreciation, the companion account is a plant asset account. For example, the plant asset account Building would have a contra account titled Accumulated Depreciation—Building. The plant asset account holds the original cost of the asset and has a normal debit balance. The contra account, Accumulated Depreciation, holds the portion of the cost of the asset that has been depreciated and has a normal credit balance. The difference between these two amounts is called the asset's **book value**. The adjusting entry for depreciation always debits (increases) the depreciation expense account and credits (increases) the Accumulated Depreciation account. The different methods of determining how much depreciation expense is recognized will be discussed in a later chapter. Let's look at an example, where Travis's Travel Center owns a building that cost $100,000 and has an estimated useful life of 20 years. This means that Travis is going to expense the cost of this building over a 20-year period. Let's take a look at the first three years:

Building	Accumulated Depreciation--Building	
100,000 (cost)	5,000 Yr 1 Adj.	Balance Sheet
	5,000 Yr. 2 Adj.	
	5,000 Yr. 3 Adj.	
	15,000 Bal.	

Depreciation Expense --Building		Income Statement
Adj. Yr. 1 5,000		
Adj. Yr. 2 5,000		
Adj. Yr. 3 5,000		

Take note of the following:

> As the Building is depreciated, the original cost of the asset is not affected.
> Each year the balance in the Accumulated Depreciation account increases by the amount of depreciation expense that is recognized each year. At the end of the third year, the balance in the Accumulated Depreciation account is $15,000. The balance in the Accumulated Depreciation account is subtracted from the cost in the Building account to determine the asset's book value of $85,000 or ($100,000 - $15,000). The book value represents the portion of the cost of the asset that has not been depreciated and is the amount reported on the balance sheet. See Exhibit 3-5 for the proper presentation of plant assets and their related accumulated depreciation accounts on the balance sheet.
> The amount of depreciation expense each year is determined by taking the cost of the asset, $100,000 and dividing it by the 20 year estimated useful life.

3) An **accrued expense** is an expense that a business has incurred but has not yet paid. Accrued expenses always create liabilities. Remember all liability accounts represent amounts owed in the future. A business's most common accrued expense is salary expense for employees. If you have worked a summer job, then you know that there may be an interval of several days or even a week between the end of your pay period and the date that you receive your paycheck. If an accounting period ends during such an interval, then your employer's salary expense would be accrued for the salary that you have earned but have not yet been paid. The adjusting entry for an accrued expense always debits (increases) an expense account and credits (increases) a liability account. Other examples of accrued expenses are interest and sales commissions.

4) **Accrued revenues** have been earned, but payment in cash has not been collected. For example, Bob Bush's Appliance Repair completed $75 of repairs on a VCR on January 28, the last business day of the month, but did not receive payment until February 3. The adjusting entry for accrued revenue of $75 would be recorded on January 31 because the service was performed in the month of January. The adjusting entry is recorded for January because the revenue was earned in the accounting period in which the service was performed. The adjusting entry for accrued revenue always debits (increases) a receivable account and credits (increases) a revenue account. Another example of an accrued revenue is interest revenue.

5) **Unearned revenues** are deferred revenues that result when cash is received from a customer before work is performed. Suppose that on March 15 you pay $80 for two tickets to a concert scheduled for April 7. The concert hall will not earn the $80 until April 7. Therefore, on March 15, the concert hall will debit (increase) Cash and credit (increase) Unearned Revenue. Unearned revenue is a liability account that indicates that the concert hall now owes the concert to the ticket holders. In April, when the concert occurs, the concert hall earns the revenue and will debit Unearned Revenue and credit Revenue. Since adjusting entries are recorded on the last day of the accounting period prior to the preparation of the financial statements, even though the concert hall officially earns the revenue on April 7, it is not recorded in the accounting records until the end of the month along with all the other adjusting entries. The adjusting entry to recognize unearned revenue that has been earned will always debit (decrease) the unearned revenue account and credit (increase) a revenue account.

Date	Accounts	Debit	Credit
Mar 15	Cash	80	
	Unearned Revenue		80
	Collected revenue in advance		
Apr. 30	Unearned Revenue	80	
	Ticket Revenue		80
	To adjust for earned ticket revenue		

Unearned Revenue

	3/15 80
Adj. 4/30 80	
	4/30 Bal. 0

Balance Sheet

Ticket Revenue

	Adj. 4/30 80

Income Statement

Note:
- ➤ Each type of adjusting entry affects at least one income statement account and at least one balance sheet account.
- ➤ Adjusting entries never affect the Cash account. Adjusting entries are noncash transactions required by accrual accounting.

Helpful Hint: See Exhibit 3-8 for a summary of adjusting entries.

Objective 4 - Prepare an adjusted trial balance.

The general sequence for preparing an adjusted trial balance is:

1. **Record** business transactions in the journal as they occur. (Chapter 2)
2. **Post** transactions from the journal to the ledger. (Chapter 2)
3. **Prepare** an unadjusted trial balance. (Chapter 2)
4. **Record** adjusting entries in the journal at the end of the accounting period. (Chapter 3)
5. **Post** adjusting entries from the journal to the ledger. (Chapter 3)
6. **Prepare** the adjusted trial balance and the financial statements. (Chapter 3)

Helpful Hint: Study Exhibits 3-9 through 3-13 in your text carefully to become familiar with the process that brings you to the adjusted trial balance and the preparation of the financial statements.

Objective 5 - Prepare the financial statements from the adjusted trial balance.

The **adjusted trial balance** provides the data needed to prepare the financial statements. The financial statements should always be prepared in the following order:

1. Income Statement
2. Statement of Owner's Equity
3. Balance Sheet

The reason for this order is quite simple. The income statement computes the amount of net income. Net income is needed for the statement of owner's equity. The statement of owner's equity computes the amount of ending capital. Ending capital is needed for the balance sheet. Exhibits 3-11, 3-12 and 3-13 in your text illustrate the flow of data from the income statement to the statement of owner's equity to the balance sheet.

The income statement starts with revenues for the period and subtracts total expenses for the period. A positive result is net income; a negative result is net loss.

The statement of owner's equity starts with the amount of capital at the beginning of the period, adds any owner investments for the period, adds net income or subtracts net loss, and subtracts withdrawals. The result is the ending capital balance.

The balance sheet uses the asset and liability balances from the adjusted trial balance and the capital balance from the statement of owner's equity.

Note that none of the financial statements will balance back to the total debits and total credits on the adjusted trial balance. This is because the financial statements group accounts differently from the debit and credit totals listed on the adjusted trial balance. For example, the new balance for Capital on the balance sheet is a summary of the beginning Capital balance, any investments made by the owner during the period, the revenue and expense accounts used to obtain net income, and owner's withdrawals during the period.

Helpful Hints: What if the balance sheet does not balance?

1. Make sure that the balance sheet contains all asset and liability accounts with the correct balances. Check your math.
2. Be sure that you correctly transferred ending capital from the statement of owner's equity to the owner's equity section of the balance sheet.
3. Check to be sure that the statement of owner's equity is correct.
4. Check the income statement to be sure that all revenue and expense accounts have been recorded at the correct amounts. Check your math.

Objective A1 - Account for a prepaid expense recorded initially as an expense.

An alternative treatment for recording prepaid expenses into asset accounts (Prepaid Insurance, Supplies, Prepaid Rent, etc.) is to record them initially into an expense account (Insurance Expense, Supplies Expense, Rent Expense, etc.) If the accountant initially recorded the prepaid expense into an expense account rather than an asset account, the adjusting entry will reduce the expense account by the amount of **unexpired** insurance and create a prepaid insurance (asset) account. As an example, assume the company pays $2,400 for a one-year insurance policy on March 1. If the payment is recorded initially as an expense, the entry is

Mar. 1	Insurance Expense	2,400	
	Cash		2,400
	Purchased a one-year insurance policy		

Assuming the accounts are adjusted on December 31, the adjusting entry is

Dec. 31	Prepaid Insurance	400	
	Insurance Expense		400
	To adjust for unexpired insurance		

After the adjusting entry is posted, the accounts would appear as follows:

Insurance Expense					Prepaid Insurance			
3/1	2,400	Adj. 12/31	400		Adj. 12/31	400		
Balance	2,000				Balance	400		

The $2,000 balance in the Insurance Expense account will appear on the Income Statement, while the $400 balance in Prepaid Insurance will be listed in the asset section of the Balance Sheet. Notice the adjusting entry still affects one income statement and one balance sheet account.

Objective A2 - Account for an unearned (deferred) revenue recorded initially as a revenue.

An alternative treatment for recording unearned (deferred) revenue into a liability account (Unearned Revenue) is to record it as revenue (Fees Earned) when received. If the accountant records the unearned revenue into a revenue account when received, the adjusting entry will reduce the revenue account by the amount of unearned revenue for the period and create an unearned revenue account. As an example, assume a delivery service company receives $50,000 on December 30 for packages to be delivered on December 31 and January 2 and 3. As of the close of business on December 31, the company has earned $45,000 for packages delivered that day. If the $50,000 is recorded initially as revenue, the entry is

Dec. 30	Cash	50,000	
	Fees Earned		50,000
	Collected revenue in advance		

Assuming the accounts are adjusted on December 31, the adjusting entry is

Dec. 31   Fees Earned   5,000
                Unearned Revenue   5,000
                To adjust for unearned fees

After the adjusting entry is posted, the accounts appear as follows:

Fees Earned			Unearned Fees	
Adj. 12/31 5,000	50,000	12/30		Adj. 12/31 5,000
	45,000	Balance	Balance	5,000

The $5,000 balance in Unearned Fees would be listed in the liability section of the Balance Sheet while the $45,000 balance in Fees Earned would appear on the Income Statement.

TEST YOURSELF

All the self-testing materials in this chapter focus on information and procedures that your instructor is likely to test in quizzes and examinations. Those questions followed by an * refer to information contained in the Appendix to the chapter.

I. Matching   *Match each numbered term with its lettered definition.*

_C_ 1. Contra asset
_G_ 2. Matching principle
_A_ 3. Prepaid expenses
_I_ 4. Unearned revenue
_D_ 5. Depreciation
_E_ 6. Plant asset
_F_ 7. Revenue principle
_N_ 8. Book value

_L_ 9. Deferrals
_K_ 10. Accruals
_M_ 11. Accumulated depreciation
_O_ 12. Adjusting entries
_B_ 13. Accrued expenses
_H_ 14. Liquidation
_I_ 15. Accrued revenues
_P_ 16. Cash-basis accounting

A. A category of assets that typically expire or are used up in the near future.

B. A liability created when a business collects cash from customers in advance of providing services for the customer.

C. A type of asset account with a normal credit balance and a companion account.

D. Expense associated with spreading (allocating) the cost of a plant asset over its useful life.

E. Long-lived assets, such as land, buildings, and equipment that are used in the operations of the business.

F. The basis for recording revenues that tells accountants when to record revenues and the amount of revenue to record.

G. The guidelines for recording expenses that direct accountants to identify all expenses incurred during the period, to measure the expenses, and to match them against the revenues earned during that same period.

H. A process of discontinuing operations and going out of business.

I. Revenues that have been earned but not recorded and paid.

J. Recorded at the end of the accounting period that updates assets, liabilities, revenues and expenses.

K. A collective term for accrued expenses and accrued revenues.

L. Expenses that have been incurred but not yet recorded.

M. A balance sheet account that is credited when adjusting for depreciation.

N. The difference between a plant asset account balance and its companion account balance.

O. A collective term for prepaid expenses and unearned revenues.

P. Accounting that records transactions only when cash is received or paid.

II. Multiple Choice   *Circle the best answer.*

1. An accountant who does not recognize the impact of a business event as it occurs is probably using:

    A. accrual accounting.
    B. cash-basis accounting.
    C. income tax accounting.
    D. actual-basis accounting.

2. An example of accrual accounting is:

    A. recording the purchase of land for cash
    B. recording utility expense when the bill is paid
    C. recording revenue when merchandise is sold on account
    D. recording salary expense when wages are paid

3. Which of the following is considered an adjusting entry category?

    A. Accrued expenses
    B. Accrued revenues
    C. Depreciation
    D. All of the above

4. All of the following have normal credit balances <u>except</u>:

    A. Accumulated Depreciation.
    B. Accounts Receivable.
    C. Unearned Rent.
    D. Wages Payable.

5. The first financial statement prepared from the adjusted trial balance is the:

    A. income statement.
    B. balance sheet.
    C. statement of owner's equity.
    D. order does not matter.

6. Which of the following statements regarding the link between the financial statements is correct?

    A. Net income from the income statement goes to the balance sheet.
    B. Owner's equity from the balance sheet goes to the statement of owner's equity.
    C. Net income from the balance sheet goes to the income statement.
    D. Owner's equity from the statement of owner's equity goes to the balance sheet.

7. Bell Co. paid one year's rent on January 1 and debited Prepaid Rent for $14,400. On January 31, Bell should:

    A. credit Prepaid Rent for $13,200.
    B. debit Rent Expense for $1,200.
    C. debit Rent Expense for $13,200.
    D. credit Cash for $14,400.

8. A company has a beginning balance in Supplies $4,100. It purchases $4,200 of supplies during the period and uses $3,800 of supplies. If the accountant does not make an adjusting entry for supplies at the end of the period, then:

    A. assets will be understated by $4,500.
    B. assets will be overstated by $3,800.
    C. expenses will be overstated by $3,800.
    D. expenses will be understated by $4,500.

9. During September, a company received $10,000 cash for services rendered. In September, the company also performed $4,000 of services on account and received $3,000 cash in advance for services to be performed in October. The amount of revenue to be included on the September income statement is:

A. $10,000.
B. $14,000.
C. $13,000.
D. $17,000

10. A company correctly made an adjusting entry on December 31, 20X6 and credited Prepaid Insurance for $2,800. During 20X6 it paid $5,500 for insurance. The December 31, 20X6 balance in Prepaid Insurance was $4,000. What was the balance in the Prepaid Insurance account on January 1, 20X6?

A. $6,800
B. $1,300
C. $9,500
D. $3,300

11. Bell Co. paid one year's rent on January 1 and debited Rent Expense for $14,400. On January 31, Bell should:

A. credit Prepaid Rent for $13,200.
B. debit Rent Expense for $13,200.
C. debit Prepaid Rent for $1,200.
D. credit Rent Expense for $13,200.

12. On December 1, 20X6 Fees Earned was credited for $12,000, representing six months of revenue for the period December 1, 20X6 to June 1, 20X7. On December 31, 20X6 the company should:

A. credit Fees Earned for $10,000
B. debit Unearned Fees for $10,000
C. debit Fees Earned for $10,000
D. credit Unearned Fees for $2,000

III. Completion   *Complete each of the following statements.*

1. _____ accounting recognizes revenue when it is earned and expenses when they are incurred.
2. Adjusting entries categories include _____ , _____ , _____ , _____ , and _____ .
3. The end-of-period process of updating the accounts is called the _____ .
4. Accumulated depreciation is an example of a(n) _____ account.
5. An amount that has been earned but not yet received in cash is a(n) _____ .
6. The revenue principle provides guidance to accountants as to _____ and _____ .
7. The objectives of the matching principle are: _____ , _____ and _____ .
8. Financial statements should be prepared in the following order: 1) _____ , 2) _____ , and 3) _____ .
9. The basic time period for financial statements is _____ , while statements prepared at other times and for shorter intervals of time are called _____ .
10. What is the difference between prepaid expense and unearned revenue? _____ .

IV. Daily Exercises

1. Review the information provided in Multiple Choice question #9, but assume the bookkeeper was following cash-basis accounting. What amount would appear on the income statement as revenue for the month of September?

2. List the following in correct sequence: trial balance, statement of owner's equity, record adjusting entries, income statement, adjusted trial balance, balance sheet, post the adjustments.

     a. _____

     b. _____

     c. _____

     d. _____

     e. _____

     f. _____

     g. _____

3. Record the following transactions in the space provided. The company has a five-day workweek.

Friday, December 27   Paid the weekly wages, $4,000
Tuesday, December 31 Adjusted for two days accrued wages
Friday, January 3   Paid the weekly wages, $4,000

Date:	Accounts	Debit	Credit

4. Classify each of the following as (a) prepaid expense, (b) accrued expense, (c) unearned revenue or (d) accrued revenue.

    1. _____ AJ's Advertising Agency performed advertising design services that have not yet been recorded and collected.

    2. _____ A customer paid $5,000 in advance for advertising design services to be performed.

    3. _____ AJ's Advertising Agency purchased $300 of office supplies.

    4. _____ Fly With Us Airlines sold airline tickets for flights that will take place next month, $3,000.

    5. _____ AJ's Advertising Agency's employees have not yet been paid for hours worked.

    6. _____ Fly With US Airlines recently purchased a two-year insurance policy.

V. Exercises

1. The accounting records of Jose's Southwestern Interiors include the following unadjusted normal balances on July 31:

Accounts Receivable	$ 2,000
Supplies	525
Salary Payable	0
Unearned Revenue	1,500
Service Revenue	8,000
Salary Expense	1,575
Supplies Expense	0
Depreciation Expense	0
Accumulated Depreciation	800

The following information is available for the July 31 adjusting entries:

a. Supplies on hand, $300
b. Salaries owed to employees, $275
c. Service revenue earned but not billed, $1,100
d. Services performed which had been paid for in advance, $125
e. Depreciation, $400

Required:

1. Open the T-accounts.
2. Record the adjustments directly to the T-accounts. (Key each entry by letter.)
3. Compute the adjusted balance for each account.

Accounts Receivable	Supplies	Salary Payable

Unearned Revenue	Service Revenue	Salary Expense

Supplies Expense	Depreciation Expense	Accumulated Depreciation

2. The balance sheets for Brown's Photo Studio had the following balances after adjusting entries: (The ending balances that appear on the previous year's balance sheet become the beginning balances for the current year.)

	20X7	20X8
Supplies	$1,700	$1,075
Prepaid rent	2,400	800
Interest payable	1,100	200
Unearned revenue	3,150	4,100

Cash payments and receipts for 20X8 included

Payments for supplies	$2,500
Payments for rent	3,000
Payments of interest	1,400
Receipts from customers	81,000

How much supplies expense, rent expense, interest expense, and revenue were reported on the 20X8 income statement?

Supplies Expense _____

Rent Expense _____

Interest Expense _____

Revenue _____

3. Antonio Carlini, owner of Treat Your Feet, a shoe repair shop, began the year with capital of $25,000. During the year, the owner invested $10,000 cash in his business and transferred to the business repair equipment valued at $23,500. During the year the business earned $74,000 and the owner withdrew $3,000 each month for his personal use. Prepare a statement of owner's equity for Treat Your Feet for the year ended December 31, 20X7.

Statement of Owner's Equity

VI. Beyond the Numbers

If a business is using cash-basis accounting, what is the amount listed on the Balance Sheet for Accounts Receivable and on the Income Statement for Revenue, assuming clients have been billed $118,500 during the year and sent in payments totaling $93,000 by the end of the year?

_____

_____

_____

VII. Demonstration Problems

Demonstration Problem #1

Family Movie Center is in the business of renting VHS movies and DVD's. The trial balance for Family Movie Center at December 31, 20X9 and the data needed for year-end adjustments are as follows:

Family Movie Center
Trial Balance
December 31, 20X9

Cash	$19,415	
Accounts Receivable	90	
Prepaid Rent	1,200	
Supplies	400	
Movie Library	24,000	
Accumulated Depreciation—Movie Library		$12,000
Furniture	9,500	
Accumulated Depreciation—Furniture		3,800
Accounts Payable		1,450
Salary Payable		
Unearned Movie Rental Revenue		1,300
Jayne Gold, Capital		22,150
Jayne Gold, Withdrawals	3,000	
Movie Rental Revenue		43,365
Salary Expense	14,400	
Rent Expense	6,600	
Utilities Expense	2,800	
Depreciation Expense—Movie Library		
Depreciation Expense—Furniture		
Advertising Expense	2,660	
Supplies Expense		
Total	$84,065	$84,065

Adjustment data:

   a. Depreciation for the year:
- on the movie library, $6,000
- on the furniture, $1,900

   b. Accrued salary expense at December 31, $120.

   c. Prepaid rent expired, $600.

   d. Unearned movie rental revenues which remain unearned as of December 31, $625.

   e. Supplies on hand at December 31, $230

   f. Accrued advertising expense at December 31, $115. (Credit Accounts Payable)

Required:

1. Prepare T-accounts for those accounts listed on the trial balance that are affected by the adjusting entries. First, enter the December 31 unadjusted balances, then prepare and post the adjusting journal entries in the accounts. Key adjustment amounts by letter as shown in the text.
2. Using the form provided, enter the adjusting entries in the Adjustment columns, and prepare an adjusted trial balance, as shown in exhibit 3-10 of the text. Be sure that each account balance affected by an adjusting entry agrees with the adjusted T-account balances as calculated in Requirement 1.

Requirement 1 (T-accounts; adjusting journal entries; posting to ledger)

a.

Date	Accounts	PR	Debit	Credit
Dec. 31				

b.

Date	Accounts	PR	Debit	Credit
Dec. 31				

c.

Date	Accounts	PR	Debit	Credit
Dec. 31				

d.

Date	Accounts	PR	Debit	Credit
Dec. 31				

e.

Date	Accounts	PR	Debit	Credit
Dec. 31				

f.

Date	Accounts	PR	Debit	Credit
Dec. 31				

Requirement 2 (Adjusted trial balance)

Family Movie Center
Preparation of Adjusted Trial Balance
December 31, 20X9

Accounts	Trial Balance Debit	Trial Balance Credit	Adjustments Debit	Adjustments Credit	Adjusted Trial Balance Debit	Adjusted Trial Balance Credit
Cash	$19,415					
Accounts Receivable	90					
Prepaid Rent	1,200					
Supplies	400					
Movie library	24,000					
Accumulated Depreciation—Movie Library		$12,000				
Furniture	9,500					
Accumulated Depreciation—Furniture		3,800				
Accounts Payable		1,450				
Salary Payable						
Unearned Movie Rental Revenue		1,300				
Jayne Gold, Capital		22,150				
Jayne Gold, Withdrawals	3,000					
Movie Rental Revenue		43,365				
Salary Expense	14,400					
Rent Expense	6,600					
Utilities Expense	2,800					
Depreciation Expense—Movie Library						
Depreciation Expense— Furniture						
Advertising Expense	2,660					
Supplies Expense						
	$84,065	$84,065				

Demonstration Problem #2

Refer to the adjusted trial balance in Demonstration Problem #1 and complete the following:

1. An income statement
2. A statement of owner's equity
3. A balance sheet

79

Income Statement

Statement of Owner's Equity

Balance Sheet

SOLUTIONS

I. Matching

1. C	5. D	9. O	13. L
2. G	6. E	10. K	14. H
3. A	7. F	11. M	15. I
4. B	8. N	12. J	16. P

II. Multiple Choice

1. B   In cash-basis accounting the accountant does not record a transaction until cash is received or paid. In accrual accounting, the accountant records transactions when they occur. Income tax accounting is appropriate for the preparation of income tax returns not financial statements and there is no such thing as actual-basis accounting.

2. C   Recording revenue when the merchandise is sold is the only event listed that does not involve the receipt or payment of cash. Accordingly, it would not be recorded using cash-basis accounting and is the only item that would be recorded under accrual-basis accounting.

3. D   Adjusting entries assign revenues to the period in which they are earned and expenses to the period in which they are incurred. The five categories of adjusting entries are 1) prepaid expenses, 2) depreciation, 3) accrued expenses, 4) accrued revenues, and 5) unearned revenues

4. B   Accounts Receivable is an asset account with a normal debit balance. Accumulated Depreciation is a contra-asset account with a normal credit balance. Unearned Rent and Wages Payable are both liability accounts with normal credit balances.

5. A   Since net income is required to prepare the statement of owner's equity, the income statement should be prepared first.

6. D   The correct sequence is:
    1) Net income from the income statement goes to the statement of owner's equity.
    2) The ending Owner's equity from the statement of owner's equity goes to the balance sheet.

7. B   One month of rent will expire during January. Therefore an adjusting entry to expense for 1/12 x $14,400, or $1,200 will be recorded with the following journal entry:

Rent Expense	1,200	
Prepaid Rent		1,200

8. B   The adjusting entry that should be made at the end of the period is:

Supplies Expense	3,800	
Supplies		3,800

Failure to credit the Supplies account for $3,800 means that assets will be overstated by $3,800.

9.   B   With accrual accounting, total revenues in September will be $10,000 of revenues received in cash plus $4,000 of revenues that have been billed but not received. The $3,000 cash received for services to be performed in October represent unearned revenues that will sit on the balance sheet as a liability until the services are rendered in October.

10.   B   This problem requires you to work backward to find the solution.

Adjusted balance (given)	$4,000
Adjustment (given)	2,800
Unadjusted balance	$6,800

The unadjusted trial balance amount of $6,800 consists of the beginning balance and purchases made during the year. Since the purchases were $5,500 (given), the beginning balance must have been $1,300.

11.   D   Because the entire prepayment was placed in an expense account, and at the end of January, only one month of the rent had expired, the adjusting entry must adjust the expense account for the amount of **unexpired** rent and place that amount into a Prepaid Rent account on the balance sheet:

Prepaid Rent	13,200	
Rent Expense		13,200

> Study Tip: When prepaid expenses are initially recorded into expense accounts, the adjusting entry will credit (reduce) the expense account and debit (increase) the asset account.

12.   C   Because the $12,000 was placed into a revenue account on December 1, 20X6 the following adjusting entry is required on December 31, 20X6 to adjust the revenue account for the amount of **unearned** revenue and place that amount into the Unearned Fees account on the balance sheet:

Fees Earned	10,000	
Unearned Fees		10,000

> Study Tip: When unearned revenue is initially recorded into a revenue account, the adjusting entry will debit (reduce) the revenue account and credit (increase) a liability (unearned) account.

III. Completion

1. Accrual
2. prepaid expenses, depreciation, accrued expenses, unearned revenue, accrued revenues (order not important)
3. adjusting the accounts
4. contra asset (A contra account has two distinguishing characteristics: (1) it always has a companion account, and (2) its normal balance is opposite that of the companion account. Accumulated depreciation's companion account is property, plant and equipment.)
5. accrued revenue
6. when to record revenue, the amount of revenue to record
7. to identify expenses which have been incurred, to measure the expenses, to match the expenses with revenues earned during the same time period
8. income statement, statement of owner's equity, balance sheet (order is important)
9. one year, interim statements
10. Prepaid expense is an asset of the business that become an expense when the asset has expired or been used. Unearned revenue represents a liability for the business to perform services or deliver goods in the future and become revenue when it is earned.

IV. Daily Exercises

1. $13,000 - representing all the cash received during September.
2.
    1. trial balance
    2. record adjusting entries
    3. post adjusting entries
    4. adjusted trial balance
    5. income statement
    6. statement of owner's equity
    7. balance sheet

3.

Dec. 27	Wages Expense	4,000	
	Cash		4,000
Dec. 31	Wages Expense	1,600	
	Wages Payable		1,600
	($4,000/5 = $800/ day x 2 days)		
Jan. 3	Wages Expense	2,400	
	($4,000/5 = $800/day x 3 days)		
	Wages Payable	1,600	
	Cash		4,000

On Jan. 3, note that $1,600 of the week's wages was already recorded (accrued) on Dec. 31; therefore only $2,400 of the weekly payroll remains an expense on Jan. 3.

4.
1. (d) Accrued revenue results when services have been performed but not yet collected.
2. (c) Unearned revenue results because the cash was collected in advance of the design services being performed.
3. (a) Supplies represent a prepaid expense, an asset, that will become an expense once the supplies are used.
4. (c) Selling the tickets has created an obligation for the airline to provide the future transportation services.
5. (b) AJ's Advertising Agency has an accrued expense for the employees' wages. This reflects that the business has incurred the expense because the employees worked, but just have not been paid yet.
6. (a) An insurance policy represents a prepaid expense, an asset, that will be expensed as the policy expires.

V. Exercises

1.

Accounts Receivable	
Bal. 2,000	
(c) 1,100	
Bal. 3,100	

Supplies	
Bal. 525	
	(a) 225
Bal. 300	

Salary Payable	
	(b) 275
	Bal. 275

Unearned Revenue	
	Bal. 1,500
(d) 125	
	Bal. 1,375

Service Revenue	
	Bal. 8,000
	(c) 1,100
	(d) 125
	Bal. 9,225

Salary Expense	
Bal. 1,575	
(b) 275	
Bal. 1,850	

Supplies Expense	
(a) 225	
Bal. 225	

Depreciation Expense	
(e) 400	
Bal. 400	

Accumulated Depreciation	
	Bal. 800
	(e) 400
	Bal. 1,200

2. Remember that Beginning balance + Additions - Reductions = Ending balance

Account analyzed:

Supplies:

		Supplies purchased for cash		Supplies expense		Ending balance
Beginning balance	+		-		=	
$1,700	+	$2,500	-	?	=	$1,075

Supplies expense = $3,125

Prepaid Rent:

Beginning balance	+	Rent paid	-	Rent expense	=	Ending balance
$2,400	+	$,3000	-	?	=	$800

Rent expense = $4,600

Interest Payable:

Beginning balance	+	Interest expense	-	Cash paid for interest	=	Ending balance
$1,100	+	?	-	$1,400	=	$200

Interest expense = $500

Unearned Revenue:

Beginning balance	+	Receipts from customers	-	Revenue earned	=	Ending balance
$3,150	+	$81,000	-	?	=	$4,100

Revenue = $80,050

3.

Treat Your Feet
Statement of Owner's Equity
For the Year Ended December 31, 20X7

Carlini, Capital, 1/1/X7	$25,000
Add: Cash invested	10,000
Equipment transferred	23,500
Net income	74,000
	132,500
Less: Carlini, Withdrawals	36,000
Capital, 12/31/X7	$96,500

VI. Beyond the Numbers

The balance in Accounts Receivable would be zero. Why? Because cash-basis accounting does not record revenue when a client is billed, only when the business receives payment. Therefore, while the business may send bills to clients, they are not recorded as receivables. Since the customers sent in payments totaling $93,000, that would be the amount of revenue reported on the Income Statement for the year.

VII. Demonstration Problems

Demonstration Problem #1 Solved and Explained

Requirement 1 (T-accounts; adjusting entries; posting to ledger)

a.

Depreciation Expense—Movie Library

(a) 6,000	
Bal. 6,000	

Accumulated Depreciation—Movie Library

	Bal. 12,000
	(a) 6,000
	Bal. 18,000

Depreciation Expense—Furniture

(a) 1,900	
Bal. 1,900	

Accumulated Depreciation—Furniture

	Bal. 3,800
	(a) 1,900
	Bal. 5,700

Date	Accounts	PR	Debit	Credit
Dec. 31	Depreciation Expense—Movie Library		6,000	
	Accumulated Depreciation—Movie Library			6,000
	To record depreciation expense on movie library			
	Depreciation Expense—Furniture		1,900	
	Accumulated Depreciation—Furniture			1,900
	To record depreciation expense on furniture			

Explanation of Adjustment (a)

As a long-lived plant asset (such as building, furniture, machinery, equipment) becomes less useful, its cost is systematically transferred from the asset account to a depreciation expense account. Note that the original cost of the asset remains unchanged on the books of Family Movie Center. The reduction in book value of each asset is accomplished by increasing the asset's accumulated depreciation account.

<u>Example:</u> Change in book value of furniture.

Plant Assets	Before Adjustment	Change	After Adjustment
Furniture	$9,500	0	$9,500
Less accumulated depreciation	3,800	+1,900	5,700
Book value	$5,700	-$1,900	$3,800

b.

Salary Expense		Salary Payable	
Bal. 14,400			(b) 120
(b) 120			
Bal. 14,520			Bal. 120

Dec. 31	Salary Expense		120	
	Salary Payable			120
	To accrue salary expense			

Explanation of Adjustment (b)

Amounts owed employees for salary and wages unpaid as of the close of an accounting period must be accrued. The facts indicate that $120 must be accrued to record salary expense and the related liability. As a result, Salary Expense is debited $120 (expenses are increased by debits), and Salary Payable is credited $120 (liabilities are increased by credits).

c.

Rent Expense			Prepaid Rent		
Bal. 6,600			Bal. 1,200	(c)	600
(c) 600					
Bal. 7,200			Bal. 600		

Dec. 31	Rent Expense		600	
	Prepaid Rent			600
	To record rent expense			

Explanation of Adjustment (c)

Family Movie Center must adjust the Prepaid Rent account for the portion of the rent that has expired, $600. Thus, $600 is transferred to the Rent Expense account by crediting the Prepaid Rent account (assets are reduced by credits) and debiting (expenses are recorded as debits) the Rent Expense account. The balance in the Prepaid Rent account represents the amount of prepaid rent still in force.

d.

Movie Rental Revenue			Unearned Movie Rental Revenue		
	Bal. 43,365			Bal. 1,300	
	(d) 675	(d) 675			
	Bal. 44,040		Bal. 625		

Dec. 31	Unearned Movie Rental Revenue		675	
	Movie Rental Revenue			675
	To record revenue collected in advance.			

Explanation of Adjustment (d)

When cash is collected from customers before the agreed-upon product or service is provided, a liability is created. If $675 of the $1,300 of Unearned Movie Rental Revenue remains unearned, then $675 has been earned. The liability account Unearned Rental Revenue should be debited (a liability is reduced by a debit) and Movie Rental Revenue should be credited (a revenue is increased by a credit).

e.

Supplies Expense		
(e)	170	
Bal.	170	

Supplies			
Bal.	400	(e)	170
Bal.	230		

Dec. 31	Supplies Expense		170	
	Supplies			170
	To record supplies expense.			

Explanation of Adjustment (e)

Supplies purchased for business use represent an asset until they are used. The Supplies account must be adjusted periodically to reflect supplies no longer on hand. Supplies of $230 remain on hand at December 31. Since $400 of supplies were on hand initially, it is clear that $170 of supplies have been used up ($400 - $230 = $170). Reduce the Supplies account by crediting it $170 (assets are decreased by credits) and record the $170 supplies expense by debiting Supplies Expense (expenses are increased by debits).

f.

Advertising Expense		
Bal.	2,660	
(f)	115	
Bal.	2,775	

Accounts Payable			
		Bal.	1,450
		(f)	115
		Bal.	1,565

Date	Accounts	PR	Debit	Credit
Dec. 31	Advertising Expense		115	
	Accounts Payable			115
	To record accrued advertising expense.			

Explanation of Adjustment (f)

The rationale for this entry is similar to that for the adjusting entry for accrued salary expense in (b.). Advertising Expense is increased by debiting the account (expenses are recorded by debits) and Accounts Payable is credited (liabilities are recorded by credits) to reflect the amount owed for advertising by Family Movie Center.

Requirement 2 (Adjusted trial balance)

Family Movie Center
Preparation of Adjusted Trial Balance
December 31, 20X9

Accounts	Trial Balance Debit	Trial Balance Credit	Adjustments Debit	Adjustments Credit	Adjusted Trial Balance Debit	Adjusted Trial Balance Credit
Cash	$19,415				$19,415	
Accounts Receivable	90				90	
Prepaid Rent	1,200			(c) 600	600	
Supplies	400			(e) 170	230	
Movie Library	24,000				24,000	
Accumulated depreciation—Movie Library		$12,000		(a) 6,000		$18,000
Furniture	9,500				9,500	
Accumulated Depreciation—Furniture		3,800		(a) 1,900		5,700
Accounts Payable		1,450		(f) 115		1,565
Salary Payable				(b) 120		120
Unearned Movie Rental Revenue		1,300	(d) 675			625
Jayne Gold, Capital		22,150				22,150
Jayne Gold, Withdrawals	3,000				3,000	
Movie Rental Revenue		43,365		(d) 675		44,040
Salary Expense	14,400		(b) 120		14,520	
Rent Expense	6,600		(c) 600		7,200	
Utilities Expense	2,800				2,800	
Depreciation Expense—Movie Library			(a) 6,000		6,000	
Depreciation Expense—Furniture			(a) 1,900		1,900	
Advertising Expense	2,660		(f) 115		2,775	
Supplies Expense			(e) 170		170	
	$84,065	$84,065	$9,580	$9,580	$92,200	$92,200

Demonstration Problem #2 Solved

Requirement 1

Family Movie Center
Income Statement
For the Year Ended December 31, 20X9

Revenues:		
Movie Rental revenue		$44,040
Expenses:		
Salary Expense	14,520	
Rent Expense	7,200	
Utilities Expense	2,800	
Depreciation Expense	7,900	
Advertising Expense	2,775	
Supplies Expense	170	
Total expenses		35,365
Net Income		$ 8,675

Requirement 2

Family Movie Center
Statement of Owner's Equity
For the Year Ended December 31, 20X9

Owner's Equity 1/1/X9	$ 22,150
Add: Net Income	8,675
	30,825
Less: Withdrawals	3,000
Jayne Gold, Capital 12/31/X9	$27,825

Requirement 3

Family Movie Center
Balance Sheet
December 31, 20X9

ASSETS			LIABILITIES	
Cash		$19,415	Accounts Payable	$ 1,565
Accounts Receivable		90	Salary Payable	120
Prepaid Rent		600	Unearned Movie Rental	
Supplies		230	Revenue	625
Movie Rental Library	24,000		Total Liabilities	2,310
Less: Acc. Dep.—Library	18,000	6,000	**OWNER'S EQUITY**	
Furniture	9,500		Jayne Gold, Capital	
Less: Acc. Dep.—Furniture	5,700	3,800	Total Liabilities and	27,825
			Owner's Equity	
Total Assets		$30,135		$30,135

91

Chapter 4—Completing the Accounting Cycle

CHAPTER OVERVIEW

Chapter Four introduces you to the final steps in the accounting cycle. Using the information you learned in the previous three chapters you are now ready to complete the accounting cycle, thereby preparing the financial records for the next accounting period. The learning objectives for this chapter are to

1. Prepare an accounting work sheet.
2. Use the work sheet to complete the accounting cycle.
3. Close the revenue, expense, and withdrawal accounts.
4. Classify assets and liabilities as current or long-term.
5. Use the current ratio and the debt ratio to evaluate a company.

CHAPTER REVIEW

OVERVIEW OF THE ACCOUNTING CYCLE

The **accounting cycle** is the process by which companies produce financial statements for a specific period.

The accounting cycle can be subdivided into two categories:

- Work performed during the period includes:
    1. Starting with the ledger account balances at the beginning of the period.
    2. Analyzing and journalizing daily business transactions as they occur.
    3. Posting journal entries to the accounts in the ledger.

- Work performed at the end of the period includes:
    4. Computing the unadjusted balance in each account at the end of the period.
    5. Entering the unadjusted trial balance on the work sheet, and completing the worksheet.
    6. Using the adjusted trial balance or the full work sheet as a guide, a) record and post adjusting entries, b) prepare financial statements, and c) record and post-closing entries.
    7. Preparing the post-closing trial balance.

Objective 1 - Prepare an accounting work sheet.

A work sheet is an optional tool the accountant often uses to prepare financial statements. It is not part of a formal accounting system. Remember that in Chapter 3 you learned how to prepare an adjusted trial balance. To complete the worksheet you use basically the same steps:

1. Prepare the unadjusted trial balance from the ledger accounts. <u>Make sure the debits equals the credits.</u>
2. Enter the necessary adjustments in the Adjustments column. Use lower case letters to denote each adjustment. <u>Make sure the debits equal the credits.</u>
3. Calculate the adjusted account balances. <u>Make sure the debits equal the credits.</u>

The work sheet is completed using the following steps:

1. Extend only the adjusted revenue and expense account balances to the Income Statement columns, which are located to the right of the Adjusted Trial Balance columns. **The debits will not equal the credits.** The difference between the two columns will be the total net income (loss) for the period.
2. Extend the adjusted asset, liability, and owner's equity (Capital and Withdrawals) account balances to the Balance Sheet columns, which are located to the right of the Income Statement columns. **The debits will not equal the credits.** The difference between the two columns will be the total net income (loss) for the period.
3. Enter net income (loss) as a balancing amount on both the Income Statement and the Balance Sheet columns, and compute the adjusted column totals. **The debits should now equal the credits.**

You should review Exhibits 4-2 through 4-6 in your text to be sure you understand the preparation of the worksheet.

Exhibits 4-2, 4-3, and 4-4 illustrate how to determine the adjusted trial balance using the work sheet. Once the adjusted trial balance has been prepared, Exhibit 4-5 illustrates how the adjusted revenue and expense account balances are transferred to the Income Statement columns and the adjusted asset, liability, and owner's equity account balances are transferred to the Balance Sheet columns. Note that every account from the adjusted trial balance will appear in either the Income Statement columns, or the Balance Sheet columns, but not both. At this point the debit and credit column totals are not equal in either the Income Statement or the Balance Sheet columns.

Exhibit 4-6 illustrates the final step in completing the work sheet, which is to calculate the difference between the debit and credit columns of the Income Statement and the Balance Sheet columns on the worksheet. This difference is the net income (loss) for the period and is entered as a balancing amount at the bottom of the Income Statement and Balance Sheet columns. If the transactions for the period result in net income, then the Income Statement column is debited and the Balance Sheet column is credited. If the result is a net loss, the Income Statement column is credited and the Balance Sheet column is debited. This balancing amount will bring the columns totals into equality meaning the debits will equal the credits.

Helpful Hint: Recall that net income increases owner's equity. On the work sheet, the capital account is recorded in the credit column of the balance sheet, which is consistent with the account's normal balance. Adding net income to the credit column of the balance sheet illustrates the increase in owner's equity that results from net income. Similar logic applies to a net loss, which appears on the work sheet in the debit column of the balance sheet, because a net loss decreases owner's equity, and decreases in owner's equity are recorded with a debit.

Objective 2 - Use the work sheet to complete the accounting cycle.

Once the work sheet has been completed, financial statements must be prepared, adjusting entries must be recorded, and the accounts must be closed.

Exhibit 4-7 in your text illustrates financial statements prepared from a completed work sheet. (Remember that the work sheet is an optional tool, and that the financial statements can be prepared directly from the adjusted trial balance, as you learned in Chapter 3.)

Next, it is necessary to record the adjusting entries. Since the work sheet is not a journal or a ledger, the adjustments entered on the work sheet do not adjust the accounts. Adjusting journal entries must be recorded in the journal and posted to the accounts, as shown in Exhibit 4-8 of your text. Companies often do not record adjusting entries until after the work sheet is completed.

Objective 3 - Close the revenue, expense, and withdrawal accounts.

Closing the accounts refers to the process of preparing certain accounts for the next accounting period. Closing involves journalizing and posting **closing entries** that set the balances of revenues, expenses, and owner's withdrawals to zero. Remember that when the balance sheet is prepared, the owner's equity balance that is carried forward from the statement of owner's equity includes the summary effect of the revenue, expense, and owner's withdrawal accounts. These accounts are referred to as **temporary accounts**—they measure the effect on owner's equity for a single accounting period and are set to zero at the end of each accounting period. This is in contrast to balance sheet accounts: assets, liabilities, and capital accounts, which are **permanent accounts** whose account balance carries forward into the next accounting period.

The closing process uses a special, temporary holding account called **Income Summary**. Turn to Exhibit 4-10 in your text to follow the four steps taken to close the accounts at the end of the accounting period:

1. Close the revenue accounts to the Income Summary account. The revenue accounts are the accounts that appear in the Income Statement credit column of the work sheet. Debit each revenue account for the amount of its balance (to zero it out), and credit Income Summary for the total amount of the revenues (total debits).
2. Close the expense accounts to the Income Summary account. The expense accounts are the accounts that appear in the Income Statement debit column of the work sheet. Credit each expense account for the amount of its balance (to zero it out), and debit Income Summary for the total amount of the expenses (total credits).
3. Calculate a balance in the Income Summary account and close the Income Summary account to the Capital account. Income Summary has no normal balance. It can have either a debit or credit balance.
   - If Income Summary has a credit balance, then the company has generated a net income. To close Income Summary when it has a credit balance, debit it for that amount (to zero it out) and credit the owner's capital account.
   - If Income Summary has a debit balance, then the company has generated a net loss. To close Income Summary when it has a debit balance, credit it for that amount (to zero it out) and debit the owner's capital account.

The amount of this third closing entry should agree with the net income (or loss) reported for the period on the Income Statement. It should also correlate with the balancing amounts for the Income Statement and Balance Sheet columns on the work sheet.

4. Close the Withdrawals account to the owner's capital account. The Withdrawals account is found in the Balance Sheet debit column of the work sheet. To close the owner's withdrawals account, credit it for the amount of its debit balance and debit the Capital account. Note that the Withdrawals account is neither a revenue nor an expense account, and thus is not closed to Income Summary.

Exhibits 4-9 and 4-10 in your text illustrate the closing process. Note that after the closing entries are posted, the balance in the owner's capital account in the ledger should be the same as the amount reported as the ending balance on the statement of owner's equity and the balance sheet.

The accounting cycle ends with the **post-closing trial balance**. It should contain only the ending balances of the permanent, balance sheet accounts, assets, liabilities, and capital. Exhibit 4-11 in your text illustrates a post-closing trial balance. Notice there are no revenue, expense, or withdrawals accounts on the post-closing trial balance. This is because each of these account balances is zero after the closing entries have been posted.

Reversing entries are an optional step in the accounting cycle completed after the post-closing trial balance has been prepared. Reversing entries literally reverse any previous accrual adjusting entries. (Deferrals are not reversed.) Doing so allows the accountant to record a subsequent cash payment (for a previously accrued expense) or cash receipt (for a previously accrued revenue) in a routine manner.

Study Tip: If a business uses reversing entries, you can identify the adjusting entries that need to be reversed by tracing the effect of the adjustment to the balance sheet. If the adjustment increases total assets or total liabilities on the balance sheet, the adjusting entry should be reversed.

Using a work sheet, the complete **accounting cycle** can now be summarized as follows:

1. Analyze the transaction
2. Record and post the journal entry
3. Complete an unadjusted trial balance and enter on worksheet
4. Analyze the adjustments and enter on work sheet
5. Complete the adjusted trial balance columns on the work sheet
6. Complete the work sheet by extending the account balances to the appropriate Income Statement or Balance Sheet columns.
7. Prepare the financial statements
8. Journalize and post the adjusting entries
9. Journalize and post the closing entries
10. Prepare a post-closing trial balance
11. Journalize and post the reversing entries (optional)

Objective 4 - Classify assets and liabilities as current or long term.

Assets and liabilities are classified according to their liquidity. **Liquidity** is a measure of how quickly an item can be converted into cash. The balance sheet lists assets and liabilities in the order of their relative liquidity, with Cash, as the most liquid asset, listed first.

Current assets are those assets expected to be converted into cash, sold, or consumed within a year, or within the business's normal operating cycle if longer than a year. Current assets include: 1) Cash, 2) Accounts Receivable, 3) Notes Receivable, 4) Inventory, and 5) Prepaid Expenses.

Long-term assets are all assets that are not current assets. Long-term assets include plant assets such as: 1) Land, 2) Buildings, and 3) Equipment. It should make sense to you that land, buildings and equipment would be considered long-term assets because these items typically will benefit the business for more than one year, which also supports the concept of depreciation that was discussed in Chapter 3.

Current liabilities are obligations that are due within one year or the normal operating cycle if the cycle is longer than one year. Current liabilities include: 1) Accounts Payable, 2) Notes Payable due within one year, 3) Salary Payable, 4) Unearned Revenue, and 5) Interest Payable.

Long-term liabilities are obligations that are not classified as current and are due in future years. Long-term liabilities include: 1) Notes Payable (the portion due beyond the current year) 2) Bonds Payable, and 3) Mortgages Payable.

Helpful hint: Review Exhibits 4-12 and 4-13 in your text for examples of a classified (detailed) balance sheet. When you prepare a balance sheet from this point forward, it should use the classified presentation.

Objective 5 - Use the current ratio and the debt ratio to evaluate a company.

The primary purpose of accounting is to provide reliable information for decision-making. Lenders need to be able to evaluate a company's financial information to determine whether a borrower has the ability to repay a loan before the loan is actually made. Analyzing ratios of various items drawn from a company's financial statements can help creditors assess the likelihood that a loan can be repaid. Two of the most widely used decision aids in business are the:

1. **Current ratio** measures the ability of a company to pay current liabilities (short-term debt) with current assets.

$$\text{Current ratio} = \frac{\text{Total current assets}}{\text{Total current liabilities}}$$

A strong current ratio typically will be 1.50 or greater indicating that the current assets in the numerator are significantly greater than the current liabilities in the denominator. If a company has a current ratio of 1.60, for example, this means that for every $1.00 of current liabilities, the company has $1.60 in current assets. Since current assets are those assets that can be converted into cash quickly, then it can reasonably be assumed that the company could pay its current liabilities if they all came due immediately. If a company has a current ratio of .80, this means that for every $1.00 of current liabilities, the company has $.80 in current assets. A current ratio of .80 would indicate that the company would not have the ability to pay its current liabilities should they all come due immediately.

2. **Debt ratio** measures how much of a company's total assets it has financed with debt. The debt ratio evaluates the relationship of total liabilities to total assets, and is an indication of a company's overall ability to pay its debt, both current and long-term.

$$\text{Debt ratio} = \frac{\text{Total Liabilities}}{\text{Total Assets}}$$

A strong debt ratio typically should be something less than .60 or 60%. Therefore, a company wants to show a high current ratio, but overall, it wants a low debt ratio.

TEST YOURSELF

All the self-testing materials in this chapter focus on information and procedures that your instructor is likely to test in quizzes and examinations.

I. Matching

Match each numbered term with its lettered definition.

K 1. Account format
O 2. Closing the accounts
B 3. Current liability
D 4. Liquidity
G 5. Long-term asset
J 6. Report format
H 7. Debt ratio
A 8. Work sheet

L 9. Post-closing trial balance
M 10. Accounting cycle
I 11. Closing entries
E 12. Income Summary
C 13. Long-term liability
F 14. Permanent accounts
N 15. Temporary accounts
P 16. Reversing entries

A. A columnar document that is designed to help move data from the trial balance to the finished financial statements

B. A debt due to be paid within one year or within the entity's normal operating cycle, whichever is longer

C. A liability other than a current liability

D. A measure of how quickly an item may be converted to cash

E. A temporary holding account into which revenues and expenses are transferred prior to their final transfer to the Capital account

F. Accounts that are not closed at the end of the accounting period

G. An asset other than a current asset

H. Ratio that measures a company's overall ability to pay its debts

I. Entries that transfer the revenue, expense and owner withdrawal balances to the Capital account

J. Balance sheet format that lists the assets at the top, with the liabilities and owner's equity below

K. Balance sheet format that lists the assets at the left, with the liabilities and owner's equity at the right

L. List of the ledger accounts and their balances at the end of the period after journalizing and posting the closing entries

M. Process by which accountants produce an entity's financial statements for a specific period

N. Revenue accounts, expense accounts, and withdrawals

O. Step in the accounting cycle that prepares the accounts for recording the transactions of the next period

P. An optional entry after the books are closed.

II. Multiple Choice   *Circle the best answer.*

1. Which of the following accounts will *not* appear on the post-closing trial balance?

   A. Cash
   B. Rent Expense

   C. Capital
   D. Interest Receivable

2. On a work sheet, which of the following is *not* extended from the adjusted trial balance to the balance sheet columns?

   A. Liabilities
   B. Capital

   C. Assets
   D. Revenues

3. What effect will adjusting entries usually have on the balance of the Accumulated Depreciation account?

   A. Increase
   B. Decrease

   C. No effect
   D. Cannot be determined

4. What effect will adjusting entries have on the balance of the companion plant asset account?

   A. Increase
   B. Decrease

   C. No effect
   D. Cannot be determined

5. A company has a $10,000 net loss for 20X7. This amount is entered on the work sheet as:

   A. a debit on the income statement column.
   B. a credit on the balance sheet column.

   C. a debit on the balance sheet column.
   D. both A and B.

6. Suppose a company has posted its closing entries to the Income Summary account. The account now has a debit balance. This means that the company had:

   A. net income.
   B. a net loss.
   C. net income only if there were no owner withdrawals.
   D. a net loss only if there were no owner withdrawals.

7. The DeRienzo, Withdrawals account has a balance of $3,000 before closing. What is the correct entry to close the Withdrawals account?

   A. Debit Capital and credit Withdrawals, $3,000
   B. Debit Withdrawals and credit Income Summary, $3,000
   C. Debit Withdrawals and credit Capital, $3,000
   D. Debit Income Summary and credit Withdrawals, $3,000

8. Which of the following accounts would be classified as a current asset?

   A. Accounts Payable
   B. Unearned Revenue

   C. Equipment
   D. Accounts Receivable

9. The current ratio measures:

A. the company's ability to pay all of its debt as it comes due.

C. the proportion of current liabilities to long-term liabilities.

(B.) the company's ability to pay its current liabilities with current assets.

D. the relationship of total liabilities to total assets.

10. The Income Summary has debits of $50,000 and credits of $67,000. This means that the company had:

(A.) $17,000 net income.

C. $117,000 net income.

B. $17,000 net loss.

D. $117,000 net loss.

III. Completion   *Complete each of the following statements.*

1. The accounting cycle starts with _ledger_ _____.
2. Revenue, expense, and the withdrawals accounts are called _temporary_ _____ accounts.
3. The optional summary device used for convenience in preparing financial statements is the __worksheet_____.
4. The accounts that are never closed at the end of an accounting period are called _permanent_____ accounts.
5. Revenue and expense accounts are usually closed to the _income summary_____ account.
6. The Withdrawals account is closed to _Capital_____.
7. _Liquidity_____ refers to how quickly an asset can be converted into cash.
8. The accounting cycle ends with the _income statement_____.
9. __Withdrawals_____ and ___expenses_____ decrease owner's equity.
10. The debt ratio compares _Assets_____ to _current liab_____.
11. The_____ is a measure of short-term liquidity.

IV. Daily Exercises

1. From the following list of account balances as of December 31, 20X8, present the current assets and total assets that would appear on the balance sheet.

Accounts Payable	$ 6,000
Accounts Receivable	9,000
Inventory	11,000
Notes Receivable (due in 120 days)	8,500
Notes Payable (due in 60 days)	6,500
Rent Expense	12,000
Jones, Withdrawals	3,200
Unearned Revenue	3,500
Cash	4,500
Utilities Expense	2,400
Notes Payable (due in 2 years)	18,000
Prepaid Insurance	1,200
Salaries Payable	2,400
Supplies	350
Interest Payable	1,280
Jones, Capital	37,020
Equipment	14,000
Accumulated Depreciation-Equipment	4,000
Service Revenue	20,250
Advertising Expense	1,800
Salaries Expense	6,000
Land	25,000

Balance Sheet

Current Assets:		
Cash	4500	4500
A/R		9000
N/R	11,000	8500
Inventory		11,000
Prepaid Insurance		1200
Supplies		350
Total Current Assets		34,550
Fixed Assets		
Land		25,000
Equipment	14000	
Less: Acc/Dep	(4000)	10,000
Total Assets		69,550

Revenues: 20,250
Expenses: 19,800
Net Income: 450

2. Using the information in #1 above, calculate the current ratio.

$$\frac{\text{Total Assets}}{\text{Total Liab.}} = \frac{69,550}{37,680} = 1.84 \qquad \frac{34,550}{19680} = 1.76$$

3. Using the information in #1 above, calculate the debt ratio.

$$\frac{\text{Total Liab}}{\text{Total assets}} = \frac{37680}{69,550} = 0.54 \qquad \frac{19680}{34,550} = .54$$

4. Using the information in #1 above, calculate whether the company generated net income or net loss and how much.   Net Income : $450

Net loss: 1950

5. On a work sheet, the asset and liability amounts appearing in the balance sheet columns are the same amounts listed on the financial statement; however, the amount for Capital on the work sheet is not the same figure listed on the financial statement. Why are the two amounts different?

_____
_____
_____
_____
_____
_____
_____
_____
_____

V. Exercises

1.

The Design Company
Trial Balance
December 31, 20X7

Cash	$ 13,500	
Accounts Receivable	2,500	
Prepaid Advertising	1,600	
Supplies	1,700	
Unearned Revenue		$ 1,200
Notes Payable		10,000
Tyler, Capital		5,975
Tyler, Withdrawals	1,000	
Fees Earned		8,500
Salary Expense	3,000	
Rent Expense	1,750	
Utilities Expense	625	
	$25,675	$25,675

Additional information:
   a. Supplies at year-end totaled $1,200.
   b. $1,100 of the Prepaid Advertising was expired at year-end.
   c. Unearned revenues total $700 as of December 31.
   d. Accrued salary expense, $250

Required:

1. Prepare the appropriate adjusting entries.
2. Prepare closing entries.

Requirement 1 (Adjusting entries)

GENERAL JOURNAL

Date	Accounts and Explanation	PR	Debit	Credit
A	Supplies expense		500	
	Supplies			500
B.	Prepaid Ad ex		1,100	
	Prepaid Ad			1,100
C.	Unearned service Rev.		500	
	Fees earned			500
D.	Salary expense		250	
	S/P.			250

Requirement 2 (Closing entries)

GENERAL JOURNAL

Date	Accounts and Explanation	PR	Debit	Credit
	Revenues		9000	
	Income Summary			9000
	Income summary		7225	
	expenses			7225
	Income Summary		1775	
	Capital			1775
	Capital		1000	
	W/D			1000

2. Using the information in Exercise 1, calculate the ending Tyler, Capital balance.

Beg.	$ 5975
Add: Rev.	9000
Less: Exp.	5375
W/D	3625
Ending Bal	$ 5975

3. Using the information in Exercises 1 and 2, prepare a post-closing trial balance.

The Design Company
Post-Closing Trial Balance
December 31, 20X7

	$	$
	$	$

4. List the accounting cycle in the correct sequence.

VI. Beyond the Numbers

Given the following information, answer the following questions:

Income Summary			
12/31	82,000	12/31	96,000

Capital		
Bal.	106,000
5/5	9,000
10/1	4,000

Withdrawals	
3/10	5,000
7/15	8,000
11/2	4,000

1. Where did the credits to the Capital account on 5/5 and 10/1 come from?

_____

_____

_____

2. Did the company generate net income or net loss? How much?

_____

3. Has the value of the company increased or decreased for the year? Explain.

_____

_____

_____

_____

VII. Demonstration Problems

Demonstration Problem #1

1. Below are the trial balance columns of the work sheet of Thai Production Company for the year ended November 30, 20X6. Using this trial balance, prepare the journal entries necessary to adjust the accounts of Thai Productions The additional data needed are provided below:

   a. Supplies on hand at November 30, 20X6, $1,095
   b. Depreciation expense, $2,350
   c. Accrued interest expense, $750
   d. Prepaid rent as of November 30, $6,700
   e. On November 30, Thai had accrued ticket revenue, $3,225.
   f. All but $20,450 of the unearned ticket revenue was earned at year end

Thai Production Company
Trial Balance
November 30, 20X6

Accounts	Debit	Credit
Cash	$ 21,325	
Accounts Receivable	1,555	
Prepaid Rent	11,000	
Supplies	7,395	
Equipment	78,000	
Accumulated Depreciation		$ 18,415
Accounts Payable		4,925
Note Payable		5,000
Interest Payable		
Unearned Ticket Revenue		52,560
Sujan Pradesh, Capital		88,510
Sujan Pradesh, Withdrawals	13,000	
Ticket Revenue		58,700
Salary Expense	19,900	
Rent Expense	37,000	
Interest Expense	9,225	
Depreciation Expense		
Advertising Expense	29,710	
Supplies Expense		
Total	$228,110	$ 228,110

2. Place each adjusting entry directly into the Adjustments columns of the work sheet and key each entry by letter. Complete the work sheet on page 95 using Exhibit 4-6 in your text as a guide.
3. Prepare the journal entries needed to close the accounts.

Requirement 1 (adjusting entries)

GENERAL JOURNAL

Date	Accounts and Explanation	PR	Debit	Credit
A.	Supplies expense		6300	
	Supplies.			6300
B	Dep exp		2350	
	A/P			2350
C.	Int exp.		750	
	Int Payable			750
d	Rent exp.		4300	
	Prepaid rent			4300
e	A/R		3225	
	Ticket rev.			3225
f	Unearned rev		32110	
	Ticket rev.			32110

Requirement 2 (work sheet)

Thai Production Company
Work sheet
For the Year Ended November 30, 20X6

Accounts	Trial Balance Debit	Trial Balance Credit	Adjustments Debit	Adjustments Credit	Adjusted Trial Balance Debit	Adjusted Trial Balance Credit	Income Statement Debit	Income Statement Credit	Balance Sheet Debit	Balance Sheet Credit
Cash	21,325				21,325				21,325	
Accounts Receivable	1,555		(e) 3225		4780				4780	
Prepaid Rent	11,000			(d) 4300	6700				6700	
Supplies	7,395			(A) 6300	1095				1095	
Equipment	78,000				78,000				78,000	
Accumulated Depreciation		18,415		(B) 2350		20765				20765
Accounts Payable		4,925				4925				4925
Note Payable		5,000				5000				5000
Interest Payable				(c) 750		750				750
Unearned Ticket Revenue		52,560	(f) 32110			20450				20450
Sujan Pradesh, Capital		88,510				88510				88510
Sujan Pradesh, Withdrawals	13,000				13000				13000	
Ticket Revenue		58,700		(e)3225 (f)32110		94035		94035		
Salary Expense	19,900				19900		19900			
Rent Expense	37,000		(d) 4300		41300		41300			
Interest Expense	9,225		(c) 750		9975		9975			
Depreciation Expense			(B) 2350		2350		2350			
Advertising Expense	29,710				29710		29710			
Supplies Expense			(A) 6300		6300		6300			
Total	228,110	228,110	49035	49035	234,435	234,435	109535	94035	124900	140400
Net Income (Loss)								15500	15500	
							109535	109535	140400	140400

108

Requirement 3 (closing entries)

GENERAL JOURNAL

Date	Accounts and Explanation	PR	Debit	Credit
	Revenues		94035	
	Income Sum			94035
	Income Sum		109535	
	Salary exp			19900
	Rent exp.			41300
	Int. exp.			9975
	D/exp.			2350
	Ad exp.			29710
	Supplies exp.			6300
	Capital		15500	
	I/S			15500
	Capital		(3000)	
	W/D			(3000)

Demonstration Problem #2

Refer to the completed work sheet in Demonstration Problem #1.

1. Prepare the income statement for the year ended November 30, 20X6.
2. Prepare the statement of owner's equity for the year ended November 30, 20X6. Draw the arrow that links the income statement to the statement of owner's equity.
3. Prepare a classified balance sheet at November 30, 20X6 using the report format. All liabilities are current.
4. Using the balance sheet, calculate the current ratio and the debt ratio.
5. Prepare the post-closing trial balance.

Requirement 1 (Income Statement)

Thai Production Company
Income Statement
For the Year Ended November 30, 20X6

Requirement 2 (Statement of Owner's Equity)

Thai Production Company
Statement of Owner's Equity
For the Year Ended November 30, 20X6

Requirement 3 (Balance Sheet)

Thai Production Company
Balance Sheet
November 30, 20X6

Requirement 4 (current and debt ratios)

Current ratio:

Debt ratio:

Requirement 5 (post-closing trial balance)

Thai Production Company
Post-Closing Trial Balance
November 30, 20X6

SOLUTIONS

I. Matching

1. K	4. D	7. H	10. M	13. C	16. P
2. O	5. G	8. A	11. I	14. F	
3. B	6. J	9. L	12. E	15. N	

II. Multiple Choice

1. B   The post-closing trial balance contains the ending balances of the permanent accounts only. The temporary accounts (revenues, expenses and withdrawals) have been closed, and therefore, have no balances and are not listed.

2. D   Revenues are extended to the income statement columns. Assets, liabilities, capital, and withdrawals are extended to the balance sheet columns.

3. A   The adjusting entry for depreciation is
    Depreciation Expense   XX
        Accumulated Depreciation   XX
    The credit to accumulated depreciation increases the account balance.

4. C   The adjusting entry for depreciation does not affect the balance in the plant asset account. The adjusting entry for depreciation increases Depreciation Expense and increases the balance in the Accumulated Depreciation account. The increase in Accumulated Depreciation has the effect of decreasing the total assets without modifying the historical cost of the asset.

5. C   A net loss is entered as a credit on the income statement column of the work sheet and as a debit on the balance sheet column of the work sheet. Net income is entered as a debit on the income statement column of the income statement and as a credit on the balance sheet column of the work sheet.

6. B   Closing has the effect of transferring all revenues to the credit side of Income Summary and all expenses to the debit side. If revenues are larger than expenses, income summary will have a credit balance that reflects net income. If expenses are greater than revenue, Income Summary will have a debit balance that reflects a net loss.

7. A   The entry to close withdrawals is
    Capital   XX
        Withdrawals   XX
    Note that Withdrawals is closed directly to Capital and is not closed through Income Summary.

8. D   Current assets are assets that are expected to be converted to cash, sold, or consumed during the next 12 months or within the business's normal operating cycle if longer than a year. Equipment is a long-term asset. Accounts Payable and Unearned Revenues are current liability accounts.

9. B   The current ratio measures the company's ability to pay its current liabilities as they come due.

10. A   Closing has the effect of transferring all revenues to the credit side of Income Summary and all expenses to the debit side. If revenues are larger than expenses, income summary will have a credit balance that reflects net income. If expenses are greater than revenues, Income Summary will have a debit balance that reflects a net loss.

III. Completion

1. account balances at the beginning of the period (The accounting cycle is the process by which accountants produce the financial statements for a specific period of time. The cycle starts with the beginning account balances.)
2. temporary (Revenue, expenses and withdrawals are temporary accounts. They are closed at the end of each accounting period.)
3. work sheet. (The work sheet is a columnar document that is designed to help move data from the trial balance to the finished financial statements.)
4. permanent (Permanent accounts, i.e., assets, liabilities and capital, are not used to measure income for a period and are not closed at the end of the period.)
5. Income Summary (Closing has the effect of transferring all revenues to the credit side of Income Summary and all expenses to the debit side. If revenues are larger than expenses, Income Summary will have a credit balance that reflects net income. If expenses are greater than revenue, Income Summary will have a debit balance that reflects a net loss.)
6. Capital (The entry to close withdrawals is always:

     Capital   XX
        Withdrawals   XX

Note that Withdrawals is closed directly to Capital and is *not* closed through Income Summary.)
7. Liquidity (Balance Sheets list assets and liabilities in the order of their relative liquidity.)
8. post-closing trial balance
9. Net losses, withdrawals
10. total liabilities, total assets
11. current ratio (current assets ÷ current liabilities)

IV. Daily Exercises

1. From the following list of account balances as of December 31, 20X8, present the current assets and total assets that would appear on the balance sheet.

Current Assets:		
Cash		$ 4,500
Accounts Receivable		9,000
Notes Receivable		8,500
Inventory		11,000
Prepaid Insurance		1,200
Supplies		350
Total current assets		$34,550
Fixed Assets:		
Land		25,000
Equipment	$14,000	
Less: Accumulated Depreciation	(4,000)	10,000
Total Assets		$69,550

2. Current ratio = current assets ÷ current liabilities
    Current assets = $34,550 (from #1 above)
    Current liabilities =

Accounts Payable	$ 6,000
Notes Payable	6,500
Unearned Revenue	3,500
Salaries Payable	2,400
Interest Payable	1,280
	$19,680

Current ratio = $34,550 ÷ $19,680 = 1.76. This means that for every $1.00 of current liabilities, the company has $1.76 in current assets.

3. Debt ratio = Total liabilities ÷ Total assets.
    Current liabilities = $19,680 (from #2 above)
    Long-term liabilities = $18,000 (Note payable due in 2 years)
    Total liabilities -= $37,680
    Total assets = $69,550 (from #1 above)
    Debt ratio = $37,680 ÷$69,550 = .54. This means that 54% of the company's assets are financed with debt.

4. The company has generated a net loss, $1,950. If Total Revenues = $20,250 and Total Expenses = $22,200, then $20,250-$22,200= ($1,950) net loss.

5. The Capital figure appearing on the work sheet has not been updated to reflect the effects of the income statement and withdrawals. Most account balances are updated when they are adjusted; however, the capital account is updated through the closing process. Remember, net income (from the income statement) is added to Capital on the Owner's Equity Statement. The ending balance amount from the Owner's Equity Statement is the updated amount listed on the Balance Sheet.

V. Exercises

1.

The Design Company

Trial Balance
December 31, 20X7

	Debit	Credit
Cash	$ 13,500	
Accounts Receivable	2,500	
Prepaid Advertising	1,600	
Supplies	1,700	
Unearned Revenue		$ 1,200
Notes Payable		10,000
Tyler, Capital		5,975
Tyler, Withdrawals	1,000	
Fees Earned		8,500
Salary Expense	3,000	
Rent Expense	1,750	
Utilities Expense	625	
	$25,675	$25,675

Additional information:
- e. Supplies at year-end totaled $1,200.
- f. $1,100 of the Prepaid Advertising was expired at year-end.
- g. Unearned revenues total $700 as of December 31.
- h. Accrued salary expense, $250

Requirement 1

Date		Accounts and Explanation	PR	Debit	Credit
	a.	Supplies Expense ($1,700- $1,200)		500	
		Supplies			500
		To record supplies used			
	b.	Advertising Expense		1,100	
		Prepaid advertising			1,100
		To record expired advertising.			
	c.	Unearned Revenues		500	
		Fees Earned ($1,200 - $700)			500
		To record fees earned			
	d.	Salary Expense		250	
		Salary Payable			250
		To record accrued salary expense			

Requirement 2

Date	Accounts and Explanation	PR	Debit	Credit
	Fees Earned ($8,500 + $500)		9,000	
	Income Summary			9,000
	Income Summary		7,225	
	Salary Expense ($3,000 + $250)			3,250
	Rent Expense			1,750
	Utilities Expense			625
	Supplies Expense			500
	Advertising Expense			1,100
	Supplies Expense and Advertising Expense from the adjusting entries must be included.			
	Income Summary		1,775	
	Tyler, Capital			1,775
	Income Summary had a credit balance of $1,775 before this entry ($9,000 credit - $7,225 debit).			
	Tyler, Capital		1,000	
	Tyler, Withdrawals			1,000

2.

Beginning Capital	$5,975
Plus: Net Income	1,775
	7,750
Less: Withdrawals	(1,000)
Ending Capital	$6,750

3.

The Design Company
Post-closing Trial Balance
December 31, 20X7

Cash	$13,500	
Accounts receivable	2,500	
Prepaid advertising	500	
Supplies	1,200	
Salary Payable		$ 250
Unearned revenue		700
Notes payable		10,000
Tyler, Capital		6,750
Totals	$17,700	$17,700

4.

1. Start with the balances in the ledger at the beginning of the period.
2. Analyze and journalize transactions as they occur.
3. Post entries to the ledger accounts.
4. Compute the unadjusted balance in each account at the end of the period.
5. Enter the trial balance on the work sheet, and complete the work sheet.
6. Prepare the financial statements.
7. Journalize and post the adjusting entries and the closing entries.
8. Prepare a post-closing trial balance.

VI. Beyond the Numbers

Income Summary			
12/31	82,000	12/31	96,000
12/31	14,000		
	-0-		

Capital				
12/31	17,000	Bal.	106,000	
		5/5	9,000	Net increase
		10/1	4,000	$10,000
		12/31	14,000	
		Bal.	116,000	

Withdrawals			
3/10	5,000	12/31	17,000
7/15	8,000		
11/2	4,000		
	-0-		

1. Where did the credits to the Capital account on 5/5 and 10/1 come from?
   Credits that appear in the Capital account during an accounting period represent additional capital contributions by the owner.

4. Did the company generate net income or net loss? How much?
   The company generated net income in the amount of $14,000. This is determined by evaluating the Income Summary account. The credit represents the total revenues, $96,000 and the debit represents total expenses, $82,000.

5. Has the value of the company increased or decreased for the year? Explain.
   The value of the company has increased by $10,000. This increase is determined by analyzing the overall change in the owner's Capital account, or owner's equity.

VII. Demonstration Problems

Demonstration Problem #1 Solved and Explained

Requirement 1

(a) Nov. 30   Supplies Expense   6,300
                        Supplies   6,300
    To record supplies expense.

Calculation:

Supplies at the beginning of accounting period	$7,395
Supplies at the end of the accounting period	1,095
Supplies Expense (used up)	$6,300

A business must adjust its Supplies account to reflect supplies used up during each accounting period. Supplies are assets that are used to operate the business. When supplies are used in the business, the amount used up during the period must be transferred from the asset account, Supplies to the expense account, Supplies Expense. To decrease the asset, credit Supplies. To record the expense, debit Supplies Expense.

(b) Nov. 30   Depreciation Expense   2,350
                        Accumulated Depreciation - Equipment   2,350
    To record depreciation expense.

To reflect the decline in usefulness of long-lived assets, a portion of the asset's cost is systematically transferred from the asset to expense. Depreciation Expense is debited (expenses are recorded with debits) and the contra asset account Accumulated Depreciation - Equipment is credited (decreases in assets are recorded by credits).

(c) Nov. 30   Interest Expense   750
                        Interest Payable   750
    To record accrued interest expense.

Accrued interest is interest that is owed but will not be paid within the current accounting period. An adjusting entry must be made to reflect the fact that the company owes money for interest, thereby updating the interest payable account, and to properly match the expense to revenues in the period when the expense was incurred. Credit Interest Payable to reflect the increase in the liability account, and debit Interest Expense to record the increase in expense.

(d) Nov. 30   Rent Expense   4,300
                        Prepaid Rent   4,300
    To record rent expense.

Prepaid rent must be decreased to adjust its balance for the amount of rent that has expired. Decrease the asset account, Prepaid Rent by crediting it, and increase Rent Expense by debiting the account.

Calculation:

Prepaid Rent at the beginning of accounting period	$11,000
Prepaid Rent at the end of the accounting period	6,700
Rent Expense (used up)	$4,300

(e) Nov. 30 Accounts Receivable   3,225
    Ticket Revenue   3,225
  To record admissions revenue.

Tickets sold on account in the last day or two of the month are occasionally not recorded for several days. To recognize this revenue in the proper accounting period, an adjusting entry must be made to increase the Ticket Revenue account (by crediting it) and increase the Accounts Receivable (by debiting it). This is an example of accrued revenue.

(f) Nov. 30 Unearned Ticket Revenue   32,110
    Ticket Revenue   32,110
  To record ticket revenue.

Advance payment is a liability because the business owes the customer a service or product. The business records the liability in an unearned revenue account. This account must be adjusted at the close of each accounting period to reflect amounts earned during the period. Note that the liability Unearned Ticket Revenue is decreased by transferring $32,110 to the Ticket Revenue account. The unearned revenue, a liability, became revenue once the agreed-on service was performed.

Calculation:

Unearned ticket revenue at the beginning of the period	$52,560
Unearned ticket revenue at the end of the period	20,450
Revenue Earned	$32,110

Work Sheet:

If the adjusting entries are prepared correctly, completion of an accurate work sheet is relatively straightforward. The work sheet makes preparation of the financial statements fast and easy. The work sheet also provides a summary of all information needed to prepare the closing entries.

Errors made in the footing of individual columns of the work sheet are revealed and, of course, corrected prior to the formal preparation of the financial statements. As a result, the work sheet is a time saver. "Cross-footing" mistakes will occur less frequently if you use a ruler. Starting at the top of the work sheet and working from left to right, cross-foot and extend one column at a time. Working methodically, and slowly if necessary, saves time in the long run. You will become more efficient with practice.

Requirement 2

Thai Production Company
Work Sheet
For the Year Ended November 30, 20X6

Accounts	Trial Balance Debit	Trial Balance Credit	Adjustments Debit	Adjustments Credit	Adjusted Trial Balance Debit	Adjusted Trial Balance Credit	Income Statement Debit	Income Statement Credit	Balance Sheet Debit	Balance Sheet Credit
Cash	21,325				21,325				21,325	
Accounts receivable	1,555		(e) 3,225		4,780				4,780	
Prepaid Rent	11,000			(d) 4,300	6,700				6,700	
Supplies	7,395			(a) 6,300	1,095				1,095	
Equipment	78,000				78,000				78,000	
Accumulated Depreciation		18,415		(b) 2,350		20,765				20,765
Accounts Payable		4,925				4,925				4,925
Note Payable		5,000				5,000				5,000
Interest Payable				(c) 750		750				750
Unearned Ticket Revenue		52,560	(f) 32,110			20,450				20450
Sujan Pradesh, Capital		88,510				88,510				88,510
Sujan Pradesh, Withdrawals	13,000				13,000				13,000	
Ticket Revenue		58,700		(e) 3,225 (f) 32,110		94,035		94,035		
Salary Expense	19,900				19,900		19,900			
Rent Expense	37,000		(d) 4,300		41,300		41,300			
Interest Expense	9,225		(c) 750		9,975		9,975			
Depreciation Expense			(b) 2,350		2,350		2,350			
Advertising Expense	29,710				29,710		29,710			
Supplies Expense			(a) 6,300		6,300		6,300			
Total	228,110	228,110	49,035	49,035	234,435	234,435	109,535	94,035	124,900	140,400
Net Income (Loss)								15,500	15,550	
							109,535	109,535	140,400	140,400

121

Requirement 3

GENERAL JOURNAL

Date	Accounts and Explanation	PR	Debit	Credit
Nov. 30	Ticket Revenue		94,035	
	Income Summary			94,035
	Income Summary		109,535	
	Salary Expense			19,900
	Rent Expense			41,300
	Interest Expense			9,975
	Depreciation Expense			2,350
	Advertising Expense			29,710
	Supplies Expense			6,300
	Sujan Pradesh, Capital		15,500	
	Income Summary			15,500
	Sujan Pradesh, Capital		13,000	
	Sujan Pradesh, Withdrawals			13,000

Closing entries zero out revenue, expense, and withdrawal accounts by transferring their amounts to the capital account. Revenues and expenses undergo the intermediate step of being transferred to a "holding" account called Income Summary.

The closing procedure can be broken down into four steps:
1. Close Revenues to Income Summary
2. Close Expenses to Income Summary
3. Close Income Summary to Capital
4. Close Withdrawals to Capital

Note how the above closing entries follow this sequence.

All information required for the first three closing entries can be taken directly from the Income Statement columns of the work sheet. Look at the Income Statement columns. Compare the revenue and expense figures with the first two closing entries, and compare the net loss figure with the third entry.

Demonstration Problem #2 Solved and Explained

Requirement 1

Thai Production Company
Income Statement
For the Year Ended November 30, 20X6

Revenues:		
Ticket Revenue		$94,035
Expenses:		
Salary Expense	$19,900	
Rent Expense	41,300	
Interest Expense	9,975	
Depreciation Expense	2,350	
Advertising Expense	29,710	
Supplies Expense	6,300	
Total Expenses		109,375
Net Income (Loss)		($ 15,500)

All the information for the Income Statement can be taken directly from the Income Statement columns of the work sheet.

Requirement 2 (Statement of Owner's Equity)

Thai Production Company
Statement of Owner's Equity
For the Year Ended November 30, 20X6

Sujan Pradesh, Capital 11/30/X5	$ 88,510
Less: Net Loss	(15,500)
	73,010
Less: Withdrawals	13,000
Sujan Pradesh, Capital 11/30/X6	$ 60,010

Beginning capital and withdrawals can be taken directly from the Balance Sheet columns of the work sheet. Net income can be taken from the Income Statement. Ending capital is then calculated. The ending capital for this period will appear as the beginning capital on next year's work sheet and statement of owner's equity.

Requirement 3 (Balance Sheet)

Thai Production Company
Balance Sheet
November 30, 20X6

ASSETS

Current Assets:

Cash	$21,325	
Accounts Receivable	4,780	
Prepaid Rent	6,700	
Supplies	1,095	
Total Current Assets		$33,900

Plant Assets:

Equipment	78,000	
Less: Accumulated Depreciation	(20,765)	57,235
Total Assets		$91,135

LIABILITIES

Current Liabilities:

Accounts Payable	$4,925
Notes Payable	5,000
Interest Payable	750
Unearned Ticket Revenue	20,450
Total Liabilities	31,125

OWNER'S EQUITY

Sujan Pradesh, Capital	60,010
Total Liabilities and Owner's Equity	$91,135

Requirement 4

Current ratio = current assets ÷ current liabilities
　　　　　　 = $33,900 ÷ $31,125 = 1.09 (rounded)

Debt ratio = total liabilities ÷ total assets
　　　　　 = $31,125 ÷ $91,135 = 0.34 (rounded)

Requirement 5

Thai Production Company
Post-closing Trial Balance
November 30, 20X6

Accounts	Debit	Credit
Cash	$ 21,325	
Accounts Receivable	4,780	
Prepaid Rent	6,700	
Supplies	1,095	
Equipment	78,000	
Accumulated Depreciation		$ 20,765
Accounts Payable		4,925
Note Payable		5,000
Interest Payable		750
Unearned Ticket Revenue		20,450
Sujan Pradesh, Capital		60,010
	$111,900	$111,900

Preparing a post-closing trial balance performs a final check of the closing process. If any temporary account balances (Revenue, Expense, Income Summary, or Withdrawals) appear in the post-closing trial balance, a mistake has been made in closing the accounts. On a post-closing trial balance, the only accounts you should see are the balance sheet (permanent) accounts.

Chapter 5—Merchandising Operations

CHAPTER OVERVIEW

Throughout the previous four chapters, you learned about the accounting cycle as it applies to a service business. In Chapter Five, the emphasis changes from a service business to a **merchandising business**—one that earns its revenue by selling a product, rather than a service, to its customers. Accounting for a merchandising business is a bit more complex because the merchandiser must obtain inventory, pay for it, sell it to customers, collect from customers, and then obtain more inventory. This process is referred to as the **operating cycle**. Understanding this chapter will make subsequent chapters, particularly Chapters 6 and 9 easier to comprehend. The learning objectives for this chapter are to

1. Account for the purchase of inventory.
2. Account for the sale of inventory.
3. Use sales and gross profit to evaluate a company.
4. Adjust and close the accounts of a merchandising business.
5. Prepare a merchandiser's financial statements.
6. Use the gross margin percentage and inventory turnover to evaluate a business.

CHAPTER REVIEW

Objective 1 - Account for the purchase of inventory.

The difference between a service business and a merchandising business is a merchandiser sells a product referred to as inventory, where a service business provides, or sells, a service. For merchandising businesses, inventory is one of the largest and most important assets. When inventory is purchased, the merchandiser acquires the asset—inventory—and holds it until it is sold to customers.

When a merchandiser decides to purchase inventory, it sends a purchase order to its supplier. The supplier ships the merchandise and sends an invoice, or bill, to the merchandiser. After the inventory has been received and inspected, the merchandiser pays the supplier.

There are two types of discounts a supplier might extend to the buyer:

- **A quantity discount** offers a buyer the option of purchasing a larger number of units and, by doing so, obtaining a lower per unit cost. The amount of a quantity discount is never recorded in the accounting records. Quantity discounts are offered and deducted prior to the purchase and establish the purchase price for the order.

- **A purchase discount** offers the buyer the option of paying an invoice early and, by doing so, takes advantage of the offered reduction in the total price paid for the merchandise. Purchase discounts are offered after the purchase and are only recorded when the purchaser takes advantage of the discount within the allowed discount period. A purchase discount would be expressed as a part of the credit terms of the sale. The terms might be 2/10, n/30. This means that the purchaser may take a 2% discount on the amount owed if the invoice is paid within 10 days of the invoice date, excluding freight charges, if any. If the invoice is not paid within 10 days of the invoice date, then the purchaser has not taken advantage of the discount, the option expires, and the buyer must pay the invoice in full within 30 days of the invoice date. If a discount is offered, it is always advantageous for the buyer to take the discount because the discount represents a savings of 2% over a period of 20 days (assuming a 30 day month). This savings represents an effective annual rate of 36.5%, calculated as follows:

# of days in a year / # of days outside of discount period x discount = annual rate

or, 365 days in a year / 20 days of savings x 2% = 36.5% annual rate

This means that over a year's time, if the buyer takes advantage of the discount every month, the business will save approximately 36.5% on the total cost of its inventory. While 2% does not look like much each month, as you can see, it represents a significant savings over a year.

If the terms of the sales are n/30, then no discount is offered and the buyer must pay the invoice within 30 days of the invoice date.

Review the following sequence of transactions and explanations:

Purchase of inventory on account:
Inventory	500	
Accounts Payable		500
Purchased inventory on account, terms 1/15, n/30		

If the amount owed is paid within discount period:
Accounts Payable	500	
Cash [$500-($500 x .01)]		495
Inventory ($500 x .01)		5

If paid after discount period:
Accounts Payable	500	
Cash		500

Anytime a supplier ships goods to the merchandiser, someone must pay for the shipping costs that may also be referred to as freight charges. The entity responsible for paying the freight charges is determined by the shipping terms at the time the purchase is made.

- If the shipping terms are **FOB shipping point**, then the buyer is responsible for paying the freight charges. FOB shipping point indicates that title to the goods transfers to the buyer at the shipping point and therefore, the buyer must pay the shipping charges. Shipping costs incurred by the buyer are termed **freight-in** and are debited to the inventory account. Freight charges paid by the buyer represent an additional cost to the buyer for the inventory and are added to the cost of the asset that appears on the balance sheet.
- If the shipping terms are **FOB destination**, then the seller is responsible for paying the freight charges since title to the goods will not transfer until the goods reach the destination, or the buyer's warehouse. Shipping costs incurred by the supplier are called freight-out and accounted for as delivery expense that appears on the income statement.

Sometimes the buyer will need to return a portion of the purchase to the seller or the buyer may request an allowance for goods that are defective, damaged, or the wrong item. **Purchase returns and allowances** are credited directly to the inventory account and reflect a reduction in the cost of merchandise acquired. A purchase return is where the buyer actually returns the goods to the supplier. A purchase allowance is where the buyer keeps the merchandise, and the supplier gives the buyer an allowance, or cost reduction for the merchandise.

The two main accounting systems used for keeping track of merchandise inventory within the accounting records are the **periodic system** and the **perpetual system**. The major difference between the two is the availability, within the accounting records, of an up-to-date value for merchandise inventory on hand. When a perpetual system is used, this value is available continuously, whereas the periodic system can only determine a value when an actual physical count is made. Taking a physical count called taking inventory can be time consuming and expensive for a business to perform. With the increasing use of computers, more and more businesses have changed their systems from periodic to perpetual. For this reason, we use the perpetual system in our discussion of merchandise businesses and cover the periodic system in the chapter supplement.

Objective 2 - Account for the sale of inventory.

After a company buys its inventory, the next step is to sell the goods. The merchandiser now shifts into the role of the seller. When inventory is sold to customers, the amount of the sale is referred to as Sales Revenue, or simply Sales. Remember, revenue is generated when the business does what it is in the business of doing, which, in this case, is selling goods. Keep in mind that when a merchandiser purchases inventory, it is an asset. Once the inventory is sold to customers, it is no longer held by the merchandiser for sale, so it is no longer an asset. The cost of the inventory that has been sold to customers becomes Cost of Goods Sold, an expense. When merchandise is sold and a perpetual inventory system is in use, two entries are required, as follows:

Sale of inventory on account:		
1) Accounts Receivable	700	
Sales		700
Sold inventory on account, terms 2/15, n/30		
2) Cost of Goods Sold	500	
Inventory		500
Recorded the cost of goods sold		

- Entry 1 records the sale at the selling price. The selling price will be some amount greater than the cost of the goods that are sold.
- Entry 2 transfers the cost of the items sold from the Inventory account (an asset) to the Cost of Goods Sold account (an expense).

As mentioned earlier, sellers offer discounts to encourage prompt payment. By offering the sales discount, the seller is willing to accept less cash to entice its customer to pay for the goods within 10 days, in this example. If the customer chooses to take advantage of the sales discount, then on the seller's books, the entry to record the collection within the discount period is

If the amount owed by the customer is collected within the discount period:

Cash [$700-($700 x .02)]	686	
Sales Discount ($700 x .02)	14	
Accounts Receivable		700

If collected after discount period:	700	
Cash		
Accounts Receivable		700

The seller may also have to accept a return or grant an allowance. The entries to record a return of merchandise is:

Sales Return and Allowances	XX	
Accounts Receivable		XX
Inventory	XX	
Cost of Goods Sold		XX

The entry to record the granting of an allowance is:

Sales Return and Allowances	XX	
Accounts Receivable		XX

Sellers rarely debit either discounts or returns and allowances directly to the Sales account. The use of a Sales Discount account and a Sales Returns and Allowances account allows a merchandiser to track how much of the business's overall sales are reduced by extending sales discounts, and from returns or allowances. Sales Discount and Sales Returns and Allowances are contra-revenue accounts that are contra to the Sales account.

Objective 3 – Use sales and gross profit to evaluate a company.

Managers and investors evaluate a business's profitability by analyzing net sales revenue, cost of goods sold, and gross profit. **Net Sales,** the amount that appears on the income statement, is computed as follows:

Sales Revenues (credit balance)
- Sales Discounts (debit balance)
- Sales Returns and Allowances (debit balance)
= Net Sales (a calculation, not an account)

The difference between the amount of the sale (determined by the selling price) and the cost of the inventory sold, called Cost of Goods Sold is called the **Gross Profit** or Gross Margin.

Gross Profit = Sales - Cost of Goods Sold

Helpful Hint: Review page 177 in your textbook.

Gross profit is a measure of how successful a business is at selling its inventory to generate a profit. A merchandising business must sell its inventory at a selling price that is greater than it's cost to generate gross profit. And, the gross profit must be sufficient to also cover the business's operating expenses in order to generate net income. This is illustrated in Exhibit 5-1 in your textbook where the income statement of a service company is compared to the income statement of a merchandising company.

Objective 4 - Adjust and close the accounts of a merchandising business.

Adjusting entries for a merchandiser are the same as those for a service business, except there is one additional adjusting entry for any discrepancy between the accounting records for inventory and the physical count for the inventory.

The general form of the **closing entries** for a merchandiser is basically the same as for a service business except now there are some additional accounts that must be closed.

When a difference exists between the balance in the Inventory account and the result of a physical count of merchandise still on hand, the inventory account will need to be adjusted so its balance agrees with the physical count. In most cases, this adjusting entry will always affect the Inventory and the Cost of Goods Sold accounts and appear as follows:

**When the physical count of the inventory reports
less inventory on hand than the Inventory
account reports in the accounting records:**

Cost of Goods Sold	XX	
Inventory		XX
To decrease the Inventory account to match the physical count		

**When the physical count of the inventory reports
more inventory on hand than the Inventory
account reports in the accounting records:**

Inventory	XX	
Cost of Goods Sold		XX
To increase the Inventory account to match the physical count		

The format for the **work sheet** is identical to the one introduced in Chapter 4, and the steps in completing the work sheet are the same. The closing process also remains unchanged, as follows:

1. Income Statement credit balances are transferred to the Income Summary account.

2. Income Statement debit balances are transferred to the Income Summary account. The debit balances will now include the Cost of Goods Sold account, Sales Discounts account, and Sales Returns and Allowances account. (Remember: Sales Discounts and Sales Returns and Allowances are contra-revenue account, not expense accounts.)
3. The Income Summary account is closed to the Capital account. (Remember, the amount of this third closing entry must agree with net income or net loss.)
4. The Withdrawals account is closed to the Capital account.

Objective 5 - Prepare a merchandiser's financial statements.

The major difference between the financial statements of a merchandiser and those of a service business is the presence of Inventory on the merchandiser's balance sheet and Cost of Goods Sold on the merchandiser's income statement.

For many businesses, Inventory will be the largest current asset on the Balance Sheet. Cost of Goods Sold will be the largest expense item on the Income Statement. In addition, the Income Statement will generally report operating expenses in two categories:

- **Selling Expenses.** Those costs directly related to marketing the company's products.
- **General Expenses.** Other operating costs incurred in the major line of business, and are not directly related to selling the products.

Finally, non-operating revenues and expenses (called Other revenues and expenses) are listed separately. Other revenues and expenses result from activities that a business might encounter in the normal course of doing business, but they do not result from the entity's main line of business. These distinctions allow the user of the financial statements to clearly differentiate between operating income, the income generated from the entity's main line of business, and net income, the bottom line income generated from all sources.

The Income Statement can be presented in either a **multiple-step format** or a **single-step format**. The multiple-step format clearly establishes significant relationships within the statement. Exhibit 5-7 is an example of a multiple-step income statement. The single-step format groups together all revenues, then groups together all expenses and, in a single computation, deducts the expenses from the revenues. Exhibit 5-8 is an example of a single-step format. You should also notice that the single-step format is similar to the income statements you have studied throughout Chapters 1-4.

Objective 6 - Use the gross margin percentage and inventory turnover ratios to evaluate a business.

A key measure of profitability for a merchandiser is the **gross margin percentage**. The gross profit percentage measures how much gross profit is generated by every dollar of sales revenue.

$$\text{Gross profit percentage} \quad = \quad \frac{\text{Gross profit}}{\text{Net Sales Revenues}}$$

Inventory turnover measures the number of times a company sells its average level of inventory during a year.

$$\text{Inventory turnover} \quad = \quad \underline{\text{Cost of goods sold}}$$

$$\text{Average inventory} = \frac{\text{Beginning inventory} + \text{Ending inventory}}{2}$$

Helpful hint: Review Exhibits 5-9 and 5-10 in your text.

TEST YOURSELF

All the self-testing materials in this chapter focus on information and procedures that your instructor is likely to test in quizzes and examinations. Those questions followed by an *S* refer to information contained in the Appendix to the chapter.

I. Matching   *Match each numbered term with its lettered definition.*

P ____ 1. Cost of Goods Sold
L ____ 2. Income from operations
M ____ 3. Multiple-step income statement
J ____ 4. Operating expenses
G ____ 5. Sales returns and allowances
K ____ 6. Single-step income statement
F ____ 7. Purchase returns & allowances
C ____ 8. Purchase discount
B ____ 9. Sales discount

H ____ 10. Gross profit
D ____ 11. Invoice
O ____ 12. Net sales
N ____ 13. Net purchases
I ____ 14. Other expense
E ____ 15. Sales revenue
A ____ 16. Quantity discount

A. A discount from supplier to merchandiser that lowers the price per item for volume purchases
B. A reduction in the amount receivable from a customer that is offered by the seller as an incentive for the customer to pay promptly
C. A reduction in the cost of inventory that is offered by a seller as an incentive for the customer to pay promptly
D. A seller's request for payment of a purchase
E. Amount that a merchandiser earns from selling inventory
F. Decreases in a buyer's debt that result from returning merchandise to the seller or receiving an allowance on the amount owed
G. Decreases in the seller's revenue from a customer's return of merchandise or from granting to the customer an allowance from the amount the customer owes
H. Excess of sales revenue over cost of goods sold
I. Expense that is outside the main operations of a business
J. Expenses, other than cost of goods sold, that are incurred in the entity's main line of business
K. Format that contains only two sections, revenues and expenses
L. Gross profit less operating expenses
M. Income statement format that lists the figures within subsections and presents intermediate subtotals, such as gross profit and income from operations
N. Purchases less purchase discounts and purchases returns & allowances
O. Sales revenue less sales discounts and sales returns & allowances
P. An account in the perpetual system; a calculation in the periodic system that represents the cost of inventory that the business sold to its customers.

II. Multiple Choice   *Circle the best answer.*

1. Which of the following companies would *not* be considered a merchandising entity?

   A. The Gap
   B. A Ford dealership

   C. Sears
   D. Alltel

2. A company will have a net loss if:

   A. cost of goods sold exceeds operating expenses.
   B. operating expenses exceed gross profit.

   C. sales exceed gross profit.
   D. sales exceed operating expenses.

3. Which of the following is classified as an operating expense?

   A. Cost of Goods Sold
   B. Rent Expense

   C. Sales Discount
   D. Interest Expense

4. A debit to Sales Returns and Allowances will:

   A. increase Inventory.
   B. increase Net Purchases.

   C. increase Net Sales.
   D. decrease Net Sales.

5. When using a perpetual inventory system, which account will capture all costs associated with the purchase of inventory?

   A. Purchases
   B. Purchase Discounts

   C. Inventory
   D. Purchase Returns and Allowances

6. A company purchases 30 DVD players systems that sell for $500 each. There is a $300 freight charge added to the invoice. The supplier also offers a 1% discount if the buyer pays the invoice within 10 days. The buyer takes advantage of all discounts offered. What will the total cost of this purchase be to the buyer?

   A. $15,000
   B. $15,147

   C. $15,150
   D. $15,000

7. A company sells merchandise on June 1 for $1,800 with terms 1/15, n/30. If it receives payment for the merchandise on June 8, the entry to record the receipt would:

   A. credit Accounts Receivable $1,800.
   B. credit Inventory $18.

   C. credit Cash $1,800.
   D. debit Inventory $1,782.

8. A company purchased merchandise for $3,200 on October 1 with terms 2/10, n/30. When it paid the account on October 13, the journal entry:

   A. debited Accounts Payable $3,136
   B. credited Inventory $64

   C. debited Inventory $3,200
   D. credited Cash $3,200

9. Which of the following accounts is *not* a contra account?

A. Inventory
B. Accumulated Depreciation
C. Sales Returns and Allowances
D. Sales Discounts

10. Gross Profit plus Cost of Goods Sold equals:

A. Net Income.
B. Cost of Goods Available for Sale.
C. Net Sales.
D. Operating Income.

III. Completion   *Complete each of the following statements.*

1. A merchandising entity earns its revenues by _____.
2. The largest single expense for most merchandisers is _____.
3. A seller's request for payment is called a(n) _____.
4. The major difference between a merchandiser's balance sheet and a service entity's balance sheet is _____.
5. The largest single current asset for most merchandisers is _____.
6. Sales minus Cost of Goods Sold is called _____.
7. A company credits the Inventory account when merchandise is sold. It is using a _____ _____ inventory system.
8. The four sections found on a multiple-step income statement for a merchandising business are _____, _____, _____, and _____.
9. The gross margin percentage measures _____ _____.
10. Inventory turnover measures _____ _____.

IV. Daily Exercises

1. Record the following transactions in the space provided.

   7/4   Purchased merchandise on account from Traders, Inc., $1,500; term 2/10, n/60, FOB shipping point, freight of $75 added to the invoice.

   7/10   Returned $300 of merchandise to Traders, Inc.

   7/14   Sent a check to Traders, Inc. for the balance due.

Date	Accounts and Explanation	PR	Debit	Credit

2. Record the following transactions in the space provided.

   8/11   Sold merchandise on account to J. Starrs, $2,000; term 4/15, n/45. The cost of the sale was $750.

   8/16   Accepted a return of $400 from J. Starrs. The cost of the merchandise was $150.

   8/18   Granted an allowance of $75 for a portion of the order that was damaged during shipping.

   8/21   Received a check from J. Starrs for the amount due.

Date	Accounts and Explanation	PR	Debit	Credit

Date	Accounts and Explanation	PR	Debit	Credit

V. Exercises

1. The following information is available for Johnson's Jade Emporium for 20X7:

Beginning Inventory	$ 6,000
Ending Inventory	4,700
Operating Expenses	3,500
Cost of Goods Sold	31,500
Sales Discounts	600
Sales	43,000
Sales Returns and Allowances	200
Interest Expense	150

Required: Calculate the following for 20X7:

1. Net sales:

2. Gross profit:

3. Income from operations:

4. Net Income:

5. Gross profit percentage:

6. Inventory turnover:

2. Use the following information from Fedelina's Fedoras for 20X8 to prepare an income statement through gross profit on sales:

Depreciation Expense	$ 700
Interest Expense	1,100
Interest Revenue	1,000
Inventory	1,500
Cost of Goods Sold	7,790
Rent Expense	600
Sales Discounts	100
Sales Returns & Allowances	50
Sales Revenues	12,175
Withdrawals	250

3. Using the information in #2 above, prepare the necessary closing entries.

Date	Accounts and Explanation	PR	Debit	Credit

VI. Beyond the Numbers

A business is offered the purchase discount term 1/15, n/45. At the same time, the business can borrow money from its bank at 10% interest. Assuming the business does not have sufficient cash on hand to take advantage of the discount, which would be less expensive—to lose the discount or to borrow the needed cash from the bank and take the discount? Support your answer.

_____
_____
_____
_____
_____

VII. Demonstration Problems

Demonstration Problem #1

On March 1, Cronies & Fish, Inc. had the following account balances:

Cash	$ 20,000	
Accounts receivable	34,000	
Inventory	44,000	
Other current assets	15,000	
Property, plant, and equipment (net)	180,000	
Account payable		$ 37,000
Long-term liabilities		104,000
Capital		152,000
Totals	$293,000	$293,000

During March, the following merchandise purchase and sales transactions occurred:

a. Sold merchandise on account to Divas, $18,000; the cost of the merchandise was $8,400.
b. Purchased merchandise on account from Taylor, $9,600, terms 1/10, n/30, FOB shipping point.
c. Received a freight bill for the Taylor purchase, $275, terms n/10.
d. Sold merchandise on account to Lahni, $7,500; the cost of the merchandise was $1,650.
e. Paid the freight bill on the Taylor purchase (#c above).
f. Received payment from Divas (#a above) within the discount period.
g. Lahni returned $1,300 of merchandise; the cost of the merchandise was $450.
h. Paid Taylor (#b above) within the discount period.
i. Sold merchandise on account to Simmons, Inc., $10,200; the cost of the merchandise was $4,300.
j. Purchased merchandise on account from Carter Co., $11,240, terms 3/20, n/60.
k. Received payment from Lahni (#d and #g above) within the discount period.
l. Returned $1,400 of merchandise to Carter.
m. A $600 allowance was granted to Simmons (#i above).
n. Paid Carter (#j and #l above) within the discount period.
o. Simmons, Inc. paid the balance due (#i and #m above) but did not earn a discount.
p. Sold merchandise on account to Ferini Co., $12,750; the cost of the merchandise was $6,750.

Additional information:

1. The terms of all sales are 2/10, n/30, FOB destination.
2. Cronie & Fish, Inc. uses a perpetual inventory system.
3. Round amounts to the nearest dollar, where necessary.

Required:

1. Place the opening balances into the T-accounts, identifying each by date.
2. Record the transactions in the journal (omit explanations).
3. Post the entries to the T-accounts, identifying each by letter.
4. Balance the accounts and prepare a trial balance.
5. Calculate the gross margin percentage.

Requirements 1, 3, and 4

Cash	Accounts receivable	Inventory

Other current assets	Property, plant and equipment, net	Accounts payable

Long-term liabilities	Capital	Sales

Sales discount	Sales returns & allowance	Cost of goods sold

Requirement 2

Date	Accounts	PR	Debit	Credit

Date	Accounts	PR	Debit	Credit

Requirement 4

Accounts	Debit	Credit

Requirement 5

_____

_____

_____

Demonstration Problem #2

Using the completed work sheet for DuMont Company on the following page:

1. Prepare a multiple-step income statement, statement of owner's equity, and balance sheet.
2. Journalize the adjusting entries (identify each by letter) and closing entries.
3. Prepare a post-closing trial balance.
4. Prepare a single-step income statement.
5. Calculate the gross margin percentage.
6. Calculate the inventory turnover ratio. The beginning inventory was $36,000.

DuMont Company
Work Sheet
For the Year Ended December 31, 20X5

Accounts	Trial Balance Debit	Trial Balance Credit	Adjustments Debit	Adjustments Credit	Income Statement Debit	Income Statement Credit	Balance Sheet Debit	Balance Sheet Credit
Cash	18,250						18,250	
Accounts receivable	20,100						20,100	
Inventory	44,000			(g) 2,000			42,000	
Supplies	2,850			(a) 2,000			850	
Prepaid advertising	10,000			(b) 4,800			5,200	
Equipment	92,500						92,500	
Accumulated depreciation		43,500		(d) 8,300				51,800
Accounts payable		23,765						23,765
Salary payable				(e) 990				990
Interest payable				(f) 255				255
Unearned sales revenue		1,560	(c) 1,000					560
Note payable, long-term		75,000						75,000
Eric DuMont, Capital		38,100						38,100
Eric DuMont,	19,750						19,750	
Sales revenue		300,460		(c) 1,000		301,460		
Sales discounts	8,700				8,700			
Sales returns and allowances	2,610				2,610			
Cost of Goods Sold	146,410		(g) 2,000		148,410			
Salary expense	75,100		(e) 990		76,090			
Rent expense	19,000				19,000			
Depreciation expense			(d) 8,300		8,300			
Utilities expense	7,125				7,125			
Supplies expense			(a) 2,000		2,000			
Interest expense	2,750		(f) 255		3,005			
Advertising Expense	13,240		(b) 4,800		18,040			
Total	482,385	482,385	19,345	19,345	293,280	301,460	198,650	190,470
Net income (loss)					8,180			8,180
					301,460	301,460	198,650	198,650

Requirement 1 (Financial Statements)

Income Statement

Statement of Owner's Equity

Balance Sheet

ASSETS		LIABILITIES	
		OWNER'S EQUITY	

Requirement 2 (adjusting and closing entries)

Date	Accounts	PR	Debit	Credit

Date	Accounts	PR	Debit	Credit

Requirement 3 (Post-closing Trial Balance)

Post-closing Trial Balance

Requirement 4 (Single-step Income Statement)

Income Statement

Requirement 5 (Gross margin)

_____

_____

_____

Requirement 6 (Inventory turnover ratio)

_____

_____

_____

SOLUTIONS

I. Matching

1. P	5. G	9. B	13. N
2. L	6. K	10. H	14. I
3. M	7. F	11. D	15. E
4. J	8. C	12. O	16. A

II. Multiple Choice

1. **D** A merchandising entity earns its revenue by selling products. Of the entities listed, all sell products except the Alltel, the telephone company that sells a service.

2. **B** The basic income statement formula for a merchandising company is:

    Sales
    - Cost of goods sold
    = Gross margin
    - Operating expenses
    = Net income or (net loss)

    For a company to have a net loss, operating expenses must be greater than gross margin.

3. **B** Cost of goods sold is the cost of inventory that the company sold to customers. The account Sales Discounts is a contra-revenue account and interest expense is "other expense."

4. **D** Sales Returns and Allowances is a contra account to the Sales account. A credit to Sales Returns and Allowances increases its balance. Since it is contra to the Sales account, Sales Returns and Allowances will decrease net sales.

5. **C** When a perpetual inventory system is used, the inventory account will be updated for every transaction that has an effect on the overall cost of inventory. Freight-in will increase the cost of inventory, where purchase discounts, and purchase returns and allowances will decrease the cost of inventory. The individual Purchases, Purchase Discounts, and Purchase Returns and Allowances accounts are only used under a periodic inventory system.

6. **C** The total amount owed for the DVD players is $15,300:

30 DVD players x $500 each =	$15,000
+ Freight charges	300
Total cost of purchase prior to discount	$15,300
After discount is taken:	
Purchase price of DVD players	$15,000
Amount of discount: $15,000 x .01 =	(150)
Cost of DVD players after discount	$14,850
+Freight in	300
Total cost of purchase after discount	$15,150

7. A The terms 1/15, n/30 mean that a 1% discount is available if payment is received within fifteen days of the invoice date; otherwise the net amount of the invoice is due in 30 days. Since payment is received within the fifteen-day discount period, the journal entry to record the payment is:

Cash	1,782	
Inventory	18	
Accounts Receivable		1,800

8. D The terms 2/10,n/30 mean that a 2% discount is available if payment is made within ten days of the invoice date; otherwise the net amount of the invoice is due in 30 days. Since payment was not made within the ten-day discount period the net amount is due. The journal entry to record the payment is:

Accounts Payable	3,200	
Cash		3,200

9. A A contra account has two distinguishing characteristics: 1) it always has a companion account, and 2) its normal balance is opposite that of the companion account. Items B, C, and D are contra accounts. Only item A, Inventory, is not a contra account.

10. C You are required to work backwards. Since Net Sales - Cost of Goods Sold = Gross Margin; therefore, Net Sales = Gross Margin + Cost of Goods Sold.

III. Completion

1. selling products. This is in contrast to the entities studied through Chapter 4 that earned revenue by selling a service.
2. Cost of Goods Sold. Cost of goods sold represents the cost of the goods a business has sold to its customers.
3. invoice. To the seller, the invoice results in a sale being recorded. To the purchaser, the same invoice results in a purchase being recorded.
4. the Inventory account. The merchandiser earns revenue by selling a tangible product, inventory. The service entity earns its revenue by selling an intangible service.
5. Inventory.
6. Gross Profit or Gross Margin. The basic income statement formula for a merchandising company is:

> Sales
> - Cost of Goods Sold
> = Gross margin
> - Operating expenses
> = Net income (Net loss)

7. perpetual. Under the perpetual system, all merchandise is debited to the Inventory account when acquired and credited to the Inventory account when sold.
8. The four sections are: 1) Revenue from Sales, 2) Cost of Goods Sold, 3) Operating Expenses, 4) Other Revenue and Expenses
9. how much gross profit is generated by every dollar of sales revenue
10. the number of times a company sells its average level of inventory during a year.

IV. Daily Exercises

1.

7/4	Inventory	1,575	
	Accounts Payable		1,575
7/10	Accounts Payable	300	
	Inventory		300
7/14	Accounts Payable	1,275	
	Inventory		24
	Cash		1,251

Note: The cash discount applies only to the original purchase less the return. It does not apply to the freight charge.

2.

8/11	Accounts Receivable	2,000	
	Sales		2,000
	Cost of Goods Sold	750	
	Inventory		750
8/16	Sales Returns and Allowances	400	
	Accounts Receivable		400
	Inventory	150	
	Cost of Goods Sold		150
8/18	Sales Returns and Allowances	75	
	Accounts Receivable		75
8/21	Cash	1,464	
	Sales Discount	61	
	Accounts Receivable ($2,000-$400-$75)		1,525

With a perpetual inventory system, sales and sales returns require double entries—one to record the sale (or return) and a second entry to update the inventory account. Recording an allowance does not require a second entry to update the inventory, because no inventory is returned to the seller.

V. Exercises

1.

Requirement 1

Sales - Sales Returns & Allowances - Sales Discount = Net Sales
$43,000 - $200 - $600= $42,200

Requirement 2

Net Sales - Cost of Goods Sold = Gross Profit (or Gross Margin)
$42,200 - $31,500 = $10,700

Requirement 3

Gross Profit – Operating Expenses = Income from Operations
$10,700 - $3,500 = $7,200

Requirement 4

Income from Operations– Other Expenses = Net Income (Loss)
$7,200 - $150 = $7,050

Requirement 5

Gross Profit ÷ Net Sales
$10,700 ÷ $42,200 = 25.36%

Requirement 6

Cost of Goods Sold ÷ Average Inventory
Average Inventory = ($6,000+ $4,700) ÷ 2 = $5,350
$31,500 ÷ $5,350 = 5.9 times

2.

Revenues from Sales			
Sales		$12,175	
Less: Sales Discount	$100		
Sales Returns/Allowance	50	150	
Net Sales			$12,025
Less: Cost of Goods Sold			7,790
Gross Profit			$4,235

4.

Date	Accounts and Explanation	PR	Debit	Credit
	Sales Revenue		12,175	
	Interest Revenue		1,000	
	Income Summary			13,175
	Income Summary		10,340	
	Cost of Goods Sold			7,790
	Interest Expense			1,100
	Sales Discounts			100
	Rent Expense			600
	Depreciation Expense			700
	Sales Returns & Allowances			50
	Income Summary		2,835	
	Capital			2,835
	Capital		250	
	Withdrawals			250

VI. Beyond the Numbers

It would be more expensive to let the discount lapse compared than to borrow the money from the bank at 10% interest. The term 1/15, n/45 means you pay 1% for extending the payment period an additional 30 days. This computes to about 12% annual interest (365 days / 30 days x .01) or about 2% more than your bank is charging. Since it will cost the business more to forego the discount than to borrow the money, the business should borrow the money in order to take advantage of the discount.

VII. Demonstration Problems

Demonstration Problem #1 Solved and Explained

Requirements 1, 3, and 4

Cash		Accounts receivable		Inventory	
Bal. 20,000	275 (e)	Bal. 34,000	18,000 (f)	Bal. 44,000	8,400 (a)
(f) 17,640	9,504 (h)	(a) 18,000	1,300 (g)	(b) 9,600	1,650 (d)
(k) 6,076	9,545 (n)	(d) 7,500	6,200 (k)	(c) 275	96 (h)
(o) 9,600		(i) 10,200	600 m)	(g) 450	4,300 (i)
Bal. 33,992		(p) 12,750	9,600 (o)	(j) 11,240	1,400 (l)
		Bal. 46,750			295 (n)
					6,750 (p)
				Bal. 42,674	

Other current assets			Property, plant and equipment, net			Accounts payable	
Bal. 15,000			Bal. 180,000			(e) 275	37,000 Bal.
						(h) 9,600	9,600 (b)
						(l) 1,400	275 (c)
						(n) 9,840	11,240 (j)
							37,000 Bal.

Long-term liabilities			Capital			Sales	
	104,000 Bal.			152,000 Bal.			18,000 (a)
							7,500 (d)
							10,200 (i)
							12,750(p)
							48,450 Bal.

Sales discount			Sales returns & allowance			Cost of goods sold	
(f) 360			(g) 1,300			(a) 8,400	450 (g)
(k) 124			(m) 600			(d) 1,650	
Bal. 484			Bal. 1,900			(i) 4,300	
						(p) 6,750	
						Bal. 20,650	

Requirement 2

a.	Accounts Receivable (Divas)		18,000	
	Sales			18,000
	Cost of Goods Sold		8,400	
	Inventory			8,400
b.	Inventory		9,600	
	Accounts Payable (Taylor)			9,600
c.	Inventory		275	
	Accounts Payable			275
d.	Accounts Receivable (Lahni)		7,500	
	Sales			7,500
	Cost of Goods Sold		1,650	
	Inventory			1,650
e.	Accounts Payable		275	
	Cash			275

154

f.	Cash		17,640	
	Sales Discount		360	
	Accounts Receivable (Divas)			18,000
g.	Sales Returns & Allowance		1,300	
	Accounts Receivable (Lahni)			1,300
	Inventory		450	
	Cost of Goods Sold			450
h.	Accounts Payable (Taylor)		9,600	
	Inventory			96
	Cash			9,504
i.	Accounts Receivable (Simmons, Inc.)		10,200	
	Sales			10,200
	Cost of Goods Sold		4,300	
	Inventory			4,300
j.	Inventory		11,240	
	Accounts Payable (Carter Co.)			11,240
k.	Cash		6,076	
	Sales Discount		124	
	Accounts Receivable (Lahni)			6,200
l.	Accounts Payable (Carter)		1,400	
	Inventory			1,400
m.	Sales Returns & Allowance		600	
	Accounts Receivable (Simmons, Inc.)			600
n.	Accounts Payable (Carter)		9,840	
	Inventory			295
	Cash			9,545
o.	Cash		9,600	
	Accounts Receivable (Simmons, Inc.)			9,600
p.	Accounts Receivable (Ferini Co.)		12,750	
	Sales			12,750
	Cost of Goods Sold		6,750	
	Inventory			6,750

Requirement 4

Cash	$33,992	
Accounts receivable	46,750	
Inventory	42,674	
Other current assets	15,000	
Property, plants, and equipment (net)	180,000	
Account payable		$ 37,000
Long-term liabilities		104,000
Capital		152,000
Sales		48,450
Sales discount	484	
Sales returns & allowance	1,900	
Cost of goods sold	20,650	
Totals	$341,450	$341,450

Requirement 5

Gross margin percentage = Gross margin ÷ Net sales
Net Sales = $48,450 - $484- $1,900 = $46,066

Gross margin = Net sales - Cost of goods sold
= $46,066 - $20,650
= $25,416

Gross margin percentage = $25416 ÷ $46,066 = 55.2% (rounded)

Points to remember:

1. When a company uses a perpetual inventory system and records a sale, two transactions are required. One transaction records the sales (at the selling price) while the second transfers the cost of the inventory sold from the Inventory account to the Cost of Goods Sold account.
2. Because of #1 above, a sales return also requires two entries. However, a sales allowance (transaction (m) in the problem) only requires one entry because no merchandise is being returned.

Demonstration Problem #2 Solved and Explained

Requirement 1

DuMont Company
Income Statement
For the Year Ended December 31, 20X5

Sales revenue		$301,460	
Less: Sales discounts	$8,700		
Sales returns & allowances	2,610	11,310	
Net Sales			$290,150
Cost of goods sold			148,410
Gross profit			141,740
Operating expenses:			
Salary Expense		76,090	
Rent Expense		19,000	
Depreciation Expense		8,300	
Utilities Expense		7,125	
Supplies Expense		2,000	
Advertising Expense		18,040	130,555
Income from operations			11,185
Other expenses:			
Interest Expense			3,005
Net income			$ 8,180

DuMont Company
Statement of Owner's Equity
For the Year Ended December 31, 20X5

Eric DuMont, Capital 1/1/20X5	$38,100
Add: Net Income	8,180
	46,280
Less: Withdrawals	19,750
Eric DuMont, Capital 12/31/20X5	$26,530

DuMont Company
Balance Sheet
December 31, 20X5

ASSETS			LIABILITIES		
Current:			Current:		
Cash	$18,250		Accounts payable	$23,765	
Accounts receivable	20,100		Salary payable	990	
Inventory	42,000		Interest payable	255	
Supplies	850		Unearned sales revenue	560	
Prepaid advertising	5,200		Total current liabilities		$ 25,570
Total current assets		$ 86,400	Long term:		
			Notes payable		75,000
Plant:			Total liabilities		100,570
Equipment	92,500				
Less: Accumulated			OWNER'S EQUITY		
Depreciation	51,800	40,700	Eric DuMont, Capital		26,530
			Total liabilities and owner's		
Total assets		$127,100	equity		$127,100

Requirement 2 (adjusting and closing entries)

	ADJUSTING ENTRIES		Debit	Credit
(a)	Supplies Expense		2,000	
	Supplies			2,000
(b)	Advertising Expense		4,800	
	Prepaid Advertising			4,800
(c)	Unearned Sales Revenue		1,000	
	Sales Revenue			1,000
(d)	Depreciation Expense		8,300	
	Accumulated Depreciation			8,300
(e)	Salary Expense		990	
	Salary Payable			990
(f)	Interest Expense		255	
	Interest Payable			255
(g)	Cost of Goods Sold		2,000	
	Inventory			2,000

		CLOSING ENTRIES			
12/31		Sales Revenue		301,460	
		Income Summary			301,460
		Close revenue to Income Summary.			
12/31		Income Summary		293,280	
		Sales Discounts			8,700
		Sales Returns and Allowances			2,610
		Cost of Goods Sold			148,410
		Salary Expense			76,090
		Rent Expense			19,000
		Depreciation Expense			8,300
		Utilities Expense			7,125
		Supplies Expense			2,000
		Interest Expense			3,005
		Advertising Expense			18,040
		Close all expenses to Income Summary.			
12/31		Income Summary ($301,460 - $293,280)		8,180	
		Eric Dumont, Capital			8,180
		Close Income Summary to capital.			
12/31		Eric DuMont, Capital		19,750	
		Eric DuMont, Withdrawals			19,750
		Close withdrawals to capital.			

Requirement 3

DuMont Company
Post-closing Trial Balance
December 31, 20X5

Cash	$ 18,250	
Accounts receivable	20,100	
Inventory	42,000	
Supplies	850	
Prepaid advertising	5,200	
Equipment	92,500	
Accumulated depreciation		$ 51,800
Accounts payable		23,765
Salary payable		990
Interest payable		255
Unearned sales revenue		560
Note payable, long-term		75,000
Eric DuMont, capital		26,530
	$178,900	$178,900

Requirement 4 (Single-step Income Statement)

DuMont Company
Income Statement
For the Year Ended December 31, 20X5

Net Sales		$290,150
Less:		
Cost of goods sold	$148,410	
Operating expenses	130,555	
Interest expense	3,005	281,970
Net income		$ 8,180

Requirement 5 (Gross margin)

Gross Profit Percentage = Gross Margin ÷ Net Sales
Gross Profit Percentage = 141,740 ÷ 290,150 = 48.9% (Rounded)

Requirement 6 (Inventory turnover ratio)

Inventory turnover ratio	=	Cost of goods sold ÷ Average inventory
	=	$148,410 ÷ [($36,000 + $42,000) ÷ 2]
	=	$148,410 ÷ $39,000
	=	3.8 times (Rounded)

Chapter 8—Internal Control and Cash

CHAPTER OVERVIEW

In Chapter 7, you learned about an accounting information system. This chapter follows that discussion by introducing you to internal control and the processes a business follows to control the organization's assets. Because cash is the most liquid asset, this chapter applies internal control concepts to cash. However, internal control applies to all assets—topics covered in the next three chapters. The learning objectives for this chapter are to

1. Define internal control.
2. Tell how to achieve good internal control.
3. Prepare a bank reconciliation and related journal entries.
4. Apply internal controls to cash receipts.
5. Apply internal controls to cash payments.
6. Make ethical judgments in business.

CHAPTER REVIEW

Objective 1 - Define internal control.

Internal control is the organizational plan and all the related measures that an entity adopts to accomplish four objectives:

1. Safeguard assets
2. Encourage employees to follow company policy.
3. Promote operational efficiency
4. Ensure accurate, reliable accounting records.

A Federal law, the **Foreign Corrupt Practice Act**, passed in 1977, requires companies under SEC jurisdiction to maintain a system of internal control. In addition, the **Sarbanes-Oxley Act of 2002** requires managers to give careful attention to internal control in their companies.

Objective 2 – Tell how to achieve internal control.

An effective system of internal control has the following components:

1. **Competent, reliable, and ethical personnel**. Paying competitive salaries, training people thoroughly, and providing adequate supervision help to promote competence.
2. **Assignment of responsibilities**. All duties to be performed must be identified, and responsibility for the performance of those duties must be assigned to appropriate people.
3. **Separation of duties**. Separation of duties limits fraud and promotes the accuracy of the accounting records. Separation of duties has two parts:
   a) separation of operations from accounting
   b) separation of the custody of assets from accounting

4. **Internal and external audits.** Auditors evaluate the system of internal control to estimate the reliability of the accounting systems. Auditors also help to spot areas where improvements in internal control can be made. **Internal auditors** are employees of the company. **External auditors** are employed by public accounting firms and are hired by a business to audit its books.

5. **Documents and records.** Business documents and records are designed according to each company's needs and provide the details of business transactions. Source documents include sales invoices and purchase orders, and records include special journals and the general ledger. Good internal control requires documents to be prenumbered. A gap in the numbered sequence will call attention to a missing document.

6. **Electronic devices, computer controls and other controls.** Additional controls include electronic sensors for inventory, fireproof vaults to safeguard cash, point-of-sale terminals used to track revenues and cash, fidelity bonds to protect the business from employee theft, mandatory vacations and job rotation for employees and electronic data processing auditors for computer systems.

In order to remain competitive in today's business world, many businesses must buy and sell goods over the Internet, referred to as **e-Commerce.** Businesses that participate in e-Commerce must take security measures to protect their customers and encourage them to buy online. Some of the risks of e-Commerce are:
1. Stolen credit cards.
2. Computer viruses and Trojan horses
3. Impersonation of companies

Businesses use **encryption** of data and **firewalls** to secure e-Commerce data.

The limitations of an internal control system are determined by the opportunities available for collusion and the resources that management devotes to the system. Collusion between two or more people working together to defraud the firm may go undetected by the system of internal control. Internal control must be designed and judged in light of the costs and the benefits.

Because cash is the most liquid asset, and is relatively easy to conceal, steal, and move, a business must provide specific controls for cash. For accounting purposes, when we refer to cash, it includes currency, coins, checks, money orders, and money held in bank accounts. The bank account provides internal control over cash. Banks safeguard cash and provide detailed records of transactions.

Documents used to control bank accounts include:

- signature cards
- deposit tickets
- checks
- bank statements
- bank reconciliation

Banks send monthly statements to customers. The bank statement shows the beginning balance in the account, all transactions recorded during the month, and the ending balance. The bank also returns canceled checks with the statement.

Electronic Fund Transfer (EFT) is a system that relies on electronic impulses to account for cash transactions. EFT systems reduce the cost of processing cash transactions by reducing the documentary evidence of transactions. The monthly bank statement lists EFT deposits and EFT payments.

Monthly **bank reconciliations** are necessary because of timing differences between when cash transactions are recorded by the business and when the bank records those transactions. For example, if you mail a check to a supplier on the last day of the month, you will record the payment in the business records on that day. However, the check will not clear your bank until the supplier has received it and deposited it in his bank, sometime in the following month.

Objective 3 - Prepare a bank reconciliation and related journal entries.

The general format for a bank reconciliation is:

Balance per Bank	**Balance per Books**
Cash balance, last day of month	Cash balance, last day of month (from balance of general ledger)
+ Deposits in transit	
- Outstanding checks	+ Bank collections
± Correction of bank errors (if any)	+ Interest paid on deposits
	- Service charge
	± Correction of book errors (if any)
Adjusted bank balance =	Adjusted book balance

Adjustments to the bank balance <u>never</u> require the preparation of journal entries because they represent items that have already been recorded in the accounting records of the business, but they have not been recorded by the bank as of the date on the statement. Adjustments to the bank balance include the following items:

1. **Deposits in transit** have been recorded by the company, but have not been recorded by the bank. There is often a time lag of a day or two until the deposit is sent to the bank and posted by the bank.
2. **Outstanding checks** are checks issued by the company and recorded in the company's books, but the checks have not yet been paid (recorded) by the bank. There is a time lag of several days until the checks are cashed or deposited by the payee and sent to the maker's bank to be paid.
3. **Corrections of bank errors** are the responsibility of the bank. The bank should be notified, and the corrections should appear on the next statement.

Adjustments to the books <u>always</u> require the preparation of journal entries because they represent items that have been recorded by the bank, but they have not been recorded in the accounting records of the business. It is only by making a journal entry that these transactions are recorded in the books of the business.

Adjustments to the book balance include the following items:

1. The bank collects money on behalf of depositors. Examples are a lock-box system where customers pay directly to the bank account. A bank may also collect on a note receivable for the depositor. The bank will notify the depositor of these collections on the bank statement. The journal entry for the collection of a note receivable and the related interest is:

Cash	XXX	
Note Receivable		XX
Interest Revenue		X

2. Interest Revenue is sometimes paid to the depositor on the checking account. The journal entry to record the interest is:

Cash	XX	
Interest Revenue		XX

3. Service charges are the bank's fees for processing transactions. The journal entry for a service charge is:

Miscellaneous Expense	X	
Cash		X

4. Nonsufficient funds (NSF) checks are customer checks that have been returned by the customer's bank because the customer's account did not have sufficient funds in the account to cover the amount of the check. Checks may also be returned if the maker's account has closed, the date is stale, the signature is not authorized, the check has been altered, or the check form is improper. The amount of returned checks is subtracted from the book balance and the following journal entry is made:

Accounts Receivable-Customer A	XX	
Cash		XX

5. The cost of printing checks is handled like a service charge. The journal entry is:

Miscellaneous Expense	XX	
Cash		XX

6. Errors on the books must be handled on a case-by-case basis. If checks are recorded on the books for the wrong amount, then a correcting journal entry must be prepared to correct the original entry.

Study Exhibit 8-6 carefully. Be sure you understand the components of a bank reconciliation and the journal entries needed to correct the Cash account balance.

When reported on the balance sheet, most companies list "Cash and equivalents"—this includes cash and other items similar enough to be included with cash (such as petty cash, short-term time deposits, and certificates of deposit).

Objective 4 - Apply internal controls to cash receipts.

The objective of internal control over cash receipts is to ensure that all cash is deposited in the bank. Companies receive cash over the counter and through the mail. Each source of cash calls for its own set of controls.

A cash register is a good device for management to control cash received in a store. Positioning the machine so that customers see the amounts rung up discourages cashiers from overcharging customers and pocketing the excess over actual prices. Issuing receipts requires cashiers to record the sale. Comparing actual receipts to cash register tapes maintained by the machine discourages theft.

For payments received from customers by mail, separation of duties among different people promotes good internal control. The mailroom clerk should open all mail and record incoming payments. The mailroom clerk should deliver checks to the cashier for deposit, and send remittance advices to the accounting department for posting. Comparison of mailroom totals, cashier totals, and accounting totals should be made daily.

Where large numbers of cash transactions occur, there is often a small difference between actual cash received and cash recorded. An account entitled **Cash Short and Over** is used to account for such differences. The account is used as a balancing account for the journal entry and is debited for cash shortages and credited for cash overages. An example of the journal entry to record an overage is:

Cash (from cash drawer)	20,010	
Cash Short and Over (plug)		10
Sales (from cash register tape)		20,000

A debit balance in Cash Short and Over appears on the income statement as a miscellaneous expense; a credit balance in Cash Short and Over appears as Other Revenue. A large debit or credit balance in the account (representing shortage or overage) should be investigated promptly.

Objective 5 - Apply internal controls to cash payments.

Internal controls over cash payments are as important as controls over cash receipts. Companies make most payments by check. They also may make smaller payments from a petty cash fund. However, before a check can be issued, additional control procedures have occurred. Before a check is written to pay for a purchase, the payment packet should include: approved purchase orders, receiving reports verifying that goods received conform to the purchase order, an invoice which agrees with both the purchase order and receiving report. When all of these documents agree, then a check can be issued for payment. (See Exhibit 8-9 and 8-10 in your text.) Additionally, many companies require two signatures before a check can be sent.

Businesses keep a **petty cash** account to have cash on hand for minor expenses that do not warrant the time required to write a check. Such minor expenses may include taxi fares, local delivery costs, and small amounts of office supplies.

Suppose a petty cash fund of $200 is established. The cash is placed under the control of a custodian and the following entry is made:

| Petty Cash | 200 | |
| Cash | | 200 |

This same entry is also used to increase the amount in the fund, say from $200 to $300:

| Petty Cash | 100 | |
| Cash | | 100 |

Cash from the fund is disbursed using petty cash tickets, which document each disbursement. Cash on hand plus the total of the petty cash tickets should always equal the fund balance. This is referred to as an **imprest fund**. If the fund comes up short, debit Cash Short and Over. If the fund comes up over, credit Cash Short and Over.

The petty cash fund must be periodically replenished, particularly on the balance sheet date. A check is drawn for the amount of the replenishment. An entry is made as follows:

| Various accounts listed on petty cash tickets | XX | |
| Cash | | XX |

Note: Once the fund is established, no entry is made to the Petty Cash account except to change the total amount in the fund. The expenses on the petty cash tickets are recorded in the journal when the fund is replenished.

Objective 6 - Make ethical judgments in business.

Most businesses have codes of ethics to which their employees are expected to conform. In addition, the accounting profession has the AICPA Code of Professional Conduct and the Standards of Ethical Conduct for Management Accountants. In many situations, the ethical course of action is clear. However, when this is not the case, the following steps may prove helpful:

1. Determine the facts
2. Identify the ethical issues
3. Specify the alternatives
4. Identify the people involved
5. Assess the possible consequences
6. Make the decision

Review the decision guidelines at the end of Chapter 8.

TEST YOURSELF

All the self-testing materials in this chapter focus on information and procedures that your instructor is likely to test in quizzes and examinations.

I. Matching   *Match each numbered term with its lettered definition.*

L	1. External auditors			
M	2. Firewall		G	9. Collusion
D	3. Bank statement		K	10. Bank collection
F	4. Separation of duties		N	11. Bank reconciliation
H	5. Electronic fund transfer		A	12. Deposit in transit
B	6. Nonsufficient funds check		I	13. Imprest system
C	7. Outstanding check		O	14. Internal control
J	8. Service charge		E	15. Petty cash

A. A deposit recorded by the company but not by the bank

B. A check for which the payer's bank account has insufficient money to pay the check

C. A check issued by a company and recorded on it's books but not yet paid by the bank

D. A document prepared by the bank that shows the beginning and ending balances in a depositor's account and lists the month's transactions that affect the account

E. A fund containing a small amount of cash that is used to pay minor expenditures

F. A component of internal control where management divides responsibility between two or more people

G. Where two or more people work together as a team to defraud a company

H. A system that accounts for cash transactions by electronic impulses rather than paper documents

I. A method of accounting for petty cash by which the balance in the Petty Cash account is compared to the sum of cash on hand plus petty cash disbursement tickets

J. Bank's fee for processing a depositor's transactions

K. Collection of money by the bank on behalf of a depositor

L. Employed by public accounting firms; hired to audit a client's books

M. A control device used to prevent access to a network by non-members

N. Process of explaining the difference between a depositor's accounting records and the bank's records related to a depositor's bank account

O. The organizational plan and all related measures adopted by an entity to safeguard assets, ensure accurate and reliable accounting records, promote operational efficiency, and encourage adherence to company policies

II. Multiple Choice   *Circle the best answer.*

1. Jason Laramy handles cash receipts and has the authority to write off accounts receivable. This violates separation of:

   A. custody of assets from accounting.
   B. operations from accounting.

   C. duties within the accounting function.
   D. authorization of transactions from custody of related assets.

2. Felipe Toledo from the purchasing department also oversees the annual inventory of the company's warehouse. This violates separation of:

   A. custody of assets from accounting.
   B. operations from accounting.

   C. duties within the accounting function.
   D. authorization of transactions from custody of related assets.

3. When preparing a bank reconciliation, which of the following items do *not* require a journal entry?

   A. Interest collected on notes receivable
   B. Outstanding checks

   C. EFT payment of note payable
   D. Bank service charge

4. The journal entry to record an NSF check returned by the bank is:

   A. debit Cash, credit Accounts Receivable.
   B. debit Accounts Payable, credit Cash.

   C. debit Accounts Receivable, credit Cash.
   D. debit Miscellaneous Expense, credit Cash.

5. Which of the following is *not* an internal control procedure for cash receipts?

   A. Comparing actual cash in the cash register to the totals on the cash register tape
   B. The cash drawer on the cash register only opens when the clerk enters an amount on the keypad.
   C. Paying bills by check
   D. Enabling customers to see amounts entered on cash receipts

6. A debit balance in Cash Short and Over is reported on the income statement as:

   A. Other Revenue
   B. Cost of Goods Sold

   C. General Expenses
   D. Miscellaneous Expenses

7. Which of the following documents is prepared first?

   A. Invoice
   B. Receiving report

   C. Purchase order
   D. Check

8. Which of the following documents is prepared last?

   A. Invoice
   B. Receiving report

   C. Purchase order
   D. Check

9. Which of the following would *not* be paid out using a petty cash fund?

A. Postage
B. Computer equipment
C. Gasoline for delivery truck
D. Pencils from local office supply

10. Which of the following is *not* an internal control for cash?

A. Fidelity bonds
B. Point-of-sale terminal
C. Electronic sensors
D. Fireproof vault

III. Completion   *Complete each of the following statements.*

1. Bank reconciliation is prepared by the depositor to explain the difference between the cash balance on the books and the cash balance shown by the bank.
2. Under the Foreign Corrupt Practices Act, _____ is (are) responsible for maintaining adequate internal controls.
3. Internal auditors are regular employees of a business; External auditors are independent of the business.
4. In a good internal control system, has the following objectives:
   a.) Separation of duties
   b.)
   c.)
   d.)

5. The documents used to control a bank account are:
   a.) Service charge
   b.) Bank errors
   c.)
   d.)
   e.)

6. When setting up a petty cash fund, the first step is to deposit money .
7. Separation of duties includes operational and financial .
8. When preparing the bank reconciliation, outstanding checks are subtracted from the Bank .
9. Fidelity Bonds insure a company against theft by an employee.
10. cash short + over is a temporary account used to reconcile discrepancies that result from cash transactions.

IV. Daily Exercises

1. Indicate how each of the following items is treated in a bank reconciliation. Use *AB* for additions to the bank balance; *AC* for additions to the company's book balance; *DB* for deductions from the bank balance; and *DC* for deductions from the firm's book balance.

    _AC_ a. A deposit for $175 was not recorded in the books
    _AC DC_ b. A check for $45 was entered in the books as $54
    _AC_ c. Bank collection of a note receivable plus accrued interest
    _DC_ d. Bank service charges
    _DB AB_ e. A deposit was credited by the bank to the firm's account in error
    _AB_ f. Deposits in transit
    _AC_ g. Interest earned on checking account
    _DB_ h. Outstanding checks
    _DC_ i. NSF checks
    _DC_ j. EFT payment of utility bill
    _DC_ k. Charge for check reorder

2. Examine your answers in Daily Exercise #1 and indicate which reconciling items will require a journal entry.

3. A small heating and air conditioning company maintains a $300 imprest petty cash fund. At the end of the month, there were receipts for miscellaneous expenditures totaling $275 and $20 in coins and currency. In the space below, record the entry to replenish the fund. Was the petty cash fund short or over, or was it in balance?

Date	Accounts and Explanation	PR	Debit	Credit

4. There are four circumstances where the account Petty Cash is used in a journal entry. What are they?
    a. _____
    b. _____
    c. _____
    d. _____

IV. Exercises

1. Lee's bank statement gave an ending balance of $815.00. Reconciling items include: deposit in transit, $260.00; service charge, $12.00; outstanding checks, $198.00; and interest earned on her checking account, $2.00. What is the adjusted bank balance after the bank reconciliation is prepared?

2. Using the information in Exercise 1 above, what was the unadjusted ending balance in Lee's checking account?

3. During the month of November, Philip's Photo Co., had the following transactions in its Petty Cash fund.

   11/1   Established Petty Cash fund, $275
   11/6   Paid postage, $35
   11/8   Paid freight charges, $15
   11/11   Purchased office supplies, $40
   11/22   Paid miscellaneous expenses, $66
   11/30   Replenished the Petty Cash fund ($167 was in the fund)

   Prepare the journal entries required by each of the above transactions.

Date	Accounts and Explanation	PR	Debit	Credit

VI. Beyond the Numbers

At the Fat Lady Sings Opera House, you notice that there is a box office at the entrance where the cashier receives cash from customers. Once the customers pay, the cashier presses a button and a machine ejects serially numbered tickets that are given to the customers. To enter the opera house, a customer must present his or her ticket to the door attendant. The attendant tears the ticket in half and returns the stub to the customer. The other half of the ticket is dropped into a locked box.

1. What internal controls are present in this scenario?
2. What should management do to make these controls more effective?
3. How can these controls be rendered ineffective?

_____
_____
_____
_____
_____
_____
_____
_____
_____
_____

VII. Demonstration problems

Demonstration Problem #1

The following petty cash transactions occurred in Oct:

10/1	Management decided to establish a petty cash fund. A check for $300 was written and cashed with the proceeds given to Betty Jones, who was designated custodian of the fund.
10/1	James Silverman, the owner of the business immediately took $25 for lunch money.
10/4	$15.95 was disbursed to reimburse an employee for an air-express package paid for with personal funds.
10/6	COD freight charges on Supplies were paid, $25.00.
10/9	$37 was spent on postage stamps while the postage meter was being repaired.
10/11	The owner "borrowed" another $30 from the fund.
10/12	COD freight charges on merchandise were paid, $45.
10/13	Because the fund was running low on cash, Ms. Jones requested a check to replenish the fund. As there was $122.05 on hand, Ms. Jones requested a check for $177.95. However, her supervisor authorized a check for $277.95 so sufficient funds would be on hand and only require monthly replenishment.
10/16	The monthly charge for the office newspaper was paid, $22.50
10/19	COD charges on merchandise were paid, $43.
10/20	The owner took $100 from the fund.
10/22	Ms. Jones took $25 from the fund to purchase coffee and supplies for the office coffee room.
10/25	The owner's spouse arrived by taxi. The fare of $22 plus a $5 tip was paid from the petty cash fund.
10/26	$75 was paid from the fund to have the front windows washed.

10/28   A coworker did not have lunch money. Ms. Jones gave the coworker $20 from the fund and took a post-dated check for that amount.

10/31   The. company decided to replenish the fund on the last working day each month. There was $84.50 left in the fund.

Required:

1. Record the appropriate transactions in the General Journal.
2. Post any entries to the Petty Cash account.

Requirement 1(General Journal entries)

Date	Accounts and Explanation	PR	Debit	Credit

Requirement 2 (Post entries to Petty Cash Fund)

Petty Cash Fund

Demonstration Problem #2

Selected columns of the cash receipts journal and the check register of Shell Co. appear as follows on March 31, 20X9:

Cash Receipts Journal (Posting reference is CR)		Check Register (Posting reference is CD)	
Date	Cash Debit	Check No.	Cash Credit
Mar. 3	$ 175	716	$ 322
7	710	717	2,244
12	428	718	544
14	880	719	576
24	3,715	720	509
28	1,525	721	501
31	428	722	817
		723	282
		724	1,074
Total	$ 7,861	Total	$ 6,869

The cash account of Shell Co. shows the following information on March 31, 20X9:

Cash

Date	Item	PR	Debit	Credit	Balance
Mar. 1	Balance				$ 6,753
31		CR 1	7,861		14,614
31		CD 2		6,869	7,745

Shell Co. received the following bank statement on March 31, 20X9:

Bank Statement for Shell Co.

Beginning balance		$ 6,852
Deposits and other credits:		
Mar 4	175	
8	710	
11	1,308	BC
13	428	
15	880	
25	3,715	
31	13	INT
	7,229	
	$14,081	

Checks and other debits:

Mar. 3	$ 572	
7	322	
11	2,244	
12	544	
15	576	
20	135	NSF
24	509	
30	817	
31	22	SC
	5,741	
Ending balance:	$8,340	

Legend:

BC = Bank Collection	NSF = Nonsufficient Funds Check
SC = Service Charge	INT = Interest Earned

Additional data for the bank reconciliation:

1. The $1,308 bank collection on Mar. 11 includes $108 interest revenue. The balance was attributable to the collection of a note receivable.
2. The correct amount of Check Number 716 is $223, a payment on account. The Shell Co. bookkeeper mistakenly recorded the check in the check register as $322.
3. The NSF check was received from Fred's Motor Co.
4. The bank statement includes a $572 deduction for a check drawn by Morton Co. The bank has been notified of its error.
5. The service charge consists of two charges: $12 for the monthly account charge and $10 for the NSF check.

Required:

1. Prepare the bank reconciliation of Shell Co. on March 31, 20X9.
2. Record the entries based on the bank reconciliation. Omit explanations.

Requirement 1 (Bank reconciliation)

Shell Co.
Bank Reconciliation
March 31, 20X9

Requirement 2 (Entries based on bank reconciliation)

Date	Accounts and Explanation	PR	Debit	Credit

SOLUTIONS

I. Matching

1. L	4. F	7. C	10. K	13. I
2. M	5. H	8. J	11. N	14. O
3. D	6. B	9. G	12. A	15. E

II. Multiple Choice

1. A Handling cash receipts and having authority to write off accounts receivable puts the person in a position to illegitimately write off an account on which payment has been received and pocket the cash. This is a violation of separation of custody of assets from accounting. Laramy has custody of the cash receipts and as well as accounting duties related to that cash.

2. B When one person has a role in the daily operations of the business, such as purchasing, and has authority to oversee the annual inventory count, this violates the separation of operations from accounting. Too much control might allow someone from the purchasing department to manipulate purchase records and remove goods from the warehouse without being detected.

3. B Outstanding checks are cash payments that have been recorded in the cash payments journal of the business but have not yet been recorded (or cleared) by the bank. The other items listed are items that will be reflected in the banks records, but have not yet been recorded on the books of the business.

4. C An NSF check represents a previously recorded cash receipt that has no substance and, accordingly, must be reversed; reduce cash (credit) and reestablish the receivable (debit).

5. C Paying bills by check is an internal control procedure for cash disbursements, not cash receipts. The other items listed are internal control procedures for cash receipts.

6. D A debit balance means a cash shortage exists. It is reported as a miscellaneous expense.

7. A The purchasing process starts when the purchaser sends a purchase order to the supplier.

8. D The check is prepared last.

9. B A petty cash fund is used to pay for minor expenditures. Computer equipment would not be considered a minor expenditure, and would not be purchased using a petty cash fund.

10. C Electronic sensors attempt to control inventory, not cash.

III. Completion

1. A bank reconciliation
2. management (Companies under SEC jurisdiction are required to maintain an appropriate system of internal control. This requirement is a responsibility of the management of the company.)
3. Internal; external (Internal auditors report directly to the company's president or audit committee of the board of directors. External auditors audit the entity as a whole and usually report to the stockholders.)
4. a.) Safeguard assets; b.) encourage employees to follow company policy; c.) promote operational efficiency; d.) ensure accurate, reliable accounting records. (Order does not matter.)
5. a.) Signature card; b.) deposit ticket; c.) check; d.) bank statement; e.) bank reconciliation (Order does not matter.)
6. open the fund. (A petty cash fund is opened when a check is issued to Petty Cash by debiting the Petty Cash account and crediting the Cash in Bank.)
7. separation of operations from accounting; separation of custody of assets from accounting
8. subtracted; balance per bank.
9. fidelity bonds
10. Cash Short and Over

IV. Daily Exercises

1.
a) AC	e) DB	i) DC
b) AC	f) AB	j) DC
c) AC	g) AC	k) DC
d) DC	h) DB	

2. From #1 above, items a, b, c, d, g, i, j and k will all require a journal entry.
3.
Miscellaneous Expense	275	
Cash Short and Over	5	
Cash		280

   The fund was short by $5.00.
4. The Petty Cash account is part of a journal entry when
   a. the fund is established
   b. the size of the fund is increased
   c. the size of the fund is decreased
   d. to close the fund

V. Exercises

1.

Balance per bank statement (unadjusted)	$815.00
Add:	
Deposit in transit	260.00
	1,075.00
Deduct:	
Outstanding checks	198.00
Adjusted bank balance	877.00

2. This requires you to work backwards. Start by setting up what is known and then solve for the unknown balance. Remember that the adjusted balance in the checkbook will equal the adjusted bank balance on the bank reconciliation.

Balance per checkbook (unadjusted)	?
Add:	
Interest earned	2.00
	?
Deduct:	
Service charge	12.00
Adjusted book balance *(same as adjusted bank balance from #1.)*	877.00

Unadjusted Book balance + 2.00 - 12.00 = 877.00
Unadjusted Book balance = $887.00

3.

Date	Accounts and Explanation	PR	Debit	Credit
11/1	Petty Cash		275	
	Cash in Bank			275
11/30	Miscellaneous Expense		16	
	Postage Expense		35	
	Delivery Expense		15	
	Supplies (an asset)		40	
	Cash Short and Over		2	
	Cash in Bank			108

Note: You make an entry to record the various expenses only when the Petty Cash fund is replenished at the end of the month.

VI. Beyond the Numbers

1. Notice that there is separation of duties—one person issues the ticket and collects the money, and the other person oversees the admission to the opera house. Thus, a ticket is necessary to gain entrance.

   The tickets are serially numbered. Management can determine the amount of cash that should be in the drawer by multiplying the price of each ticket by the number of tickets issued.

2. To make the controls effective, management should 1) record the serial number of the first and last ticket sold on each cashier's shift, 2) maintain control over the unsold tickets, and 3) count the cash at the beginning and end of each shift. Also, management can compare the number of customers in the audience with the number of tickets taken at the door.

3. The controls are ineffective if there is collusion by the cashier and the door attendant. The door attendant may choose to keep the entire ticket instead of tearing it in half. The ticket is then given to

the cashier to be sold again. The cashier can then pocket the cash received for the "used" tickets. Remember, internal controls are ineffective if collusion exists.

VII. Demonstration Problems

Demonstration Problem #1

Requirement 1

Only three journal entries were required for this problem! Remember, the purpose of a petty cash fund is to make small disbursements while avoiding the time and cost of writing checks. Therefore, entries are only recorded when a fund is established, when the fund balance is changed, and when the fund is replenished.

10/1	Petty Cash	300.00	
	Cash in Bank		300.00
10/13	Silverman, Withdrawals	55.00	
	Postage Expense ($15.95 + $37.00)	52.95	
	Supplies	25.00	
	Inventory	45.00	
	Petty Cash	100.00	
	Cash in Bank		277.95

Amounts taken by the owner are charged to the owner's Withdrawals account. Freight charges on merchandise are debited to the Inventory account. Remember, freight charges on assets are debited to the asset account, not to an expense account. The receipts plus remaining cash did reconcile to the beginning balance of $300.00, so there was no Cash Short and Over. Since the supervisor authorized the fund to be replenished with $277.95 rather than the amount needed of $177.95, the additional $100.00 represents an increase to the petty cash fund balance.

10/31	Inventory	43.00	
	Silverman, Withdrawals	127.00	
	Accounts Receivable	20.00	
	Miscellaneous Expense ($22.50 + $25.00 + $75.00)	122.50	
	Cash Short and Over	3.00	
	Cash		315.50

The newspaper, coffee money, and window washing were all charged to Miscellaneous Expense, although they could be debited to separate accounts. The post-dated check is charged to Accounts Receivable because it represents an amount the employee owes the business. Allowing an employee to "borrow" from the petty cash fund violates effective internal control procedures and should be stopped immediately. If permitted to continue, the petty cash fund will contain nothing but a stack of post-dated checks! Finally, the receipts plus the remaining cash did not reconcile to the petty cash fund balance of $400.00, so Cash Short and Over was debited for a shortage of $3.00.

Requirement 2

		Petty Cash Fund	
10/1	300		
10/13	100		
Bal.	400		

Assuming the company is correct in its estimates that a $400 balance is sufficient for the petty cash fund, the general ledger account, Petty Cash Fund, will remain as presented above, with the $400 balance undisturbed.

Demonstration Problem #2

Requirement 1

Shell Co.
Bank Reconciliation
March 31, 20X9

BANK:		
Balance 3/31		$ 8,340
Add:		
Deposit in transit of 3/28		1,525
Deposit in transit of 3/31		428
Correction of bank error		572
		10,865
Less:		
Outstanding checks		
Check # 721	501	
Check # 723	282	
Check # 724	1,074	1,857
Adjusted bank balance 3/31		$ 9,008
BOOKS:		
Balance 3/31		$ 7,745
Add:		
Bank collection of note receivable, including interest of $108		1,308
Interest earned on bank balance		13
Error - Check #716		99
		9,165
Less:		
Bank Service charge		12
NSF check ($135 + service charge $10)		145
Adjusted book balance 3/31		$ 9,008

Explanation: bank reconciliation

1. A bank reconciliation prepared on a timely basis provides good internal control over a company's cash accounts. Comparing the cash balance in the general ledger with the cash balance maintained by the bank makes errors easy to detect.

2. The month-end balance shown in the general ledger rarely agrees with the month-end balance shown on the bank statement. The difference generally occurs for one of two reasons:

    1. Timing differences: These occur because of the time lag that occurs when one record keeper records a transaction before the other. Typical timing differences include:

        - Deposits in transit (the bank has yet to record)
        - Outstanding checks (the bank has yet to record)
        - Bank service charges (the company has yet to record)
        - Notes collected by the bank (the company has yet to record)
        - Interest earned on account (the company has yet to record)
        - NSF checks (the company has yet to record)

    2. Errors: An error must result in an adjustment by the record keeping party that made the error. If the company makes the error, a general journal entry is made. The correcting entry will include an increase or decrease to the Cash account. Note that if the bank has made the error, the proper procedure is to notify the bank promptly. Since the company's records are accurate, no journal entry is needed.

Requirement 2

Date	Accounts and Explanation	PR	Debit	Credit
a.	Cash		1,308	
	Note Receivable			1,200
	Interest Revenue			108
	Note Receivable collected by the bank.			
b.	Cash		13	
	Interest Revenue			13
	Interest earned on bank balance.			
c.	Miscellaneous Expense		12	
	Cash			12
	Bank service charge.			
d.	Accounts Receivable – Fred's Motors		145	
	Cash			145
	NSF check returned by bank plus service charge.			
e.	Cash		99	
	Accounts Payable			99
	To correct error in recording Check #716			

Explanations: Journal Entries

Entries (a) and (b) are necessary to record the increase in the cash account attributable to 1) the collection of interest and principal on the note receivable, and 2) interest earned on the account paid by the depository bank. These are timing differences that occur because of the time lag between the recording of an item on the bank's books and the books of the company. The bank has already recorded these items in its records (as evidenced by the bank statement), and the company must do so when it learns of the transaction(s).

Entries (c) and (d), which are similar to entries (a) and (b) reduce cash on the company's books. The bank has already recorded these timing differences. Entry (c) reduces cash for the account service charges for the monthly period and brings the account up to date. The entry for the NSF check is necessary to establish an account receivable for Fred's Motor Co. They had paid the company with a check that was deposited in the cash account. Because the check was returned unpaid for nonsufficient funds, the company must pursue collection of the debt and record on its books that $145 is still owed. Notice that the original amount of the check was $135, but now Fred's Motor Co. owes for the amount of the original check plus the $10 that the bank charged Shell Co. for the NSF Check.

Entry (e) represents the correction of an error. Check #716 was recorded in the cash disbursements journal as a reduction to Cash of $322 instead of $223. This error resulted in $99 too much being deducted from the company's checking account. To correct the error, $99 must be added back to the account.

Note: No entry is required for the bank error. Once notified, the bank needs to correct their books.

Chapter 19 - Introduction to Management Accounting

CHAPTER OVERVIEW

This chapter is the first of eight introducing you to management accounting. You will learn about techniques businesses use to assist management in planning and controlling activities. In this chapter you are introduced to management accounting. The learning objectives for the chapter are to

1. Distinguish financial accounting from management accounting.
2. Describe service, merchandising, and manufacturing companies and classify their costs by value-chain element.
3. Distinguish among (a) direct costs and indirect costs; and (b) full product costs, inventoriable product costs, and period costs.
4. Prepare the financial statements of a manufacturing company.
5. Identify trends in the business environment, and use cost-benefit analysis to make business decisions.
6. Use reasonable standards to make ethical judgments.

CHAPTER REVIEW

Objective 1 - Distinguish financial accounting from management accounting.

Financial accounting leads to financial statements that allow stockholders and creditors—both parties external to the business—to make investment and credit decisions. The financial statements we have discussed are the income statement, balance sheet, statement of stockholders' equity and statement of cash flows. **Management accounting** provides information to the individuals inside a business—the managers—to assist them in making decisions related to running the business. Managers have two main responsibilities:

1. **Planning** by choosing goals and deciding how to achieve them. A **budget** is a quantitative expression of the plan that helps managers coordinate their efforts to achieve the goal.
2. **Controlling** by evaluating the results of business operations by comparing the actual results to the plan.

Exhibit 19-2 in your textbook summarizes the differences between financial and management accounting.

The weighing of costs against benefits to aid decision-making is called **cost-benefit analysis**. For planning and control purposes, managers must know the costs of the products and services provided. For service businesses, the most significant cost is labor. For merchandising companies, the most significant cost will be inventory. For manufacturers, the cost of the finished product will include raw materials, labor, and all the costs related to the conversion of the raw materials into a finished good. (See Exhibit 19-3 in your text.)

Objective 2 - Describe service, merchandising, and manufacturing companies and classify their costs by value-chain element.

Service companies provide intangible services rather than tangible products. Labor makes up the largest cost for service businesses in addition to costs to develop new services, marketing costs and costs of providing customer service.

Merchandising companies resell a tangible product that they buy from suppliers. Inventory makes up the largest cost for merchandising businesses in addition to costs to research new products and locations for new stores, marketing costs, and costs of providing customer service.

Manufacturing companies use labor, plant, and equipment to convert raw materials into new, finished products. Manufacturers have three kinds of inventory:

- **Materials inventory** consists of the basic materials required to produce a finished good.
- **Work in process inventory** consists of those goods that have begun the manufacturing process, but are still in the process of being converted into a finished product.
- **Finished goods inventory** refers to those products that have been completed and are ready for sale.

The **value chain** refers to those business activities that result in value being added to a company's product. There are six elements of the value chain:

1. **Research and development:** Researching and developing new or improved products or services, or the processes for producing them.
2. **Design:** Detailed engineering of products and services, or the processes for producing them.
3. **Production or purchases:** Resources used to produce a product or service, or to purchase finished merchandise.
4. **Marketing:** Promotion of products or services.
5. **Distribution:** Delivery of products or services.
6. **Customer service:** Support provided for customers after the sale.

Review Exhibit 19-4 in your text to become familiar with the elements of the "value chain."

Objective 3 - Distinguish among (a) direct costs and indirect costs; and (b) full product costs, inventoriable product costs, and period costs.

Controlling costs throughout the entire chain is of primary importance to managers. In manufacturing, the term "cost" has a variety of meanings, determined by the context in which it is used.

Direct costs are costs which can be traced to cost objects, whereas **indirect costs** are costs which cannot be traced to cost objects. A **cost object** can be anything for which a separate measurement of cost is desired. Therefore, the important consideration in distinguishing direct from indirect costs is the specific cost object. Consider the calculator you use in this accounting course. If it is the cost object, then some of the direct costs will be its plastic casing, the container and packing material in which it was sold, the components inside which make it work, and batteries (if they were included when you purchased it). In other words, each of the costs mentioned can be traced directly to the calculator. However, these are not the only costs involved in the calculator's manufacture. For instance, the building in which the calculator was produced is also a cost, but its cost cannot be traced directly to the calculator. Therefore, the building is an indirect cost. Obviously, if the cost object changes, the assignment of costs as direct or indirect will also change.

The term **product costs** refers to the costs of producing or purchasing goods intended for sale. The two types of product costs are:

- **Full product costs** that include *all* the costs of all resources used throughout the value chain.
- **Inventoriable product costs** refer to only those costs that GAAP requires companies to treat as assets for external reporting purposes. These costs are not expensed until the product is sold.

For a merchandiser, inventoriable product costs are only those included as Inventory (an asset) until the product is sold, at which time they become part of Cost of Goods Sold. Therefore, inventoriable product costs for a merchandiser would include the actual price paid for the product plus the freight costs. Any other related costs (advertising, sales salaries, etc.) are not inventoriable. These "other" related costs are classified as **period costs**—ones that are expensed immediately and appear on the income statement in the period in which they are incurred. They never become part of the asset account Inventory. Exhibit 19-5 illustrates full product costs, inventoriable product costs and period costs for a merchandising business.

For a manufacturing company, the inventoriable product costs are more complex. This is due to the manufacturing process of taking raw materials and converting them into a finished product.

The inventoriable product costs for a manufacturing business include:

Direct materials 1) must become a physical part of the finished product and 2) their costs must be separately and conveniently traceable to the finished product.

Direct labor is the compensation of the employees who physically convert materials into finished goods.

Manufacturing overhead includes all manufacturing costs other than direct materials and direct labor. Manufacturing overhead costs include:

- **Indirect materials** are materials used to manufacture a product but are not conveniently traceable to specific finished products.
- **Indirect labor** consists of the wages and salaries of all factory workers who are not directly involved in converting material into finished goods.
- **Other indirect manufacturing overhead costs** such as plant rent, insurance, and property taxes.

Prime costs are the sum of direct materials plus direct labor.
Conversion costs are the sum of direct labor plus manufacturing overhead.

(Review carefully Exhibit 19-6 in your text.)

Objective 4 - Prepare the financial statements of a manufacturing company.

Computing cost of goods manufactured:

1) Cost of goods manufactured = Beginning work in process inventory + Total manufacturing costs - Ending work in process inventory

2) Total manufacturing costs = Direct materials used + Direct labor + Manufacturing overhead

3) Direct materials used = Beginning materials inventory + Purchases - Ending materials inventory

Familiarize yourself with Exhibit 19-11 to be sure you understand how to compute cost of goods manufactured. Study the diagram below. It will help you to understand the flow of inventory costs through a manufacturing company.

__DIRECT MATERIALS (DM)__	__WORK IN PROCESS (WIP)__	__FINISHED GOODS (FG)__

Beginning inventory-DM
+   Purchases
	Beginning inventory-WIP
	+ Direct material used
	     Direct labor
	     Manufacturing overhead
		Beginning inventory-FG
		+ Cost of goods manufactured

Direct materials
   available for use
-   Ending inventory-DM
	Total manufacturing costs
	   to account for
	- Ending inventory-WIP
		Goods available for sale
		- Ending inventory-FG

Direct materials
  used
	Cost of goods
	  manufactured
		Cost of goods sold

All of the costs that flow through manufacturing inventories are **inventoriable costs**. **Period costs** are not traced through the inventory accounts. They are accounted for as operating expenses and include selling expenses and general and administrative expenses.

Study the Decision Guidelines titled *Building Blocks of Management Accounting* to further your understanding of the concepts introduced through Objective 4.

Objective 5 – Identify trends in the business environment, and use cost-benefit analysis to make business decisions.

Business operations and management accounting are being influenced by the following trends in the business environment:

1. A shift towards a service economy
2. Competing in the global marketplace
3. Time-based competition (including electronic commerce and just-in-time management)
4. Total quality management

As the economy becomes more service oriented, managers will need increasing amounts of information about the costs of providing services thereby enabling the companies to more competitively price those services.

Global markets provide a more competitive business environment requiring companies to possess more accurate information for decision-making. Companies must decide whether to expand into foreign countries and consider the costs of manufacturing their products domestically versus the costs of manufacturing abroad.

Time-based competition refers to meeting the demands of consumers who demand quality and want the products they order delivered quickly. The Internet, electronic commerce (e-commerce), email and express delivery have enhanced the speed at which business is conducted. **Supply chain management** is the exchange of information between suppliers and customers in an effort to reduce costs, improve quality, and speed delivery of goods and services from suppliers, through the company itself, and on to customers. The **just-in-time (JIT) management philosophy** has been adopted by many companies. Originally developed in Japan by Toyota, JIT emphasizes scheduling production precisely to meet demands thereby eliminating the costs associated with excess raw materials and finished goods inventory. Doing so means the **throughput time** (the length of time from the purchase of raw materials to the actual sale of a finish product) is drastically reduced. Obviously, the shorter the time commitment, the lower the costs. Careful analysis, frequently using present value tables, can assist managers in analyzing the costs and benefits of adopting JIT.

As competition becomes global, customers will be attracted to those products providing the highest quality. **Total quality management** is a philosophy whereby employees not only strive for top quality, but also attempt to insure their success through a program of continuous improvement. Ethical behavior is a key indicator of quality.

Objective 6 – Use reasonable standards to make ethical judgments.

Everyone is faced with ethical dilemmas. Occasionally, the correct decision (i.e., the ethical decision) is not always clear-cut, particularly when there might be adverse consequences to your decisions. Both the Institute of Management Accountants (IMA) and the American Institute of Certified Public Accountants (AICPA) have adopted Standards of Ethical Conduct that serve as guidelines for accounting professionals. The IMA Standards of Ethical Conduct for Management Accountants include competence, confidentiality, integrity and objectivity.

TEST YOURSELF

All the self-testing materials in this chapter focus on information and procedures that your instructor is likely to test in quizzes and examinations.

I. Matching   *Match each numbered term with its lettered definition.*

_____ 1. Budget
_____ 2. Direct labor
_____ 3. Direct materials
_____ 4. Manufacturing overhead
_____ 5. Indirect materials
_____ 6. Indirect labor
_____ 7. Continuous improvement
_____ 8. Cost-benefit analysis
_____ 9. Period costs
_____ 10. Inventoriable product cost

_____ 11. Supply chain management
_____ 12. Materials inventory
_____ 13. Conversion costs
_____ 14. Just-in-time production
_____ 15. Total quality management
_____ 16. Value chain
_____ 17. Work in process inventory
_____ 18. Finished goods inventory
_____ 19. Prime costs
_____ 20. Cost object

A. Companies exchange of information between suppliers and customers in an effort to reduce costs, improve quality, and speed deliver of goods and services from suppliers, through the company itself, and on to customers.
B. Sequence that adds value to a firm's products or services
C. Direct labor plus manufacturing overhead
D. The weighing of costs against benefits to aid in decision making
E. All manufacturing costs other than direct materials and direct labor
F. A philosophy requiring employees to continually look for ways to improve performance
G. All costs of a product that are regarded as an asset for financial reporting
H. Quantitative expression of a plan of action that helps managers to coordinate and implement that plan
I. Completed goods that have not yet been sold
J. Cost of salaries and wages for the employees who physically convert materials into the company's products
K. Costs that are never traced through the inventory accounts
L. Manufacturing labor costs which are difficult to trace to specific products
M. Goods that are in production but not complete at the end of the period
N. Manufacturing materials whose costs cannot easily be traced to a particular finished product
O. Material that becomes a physical part of a finished product and whose cost is separately and conveniently traceable through the manufacturing process to finished goods
P. Materials on hand to be used in the manufacturing process
Q. A system in which a company schedules production just in time to satisfy needs
R. A philosophy of satisfying customers by providing them with superior products and services
S. Anything for which a separate measurement of costs is desired
T. Direct materials plus direct labor

II. Multiple Choice   *Circle the best answer.*

1. If cost of goods manufactured exceeds total manufacturing costs, which of the following must be true?

   A. Finished goods inventory has increased
   B. Finished goods inventory has decreased
   C. Work in process inventory has decreased
   D. Work in process inventory has increased

2. If finished goods inventory has increased, which of the following must be true?

   A. Total manufacturing costs are more than cost of goods manufactured
   B. Total manufacturing costs are less than cost of goods manufactured
   C. Cost of goods sold is less than cost of goods manufactured
   D. Cost of goods sold is more than cost of goods manufactured

3. Which inventory account reflects the costs of products that have been started but not completed?

   A. Materials inventory
   B. Work in process inventory
   C. Finished goods inventory
   D. Manufacturing overhead

4. Total manufacturing costs equals:

   A. direct materials used plus direct labor plus manufacturing overhead.
   B. beginning finished goods inventory plus cost of goods manufactured.
   C. beginning work in process plus direct materials plus direct labor plus manufacture overhead.
   D. beginning finished goods plus cost of goods manufactured less ending finished goods inventory.

5. Which of the following would not be included in manufacturing overhead?

   A. Factory utilities
   B. Repairs to manufacturing equipment
   C. Property taxes on the factory
   D. Supplies used in the warehouse

6. If beginning finished goods inventory is $55,000, ending finished goods inventory is $40,000, and cost of goods sold is $385,000, then cost of goods manufactured must be:

   A. $480,000
   B. $400,000
   C. $370,000
   D. Cannot be determined

7. Which of the following is not an inventoriable product cost?

   A. Indirect labor
   B. Direct labor
   C. Sales commissions
   D. Direct materials

8. Which of the following accounts would not be found in a merchandiser's records?

   A. Supplies
   B. Merchandise Inventory
   C. Work in Process Inventory
   D. Depreciation Expense

9. Which of the following is a period cost?

    A. Materials used
    B. Office salary expense

    C. Depreciation expense - manufacturing
    D. Manufacturing wages expense

10. Throughput time refers to:

    A. the time between selling a product and collecting the receivable.
    B. the time between purchasing raw materials and completing the finished product.
    C. the time between purchasing raw materials and placing those materials into production.
    D. the time between purchasing raw materials and selling the finished product.

III. Completion   *Complete each of the following.*

1. The two primary responsibilities of managers are _____ and
   _____.
2. The inventory accounts of a manufacturing firm will include _____,
   _____, and _____ inventories.
3. _____ are a physical part of the finished product and their cost is
   separately and conveniently traceable through the manufacturing process.
4. Indirect materials and indirect labor are part of _____.
5. _____ are also called inventoriable costs.
6. _____ are never traced through the inventory accounts.
7. A reduction in throughput time is a feature of _____ management
   philosophy.
8. Prime costs include _____ and _____.
9. Conversion costs include _____ and _____.
10. The philosophy of delighting customers by providing them with superior products and services is
    referred to as _____.

IV. Daily Exercises

1. If cost of goods manufactured was $240,000, and beginning and ending Work in Process Inventories
   were $18,000 and $21,000 respectively, what were total manufacturing costs?

2. Work in Process Inventory increased $4,000 during the year for a manufacturing company. Total
   manufacturing costs were $305,000. What was Cost of Goods Manufactured?

3. Given the following information, calculate total Manufacturing Overhead:

Factory Building Depreciation	$ 50,000
Sales Office Expense	4,400
Factory Equipment Depreciation	21,900
Advertising Expense	51,000
Administrative Salaries	202,000
Property Taxes - Manufacturing	42,000
Depreciation on Delivery Equipment	17,000
Office Utilities Expense	8,200
Indirect Materials	2,700
Factory Equipment Repair Expense	6,600
Indirect Labor	12,500
Utilities Expense - Manufacturing	9,100

4. Given the following information, determine the amount of direct materials used.

Raw Material Inventory, 12/31	$ 15,000
Freight-In	1,200
Materials Returns	10,300
Raw Materials Inventory, 1/1	17,800
Discounts on Materials Purchases	3,480
Raw Material Purchases	109,740

5. Review the information in Daily Exercise #4 above and calculate total manufacturing costs, assuming direct labor was $67,580 and manufacturing overhead was $71,065.

6. Review the information in Daily Exercises #4 and #5 above and calculate cost of goods manufactured assuming Beginning Work in Process Inventory was $23,810 and Ending Work in Process Inventory was $19,770.

V. Exercises

1. The following information pertains to Ace Manufacturing, Inc., for 20X9:

Cost of Goods Sold	$425,000
Direct Materials Purchased	170,000
Direct Materials Used	158,000
Beginning Work in Process Inventory	6,000
Net increase in Work in Process Inventory	18,000

Finished Goods Inventory did not change.
Manufacturing Overhead is twice direct labor cost.

A. Compute Ending Work in Process Inventory.

B. Compute Cost of Goods Manufactured.

C. Compute Total Manufacturing Costs.

D. Compute Direct Labor and Manufacturing Overhead.

2. Using a check mark, indicate if the following list of accounts would appear in the records of a service, merchandising, or manufacturing business. Some of the accounts may appear in more than one business.

Accounts	Service	Merchandising	Manufacturing
Fees Earned			
Cost of Goods Sold			
Merchandise Inventory			
Freight-In			
Sales Discounts			
Advertising Expense			
Raw Materials Inventory			
Purchase Discounts			
Factory Wages			
Insurance Expense			
Prepaid Rent			
Work in Process Inventory			
Sales Returns			
Finished Goods Inventory			
Office Salary Expense			
Payroll Tax Expense			
Purchase Discounts			
Manufacturing Overhead			

3. Novis Company wants to adopt several quality improvement programs related to the manufacturing of electrical components. To implement the new programs, Novis expects to incur a cost of $5,750,000. A review of their current traditional system compared with the new programs indicates Novis could expect an initial cost savings of $5,000,000. Novis managers further predict they will yield additional benefits (cost savings) with a present value of a $1,867,250 that has a 70% probability of resulting while a lesser-cost savings with a present value of $1,387,100 has a 30% probability of occurring. Given this information, what are the total benefits expected from adopting the additional quality improvement programs?

Beyond the Numbers

Using the information provided in Exercise #3, was Novis' decision to implement additional quality improvement programs worthwhile?

_____
_____
_____
_____
_____

Demonstration Problems

Demonstration Problem #1

Lifestyle Liquids manufactures a variety of organic vegetable and fruit juice blends, all sold exclusively in health-food stores. During the current period, the following amounts were recorded:

Freight-In	$ 650
Insurance Expense – Delivery Trucks	1,400
Depreciation Expense – Manufacturing Equipment	2,770
Payroll Tax Expense – Manufacturing Wages	14,215
Utilities Expense – Manufacturing	9,970
Sales Salaries Expense	124,000
Advertising Expense	72,440
Fresh Organic Vegetables	189,600
Manufacturing Wage Expense – Direct	204,114
Research and Development Expenses	71,265
Miscellaneous Selling Expense	820
Fresh Organic Fruits	161,970
Sales Discounts	2,775
Fresh Vegetable/Fruit Returns	3,545
Manufacturing Supervisor Salaries	51,150
Product Design Expenses	81,735
Consumer Hotline Expense	36,000
Sales	1,937,400
Purchase Discounts	2,030
Sales Returns/Allowances	8,990
Fresh Herbs/Spices/Flavoring	810
Maintenance Expense – Manufacturing	14,930
Property Tax Expense – Manufacturing	28,790
Container Expense	104,720
Delivery Wages Expense	80,205

Requirement 1 – Using the format that follows, classify the above costs according to their place in the value chain. When you have finished, total each column.

| | Research | Design | Production | | | Marketing | Distribution | Customer Service |
			DM	DL	MO			
Freight-In			650				1700	
Insurance Expense – Delivery Trucks								
Depreciation Expense – Manufacturing Equipment					2670			
Payroll Tax Expense – Manufacturing Wages				14215				
Utilities Expense – Manufacturing					9920			
Sales Salaries Expense						124000		
Advertising Expense						7240		
Fresh Organic Vegetables			189600	209114				
Manufacturing Wage Expense – Direct								
Research and Development Expenses	71265							
Miscellaneous Selling Expense						820		
Fresh Organic Fruits			16197					
Sales Discounts								
Fresh Vegetable/Fruit Returns			(3545)		51125			
Manufacturing Supervisor Salaries					51150			
Product Design Expenses		91935						
Consumer Hotline Expense								36080
Sales							1900	
Purchase Discounts			(2270)					
Sales Returns/Allowances					840			
Fresh Herbs/Spices/Flavoring					840			
Maintenance Expense – Manufacturing					14930			
Property Tax Expense – Manufacturing					26790			
Container Expense			10470					
Delivery Wages Expense							28200	
Totals								

Requirement 2 – Calculate the following

    a.   Total full product costs

    b.   Total inventoriable product costs

    c.   Total prime costs

    d.   Total conversion costs

    e.   Total period costs

Demonstration Problem #2

Lifestyle Liquids had the following inventories for the period ended December 31, 20X8:

Raw Materials, 1/1	$18,680
Work in Process, 1/1	8,225
Finished Goods, 1/1	30,005
Raw Materials, 12/31	14,130
Work in Process, 12/31	7,830
Finished Goods, 12/31	34,375

Requirement 1 – In the space provided, present the annual Schedule of Cost of Goods Manufactured for Lifestyle Liquids for the year ended December 31, 20X8 using the appropriate amounts from both Demonstration Problem #1 and the inventory values listed above.

Requirement 2 – In the space provided, present the annual Income Statement for the year ended December 31, 20X8 for Lifestyle Liquids using the appropriate amounts above and from Demonstration Problem #1.

SOLUTIONS

Matching

1. H	5. N	9. K	13. C	17. M
2. J	6. L	10. G	14. Q	18. I
3. O	7. F	11. A	15. R	19. T
4. E	8. D	12. P	16. B	20. S

Multiple Choice

1.   C   Recall:

       Beginning Work in Process Inventory (WIP)
  +   Total Manufacturing Costs
  -   <u>Ending Work in Process Inventory (WIP)</u>
  =   Cost of Goods Manufactured

If cost of goods manufactured exceeds total manufacturing costs, then the net effect of Work in Process (WIP) inventory in the formula must be positive. Accordingly, beginning WIP Inventory must be greater than ending WIP Inventory. If the ending balance is smaller than the beginning balance, the inventory has decreased.

2.   C   Recall:

       Beginning Finished Goods Inventory
  +   <u>Cost of Goods Manufactured</u>
  =   Goods Available for Sale
  -   <u>Ending Finished Goods Inventory</u>
  =   Cost of Goods Sold

If Finished Goods Inventory has increased, the net effect of Finished Goods Inventory on the above formula is negative. Accordingly, Cost of Goods Sold would be less than Cost of Goods Manufactured. Answers A and B are incorrect because they do not relate to the calculation of Cost of Goods Sold.

3.   B   Materials Inventory reflects the cost of the materials needed to produce a product. Finished Goods Inventory reflects the cost of goods that have been completed. Manufacturing Overhead is one of the components of the total cost of Work In Process Inventory to include the cost of indirect materials, indirect labor, and other manufacturing overhead costs.

4.   A   Manufacturing costs is synonymous with inventoriable costs, i.e., direct materials, direct labor plus manufacturing overhead.

5.   D   Warehouse supplies are a cost incurred after the product has been manufactured and would not be included in manufacturing overhead.

6.   C   The formula is beginning finished goods inventory + cost of goods manufactured – ending finished goods inventory = cost of goods sold. $55,000 + X - $40,000 = $385,000; so X = $370,000.

7. C Inventoriable product costs = direct materials + direct labor + manufacturing overhead. Indirect labor is a component of manufacturing overhead. Sales commissions are a period cost, not a product cost.

8. C The Work in Process Inventory account relates to a manufacturer, not a merchandiser.

9. B Of those listed, only office salaries is a period cost. Materials, manufacturing depreciation, and manufacturing wages are all inventoriable costs.

10. D Throughput time refers to the time it takes a manufacturer to purchase raw materials, convert them into a finished product, and sell the finished product to the customer. Companies adopting the just-in-time system seek to decrease the throughput time on their products.

Completion

1. planning, control
2. materials, work in process, finished goods
3. Direct materials
4. manufacturing overhead
5. Product costs
6. Period costs
7. just-in-time (JIT)
8. direct materials, direct labor
9. direct labor, manufacturing overhead
10. total quality management (TQM)

Daily Exercises

1.

	Beginning Work in Process Inventory	$ 18,000
+	Total Manufacturing Costs	?
-	Ending Work in Process Inventory	21,000
=	Cost of Goods Manufactured	240,000

Total Manufacturing Costs = $243,000

2.

	Beginning Work in Process Inventory	$ X
+	Total Manufacturing Costs	305,000
-	Ending Work in Process Inventory	X + 4,000
=	Cost of Goods Manufactured	$?

X + $305,000 – (X + $4,000) = $301,000

3.

Factory Building Depreciation	$ 50,000
Factory Equipment Depreciation	21,900
Property Taxes – Manufacturing	42,000
Indirect Materials	2,700
Factory Equipment Repair Expense	6,600
Indirect Labor	12,500
Utilities Expense – Manufacturing	9,100
Total Manufacturing Overhead	$144,800

4.

Beginning Raw Materials Inventory			$17,800
Add: Raw Materials Purchases		109,740	
Freight-In		1,200	
		110,940	
Less: Returns	10,300		
Discounts	3,480	13,780	
Net Raw Materials Purchases			97,160
Raw Materials Available for Use			114,960
Less: Ending Raw Materials Inventory			15,000
Raw Materials Used			$99,960

> **Study Tip:** This format is identical to the one you learned in the Chapter 5 Appendix for cost of goods sold.

5.

Total Manufacturing Costs = Direct Materials + Direct Labor + Manufacturing Overhead

Direct Materials Used	$ 99,960
Direct Labor	67,580
Manufacturing Overhead	71,065
Total Manufacturing Costs	$238,605

6.

Cost of Goods Manufactured = Beginning Work in Process + Total Manufacturing Costs – Ending Work in Process

Beginning Work in Process Inventory	$ 23,810
Total Manufacturing Costs	238,605
	262,415
Less: Ending Work in Process Inventory	19,770
Cost of Goods Manufactured	$242,645

> **Study Tip:** Remember, "Total Manufacturing Costs" and "Cost of Goods Manufactured" are NOT synonymous terms.

Exercises

1.

A.

Ending Work in Process Inventory = Beginning Work in Process Inventory + Net increase in Work in Process Inventory

$6,000 + $18,000 = $24,000 Ending Work in Process Inventory

B.

Beginning Finished Goods (FG) Inventory + Cost of Goods Manufactured – Ending FG Inventory = COGS

Beginning FG Inventory = Ending FG Inventory

Cost of Goods Manufactured = COGS = $425,000

C.

	Beginning Work in Process Inventory	$ 6,000
+	Total Manufacturing Costs	X
-	Ending Work in Process Inventory	24,000
=	Cost of Goods Manufactured	$425,000

Total Manufacturing Costs = $443,000

D.

	Direct Materials Used	$158,000
+	Direct Labor	X
+	Manufacturing Overhead	2X
=	Total Manufacturing Costs	$443,000

$3X = $285,000$

$X = $95,000$ (Direct Labor)

$2X = $190,000$ (Manufacturing Overhead)

2.

Accounts	Service	Merchandising	Manufacturing
Fees Earned	√		
Cost of Goods Sold		√	√
Merchandise Inventory		√	
Freight-In		√	√
Sales Discounts		√	√
Advertising Expense	√	√	√
Raw Materials Inventory			√
Purchase Discounts		√	√
Factory Wages			√
Insurance Expense	√	√	√
Prepaid Rent	√	√	√
Work in Process Inventory			√
Sales Returns		√	√
Finished Goods Inventory			√
Office Salary Expense	√	√	√
Payroll Tax Expense	√	√	√
Purchase Discounts		√	√
Manufacturing Overhead			√

3.

$1,867,250 \times .7 \quad = \quad 1,307,075$

$1,387,100 \times .3 \quad = \quad 416,130$

$1,723,205	Expected Value of Additional Benefits
5,000,000	Initial Benefit
$6,723,205	Total benefits expected from adopting JIT

VI. Beyond the Numbers

The total benefits expected of $6,723,205 exceed the $5,750,000 cost by $973,205; therefore suggesting that the quality improvement efforts were worthwhile.

VII. Demonstration Problems

Demonstration Problem #1 Solved and Explained

Requirement 1

Item	Research	Design	Production			Marketing	Distribution	Customer Service
			DM	DL	MO			
Freight-In			$ 650					
Insurance Expense – Delivery Trucks							$ 1,400	
Depreciation Expense – Manufacturing Equipment					$ 2,770			
Payroll Tax Expense – Manufacturing Wages				$ 14,215				
Utilities Expense – Manufacturing					9,970			
Sales Salaries Expense						$124,000		
Advertising Expense						72,440		
Fresh Organic Vegetables			189,600					
Manufacturing Wage Expense – Direct				204,114				
Research and Development Expenses	$71,265							
Miscellaneous Selling Expense						820		
Fresh Organic Fruits			161,970					
Sales Discounts								
Fresh Vegetable/Fruit Returns			(3,545)					
Manufacturing Supervisor Salaries					51,150			
Product Design Expenses		$81,735						
Consumer Hotline Expense								$36,000
Sales								
Purchase Discounts			(2,030)					
Sales Returns/Allowances								
Fresh Herbs/Spices/Flavoring					810			
Maintenance Expense – Manufacturing					14,930			
Property Tax Expense – Manufacturing					28,790			
Container Expense			104,720					
Delivery Wages Expense							80,205	
Totals	$71,265	$81,735	$452,175	$218,329	$107,610	$197,260	$81,605	$36,000

Requirement 2

a. Total full product costs = all costs associated with the value chain

Research	$ 71,265
Design	81,735
Production – DM	452,175
Production – DL	218,329
Production – MO	107,610
Marketing	197,260
Distribution	81,605
Customer Service	36,000
Total Full Product Costs	$1,245,979

b. Total inventoriable product costs = total production costs

Direct Materials	$452,175
Direct Labor	218,329
Manufacturing Overhead	107,610
	$778,114

c. Total prime costs = direct materials + direct labor

Direct Materials	$452,175
Direct Labor	218,329
Total	$670,504

d. Total conversion costs = direct labor + manufacturing overhead

Direct Labor	$218,329
Manufacturing Overhead	107,610
Total	$325,939

e. Total period costs = total full product costs less total inventoriable product costs

Total full product costs	=	$1,245,979 (from (a) above)
Total inventoriable product costs =		778,114 (from (b) above)
Total period costs	=	$ 467,865

Demonstration Problem #2 Solved

Requirement 1

Lifestyle Liquids
Schedule of Cost of Goods Manufactured
For the Year Ended December 31, 20X8

Beginning Work in Process Inventory				$ 8,225
Add: Direct Materials				
Beginning Inventory Direct Materials		$ 18,680		
Add: Purchases		457,100		
Freight-In		650		
Total		476,430		
Less: Discounts	$2,030			
Returns	3,545	5,575		
Net Direct Material Available		470,855		
Less: Ending Direct Material Inventory		14,130		
Direct Material Used			456,725	
Direct Labor			218,329	
Manufacturing Overhead:				
Depreciation Expense – Manufacturing Equipment		2,770		
Utilities Expense		9,970		
Supervisor Salaries		51,150		
Maintenance Expense		14,930		
Property Taxes		28,790	107,610	
Total Manufacturing Costs Incurred				782,664
Total Manufacturing Costs to Account for				790,889
Less: Ending Work in Process Inventory				7,830
Cost of Goods Manufactured				$783,059

Requirement 2

Lifestyle Liquids
Income Statement
For the Year Ended December 31, 20X8

Revenues:		
Sales		$ 1,937,400
Less: Sales Discounts	$ 2,775	
Sales Returns/Allowance	8,990	11,765
Net Sales		1,925,635
Cost of Goods Sold:		
Beginning Inventory Finished Goods	30,005	
Add: Cost of Goods Manufactured	783,059	
Goods Available for Sale	813,064	
Less: Ending Inventory Finished Goods	34,375	
Cost of Goods Sold		778,689
Gross Profit		1,146,946
Less: Operating Expenses		
Research	71,265	
Design	81,735	
Marketing	197,260	
Distribution	81,605	
Customer Service	36,000	
Total Operating Expenses		467,865
Net Income		$ 679,081

Chapter 20 - Job Costing

CHAPTER OVERVIEW

In Chapter 19, you were introduced to Management Accounting and some topics unique to manufacturing operations. We now apply that information to a specific type of cost accounting system—job costing. A second type of cost accounting system will be introduced in the next chapter —process costing. The learning objectives for this chapter are to

1. Distinguish between job costing and process costing.
2. Trace materials and labor in a manufacturer's job costing system.
3. Allocate manufacturing overhead in a manufacturer's job costing system.
4. Account for completion and sales of finished goods and adjust for under- or overallocated manufacturing overhead.
5. Assign noninventoriable costs in job costing.

CHAPTER REVIEW

Objective 1 – Distinguish between job costing and process costing.

The two major types of costing systems are **job costing and process costing**. Both types share common characteristics. For instance, both systems accumulate the same type of costs – direct materials, direct labor, and manufacturing overhead. Also, both systems average these accumulated costs over the number of units produced. The major distinguishing characteristic between the two is the cost object. As the names imply, the cost object in job costing is a job (from raw materials to finished good) whereas the cost object in process costing is a specific process, for example, blending, baking, finishing, or packaging. Review Exhibit 20-3 in your text for a comparison between the two systems. Generally, job costing requires less averaging because the output is usually less – frequently only a single unit (a large construction project, for instance) or a small number of units. Process costing, in contrast, usually results in a high number of units being "processed" so costs are averaged over a larger base. In both systems, the per unit cost is calculated the same, as follows:

$$\frac{\text{Total Costs}}{\text{Total Units}} = \text{Cost per unit}$$

Also, both job and process costing can be found in service and merchandising businesses, in addition to manufacturers. Review Exhibit 20-2 in your text that presents a matrix comparing job and process costing in service, merchandising, and manufacturing businesses.

In job costing, a job cost record is used to accumulate costs for each job. Remember that manufacturing "costs" include direct materials, direct labor, and manufacturing overhead. The job cost record continues to accumulate direct materials and direct labor until the job is complete, at which time manufacturing overhead is allocated.

Objective 2 – Trace materials and labor in a manufacturer's job costing system.

A manufacturer acquires materials by sending a purchase order to a supplier. When the materials are received, a receiving report is prepared and a journal entry is recorded:

Materials Inventory	XX	
Accounts Payable		XX

A **subsidiary materials ledger** is maintained which tracks the receipt, usage, and the balance of each materials inventory item. See Exhibit 20-6.

When a job is entered into production, a **materials requisition** is prepared to have materials transferred from inventory storage to the factory floor. See Exhibit 20-7.

The cost of direct materials is debited to Work in Process Inventory, while the cost of any indirect materials is debited to Manufacturing Overhead:

Work in Process Inventory (direct materials)	XX	
Manufacturing Overhead (indirect materials)	XX	
Materials Inventory (total materials requisitioned)		XX

This entry records the transfer of both direct and indirect materials from materials inventory to the manufacturing process. At the same time, the cost of the direct materials is entered on the job cost record. See Exhibit 20-8.

A **labor time record** (Exhibit 20-9 in your text) is used to identify the employee, accumulate the time spent on a particular job and the labor cost associated with the job.

Manufacturing wages are recorded with this entry:

Manufacturing Wages	XX	
Wages Payable		XX

Based on the information from the labor time record, the balance in the Manufacturing Wages account is allocated to direct labor and indirect labor, and recorded with this entry:

Work in Process Inventory (direct labor)	XX	
Manufacturing Overhead (indirect labor)	XX	
Manufacturing Wages (total manufacturing wages)	XX	

The direct labor costs associated with each job are posted to the appropriate job cost records. Exhibit 20-10 in your text summarizes accounting for materials and labor in job costing. Also, see the Decision Guidelines titled *Job Costing: Tracing direct materials and direct labor*.

Objective 3 - Allocate manufacturing overhead in a manufacturer's job costing system.

During the year, actual overhead costs are debited to Manufacturing Overhead as they are incurred:

Manufacturing Overhead	XX	
Various Accounts		XX

At year-end, the Manufacturing Overhead account contains all the actual overhead costs of the period. Now, we must determine how to assign these overhead costs to the products that were produced. In addition, applying overhead costs to production cannot wait until the end of each year. To enable accountants to assign manufacturing overhead costs throughout the year, a **predetermined manufacturing overhead rate** is used:

$$\text{Predetermined manufacturing overhead rate} = \frac{\text{Estimated manufacturing overhead costs}}{\text{Estimated quantity of the manufacturing overhead allocation base}}$$

To allocate manufacturing overhead accurately, the allocation base should be the primary cost driver of those overhead costs. Historically, direct labor (expressed as either dollars or hours) has been the primary cost driver in many manufacturing operations. While this remains the case in some industries, increasingly the use of a different cost driver, such as machine hours, may become the primary cost driver, especially in highly automated processes. Obviously, selecting the primary cost driver accurately will insure the most realistic total cost for each job. The steps to develop a predetermined overhead rate and allocate overhead are as follows:

1. Estimate the total overhead cost for the planning period.
2. Identify the manufacturing overhead (cost) allocation base.
3. Estimate the total quantity of the overhead allocation base.
4. Compute the predetermined manufacturing overhead rate.
5. Obtain actual quantities of the overhead allocation base used by individual jobs.
6. Allocate manufacturing overhead to jobs by multiplying the *predetermined* manufacturing overhead rate by the *actual* quantity of the allocation base used by each job.

The entry to record the allocation of overhead is:

Work in Process Inventory	XX	
Manufacturing Overhead		XX

Once overhead is allocated to a job, we can compute unit cost:

$$\frac{\text{unit}}{\text{cost}} = \frac{\text{direct materials + direct labor + overhead allocated}}{\text{number of units produced}}$$

See Exhibit 20-11 for the manufacturing overhead entry on the job cost record.

Objective 4 – Account for completion and sales of finished goods, and adjust for under- or overallocated manufacturing overhead.

As jobs are completed, they are transferred to finished goods inventory:

Finished Goods Inventory	XX	
Work in Process Inventory		XX

When goods are sold, these two entries are recorded:

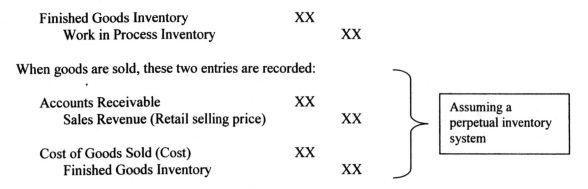

Accounts Receivable	XX	
Sales Revenue (Retail selling price)		XX
Cost of Goods Sold (Cost)	XX	
Finished Goods Inventory		XX

Assuming a perpetual inventory system

Note: The difference in these two entries represents gross profit.

Consider this T-account:

Manufacturing Overhead	
Actual	Allocated

If allocated overhead is less than actual overhead (a debit balance remains), then overhead is **underallocated**. If allocated overhead is greater than actual overhead (a credit balance remains), then overhead is **overallocated**.

Insignificant amounts of over- or underallocated overhead are closed to Cost of Goods Sold at year-end. Significant amounts of over- or underallocated overhead are distributed to Work in Process Inventory, Finished Goods Inventory, and Cost of Goods Sold.

The process for distributing a significant amount of over- or under allocated overhead is called **proration**. Proration spreads the remaining debit balance (representing an underallocation) or credit balance (representing an overallocation) to the three accounts in proportion to the balance in each.

Whether significant or insignificant, the balance of the Manufacturing Overhead account should be zero at the end of the accounting period.

Review Exhibit 20-12 in your text for a summary of job costing.

Objective 5– Assign noninventoriable costs in job costing.

Recall from Chapter 19 that inventoriable costs refer to only manufacturing costs (direct materials, direct labor, and manufacturing overhead) and not to the costs incurred in other elements of the value chain. However, these non-inventoriable costs can also be traced and allocated to jobs using the same principles introduced in the preceding sections of this chapter.

As illustrated in Exhibit 20-1, both job and process costing systems can also be used by service and merchandising businesses.

Obviously, a service business will not have any direct materials assigned to particular jobs (a lawyer advising a client, a CPA preparing a tax return, or a physician examining a patient, etc.); however, direct labor can constitute a significant portion of the fee charged for the service. In addition, every service business will incur many indirect costs (rent, utilities, insurance, salaries for support staff, etc.) and these costs need to be accurately allocated to jobs if the business owner is going to have a realistic picture of business operations.

TEST YOURSELF

All the self-testing materials in this chapter focus on information and procedures that your instructor is likely to test in quizzes and examinations.

I. Matching   *Match each numbered term with its lettered definition.*

_____ 1. Predetermined manufacturing overhead rate   _____ 8. Materials requisition
_____ 2. Job cost record   _____ 9. Overallocated overhead
_____ 3. Cost driver   _____ 10. Underallocated overhead
_____ 4. Cost allocation base   _____ 11. Cost tracing
_____ 5. Cost allocation   _____ 12. Job costing
_____ 6. Cost assignment   _____ 13. Process costing
_____ 7. Labor time record   _____ 14. Time record

A. A common denominator for systematically linking indirect costs to products
B. Any factor that affects costs
C. Document used to accumulate the costs of a job
D. Request for materials, prepared by manufacturing personnel
E. Source document used primarily by employees engaging in service activities, to trace direct labor to specific jobs
F. A credit balance in manufacturing overhead after overhead has been allocated to jobs
G. System for assigning costs to large numbers of identical units that usually proceed in a continuous fashion through a series of uniform production processes
H. Estimated manufacturing overhead rate computed at the beginning of the year
I. Source document manufacturing firms commonly use to trace direct labor to specific job cost records
J. Assigning indirect costs to cost objects
K. Assigning direct costs to cost objects
L. A general term that covers both tracing direct costs and allocating indirect costs
M. A remaining debit balance in manufacturing overhead after overhead has been allocated to jobs
N. A system for assigning costs to specific units or to a small batch of products

II. Multiple Choice   *Circle the best answer.*

1. When manufacturing labor costs are incurred, the account credited is:

   A. Manufacturing Wages.   C. Manufacturing Overhead.
   B. Wages Payable.   D. Work In Process Inventory.

2. Which of the following is not an inventoriable cost?

   A. Manufacturing Overhead   C. Delivery Expense
   B. Indirect Materials   D. Direct Labor

3. Which of the following manufacturers would be most likely to use process costing?

   A. Oil refinery   C. Aircraft
   B. Contractors   D. Furniture

4. When indirect materials are used in production:

   A. Work In Process Inventory is debited.
   B. Manufacturing Overhead is credited.
   C. Manufacturing Overhead is debited.
   D. Materials Inventory is debited.

5. When direct materials are used in production:

   A. Work In Process Inventory is credited.
   B. Manufacturing Overhead is debited.
   C. Materials Inventory is debited.
   D. Work In Process Inventory is debited.

6. When manufacturing wages are allocated, indirect labor is:

   A. Debited to Work In Process Inventory.
   B. Debited to Manufacturing Overhead.
   C. Credited to Manufacturing Overhead.
   D. Credited to Work In Process Inventory.

7. The entry to debit Cost of Goods Sold and credit Finished Goods Inventory as sales are made is recorded in:

   A. a periodic inventory system
   B. a perpetual inventory system
   C. when goods have completed the production process
   D. both B. and C.

8. Underallocated overhead implies:

   A. a credit balance in the Manufacturing Overhead account.
   B. too little overhead was applied to production.
   C. too much overhead was applied to production.
   D. Cost of Goods Sold is overstated.

9. In a service business, which of the following is an appropriate allocation base for indirect costs?

   A. Labor hours
   B. Machine hours
   C. Direct materials
   D. None of the above

10. An insignificant amount of under/over allocated manufacturing overhead should be:

    A. carried forward to the next accounting period.
    B. closed to Cost of Goods Sold.
    C. reported as an "Other expenses and revenues" on the income statement.
    D. allocated proportionately to Work In Process Inventory, Finished Goods Inventory, and Cost of Goods Sold.

III. Completion   *Complete each of the following.*

1. In a job costing system, unit cost is determined by dividing _____ by _____.

2. The document used to accumulate all the costs for each job is the _____.

3. _____ are a physical part of the finished product and their cost is separately and conveniently traceable through the manufacturing process.

4. Indirect materials and indirect labor are part of _____.

5. _____ are also called inventoriable costs.

6. _____ are never traced through the inventory accounts.

7. There are two main types of accounting systems for product costing: _____ and _____.

8. The purpose of a Materials Ledger is to _____.

9. Generally, the difference between direct and indirect labor is _____.

10. Job costing is used by companies that manufacture products _____.

IV. Daily Exercises

1. Place the following in correct sequence (use 1 through 6).

    _____ A.   Compute the predetermined manufacturing overhead rate
    _____ B.   Estimate the total overhead cost for the planning period
    _____ C.   Obtain actual quantities of the overhead allocation base used by individual jobs
    _____ D.   Select a cost allocation base
    _____ E.   Allocate manufacturing overhead to jobs
    _____ F.   Estimate the total quantity of the overhead allocation base

2. Raw Material XX had a balance of $56,500. During November, the following requisitions were processed for XX and charged to:

Job 243	$11,550
Job 256	8,210
Job 261	14,925
Factory Maintenance	775

    Record the entry assigning Raw Material XX.

3. During November, the following manufacturing labor costs were incurred and the following time tickets were assigned:

Job 243	$ 6,250
Job 256	2,340
Job 261	5,980
Factory Maintenance	16,810

Record the entry to assign November's labor costs.

4. Review the information in Daily Exercises #2 and #3 above and assume $53,200 in manufacturing overhead costs have been incurred and recorded, exclusive of indirect materials and indirect labor. If Manufacturing Overhead is allocated at a rate of 200% of Direct Materials cost, allocate Manufacturing Overhead to Jobs 243, 256, and 261. Is Manufacturing Overhead over- or underallocated?

5. Review the information in Daily Exercises #2, #3, and #4 above but assume overhead is allocated at the rate of 450% of direct labor costs. Determine the amount of manufacturing overhead to allocate to Jobs 243, 256, and 261. Is Manufacturing Overhead over- or underallocated?

V. Exercises

1. Review the information in Daily Exercises #2, #3 and #4, assuming the number of units produced for each job were:

Job 243	200 units
Job 256	120 units
Job 261	350 units

   A. Calculate the total cost and the per unit cost for each job.

   B. Record the journal entry for the completed jobs.

2. At the end of the year, the Manufacturing Overhead account appears as follows:

   Manufacturing Overhead

280,000	292,000

   A. Was overhead under- or overallocated for the year?

   Overallocated

   B. Assuming the balance in the overhead account is not significant, record the journal entry to close the account.

Mfg Overhead		12 000	
COGS			12 000

3. Given the following information, calculate total Manufacturing Overhead:

Factory Building Depreciation	$ 50,000
Sales Office Expense	4,400
Factory Equipment Depreciation	21,900
Advertising Expense	51,000
Administrative Salaries	202,000
Property Taxes - Manufacturing	42,000
Depreciation on Delivery Equipment	17,000
Office Utilities Expense	8,200
Indirect Materials	2,700
Factory Equipment Repair Expense	6,600
Indirect Labor	12,500
Utilities Expense - Manufacturing	9,100

4. Record the following journal entries in the space provided.
   a. $62,000 of direct materials was requisitioned for jobs.
   b. Direct labor costs of $32,600 were assigned to jobs.
   c. Manufacturing overhead of $18,000 was allocated to jobs.
   d. Three jobs with a total cost of $87,000 were completed.

WIP Inv	62000	
Direct mat inv		62000
WIP Inv	32600	
Wages Payable - Man Wages		32600
Direct labor WIP -inv	18000	
Man ovh		18000
Finished goods inv	87000	
WIP -inv		87000

5. Using the information in Exercise #4 above, reconstruct the Work in Process Inventory T-account and calculate the ending balance in the account, assuming a beginning balance of $12,575.

Work in Process Inventory

VI. Beyond the Numbers

Review the information in Daily Exercises #2 though #5 and comment on the appropriateness of direct materials or direct labor as the manufacturing overhead cost allocation base.

_____
_____
_____
_____
_____
_____
_____
_____
_____
_____

VII. Demonstration Problems

Demonstration Problem #1

Pat's Pottery had the following inventory balances on January 1, 20X9:

Materials Inventory	$28,000
Work in Process Inventory	41,250
Finished Goods Inventory	62,425

The Work in Process and Finished Goods Inventory accounts consisted of the following:

Work in Process:

		Direct Materials	Direct Labor	Manufacturing Overhead	Total
Job	420	$13,280	$7,100	$3,984	$24,364
Job	423	2,700	4,860	810	8,370
Job	424	5,640	1,184	1,692	8,516
				Total	$41,250

Finished Goods:

		Cost of job:
Job	419	$24,215
Job	421	21,910
Job	422	16,300
		$62,425

During the month of January 20X9, the following transactions occurred:

A. Pat purchased 900 tons of clay (materials) for $35 per ton.

B. Workers requisitioned $38,000 of direct materials for the following jobs:

420	$4,000
423	3,200
424	2,450
425	7,100
426	14,700
427	4,300
428	2,250
	$38,000

C. $4,050 of indirect materials was used.

D. The total manufacturing wages, $10,125, were incurred and assigned to production. 80% of total manufacturing wages was direct labor. (2 entries)

Time cards indicated the direct labor cost should be assigned to the jobs as follows:

420	$ 925
423	860
424	1,270
425	1,020
426	3,110
427	585
428	330
	$ 8,100

E. The following additional overhead costs were incurred: $1,600 in depreciation on manufacturing equipment and $3,765 in miscellaneous other costs (credit Accounts Payable).

F. Overhead is allocated to production at the rate of 30% of direct materials cost.

G. Jobs 420, 423, 424, 425 and 427 were completed.

H. Jobs 419, 420, 421, 422, 424, and 425 were sold on account. The total sales price for the jobs was $186,000. Assume a perpetual inventory system.

I. The balance in Manufacturing Overhead was considered insignificant.

Required:

1. Place the January 1 balances in the inventory accounts and the Work In Process Inventory and Finished Goods Inventory subsidiary ledgers.

2. Record the transactions in the general journal and post to the job T-accounts.

3. Calculate the ending balances in the inventory accounts, the job T-accounts, and manufacturing overhead.

4. Was Manufacturing Overhead overallocated or underallocated?

5. What will be the amount of Cost of Goods Sold on the January income statement?

Requirements 1, 2 & 3 (T-accounts)

	Work in Process Inventory	Finished Goods Inventory
Materials Inventory		

Work in Process Inventory Subsidiary Ledger

Job 420	Job 423	Job 424

Job 425	Job 426	Job 427

Job 428

Finished Goods Inventory Subsidiary Ledger

Job 419 | Job 420 | Job 421

Job 422

Requirement 2 (record transactions)

Date	Accounts and Explanation	PR	Debit	Credit

Requirement 3 (overhead)

Manufacturing Overhead account:

Manufacturing Overhead

_____|_____

Requirement 4 (overhead)

Manufacturing overhead is _____.

Requirement 5 (cost of goods sold)

Cost of Goods Sold

_____|_____

Demonstration Problem #2

Review your solution to Demonstration Problem #1 and present a Schedule of Cost of Goods Manufactured for Pat's Pottery for the month ended January 31, 20X9.

SOLUTIONS

I. Matching

1. H		5. J		9. F		13. G	
2. C		6. L		10. M		14. E	
3. B		7. I		11. K			
4. A		8. D		12. N			

II. Multiple Choice

1. B   Manufacturing Wages is debited when direct labor is *incurred* and Wages Payable is credited. When Manufacturing Wages are *assigned* to jobs, Manufacturing Overhead is debited for indirect labor Work in Process Inventory is debited for direct labor and Manufacturing Wages is credited.

2. C   Delivery Expense is a non-inventoriable cost.

3. A   Manufacturers producing a continuous flow of the same product use process costing. Of the manufacturers listed, the oil refinery is most likely to produce the same product in a continuous flow.

4. C   The use of indirect materials requires Materials Inventory to be reduced and Manufacturing Overhead to be increased. The journal entry is:
   Manufacturing Overhead   XX
       Materials Inventory   XX

5. D   The journal entry for the use of direct materials is:
   Work in Process Inventory   XX
       Materials Inventory   XX

6. B   Recall that manufacturing wages are cleared through a clearing account so that direct labor and indirect labor can be allocated properly. In recording the payroll allocation, Work in Process Inventory is debited for direct labor and Manufacturing Overhead is debited for indirect labor.

7. B   Only a perpetual inventory system has a Cost of Goods Sold account.

8. B   If overhead is underallocated, actual overhead costs were greater than overhead allocated to Work in Process Inventory. Accordingly, the debits to Manufacturing Overhead are greater than the credits, and Manufacturing Overhead will have a debit balance.

9. A   Labor hours are used to allocate indirect costs in a service businesses. Machine hours would be more appropriate allocation base in a manufacturing business.

10. B   When the amount of under/overallocated manufacturing overhead is insignificant it is closed to Cost of Goods Sold.

III. Completion

1. total costs assigned to a job, number of units completed (order important)
2. job cost record
3. direct materials
4. manufacturing overhead
5. Product costs
6. Period costs
7. job costing, process costing
8. maintain accurate records for each raw material
9. direct labor can be traced directly to the units being manufactured
10. as individual units or in small batches

IV. Daily Exercises

1. A. 4   D. 2
    B. 1   E. 6
    C. 5   F. 3

2. Work in Process Inventory   34,685
    Manufacturing Overhead   775
       Raw Materials Inventory   35,460

3. Work in Process Inventory   14,570
    Manufacturing Overhead   16,810
       Manufacturing Wages   31,380

4.

Total manufacturing overhead $53,200 + $775 (from Daily Exercise #2) + $16,810 (from Daily
(MOH) incurred =   Exercise #3) = $70,785

Manufacturing Overhead allocated to jobs:
Job 243   = $11,550 × 200% = $23,100
Job 256   = $ 8,210 × 200% = 16,420
Job 261   = $14,925 × 200% = 29,850
                              $69,370 Allocated to Work in Process Inventory

Total MOH incurred –Total MOH allocated to production = Over- or Underallocated Overhead
$70,785 - $69,370 = $1,415 Underallocated

4. Total manufacturing (MOH) overhead incurred = $70,785 (from Daily Exercise #4)

Manufacturing Overhead allocated to jobs:
Job 243   = $6,250 × 450% = $28,125
Job 256   = $2,340 × 450% = 10,530
Job 261   = $5,980 × 450% = 26,910
                             $65,165

Total MOH incurred –Total MOH allocated to production = Over- or Underallocated Overhead
$70,785 - $65,165 = $5,620 Underallocated

V. Exercises

1. A.

	Job 243	Job 256	Job 261
Direct Materials	$11,550	$8,210	$14,925
Direct Labor	6,250	2,340	5,980
Manufacturing Overhead	23,571	16,755	30,459
Total Costs	$41,371	$27,305	$51,364
Divided by units	÷ 200	÷ 120	÷ 350
Unit Cost	$206.86	$227.54	$146.75

B. Finished Goods Inventory   120,040
      Work in Process Inventory   120,040

This could also be recorded as separate entries for each of the three jobs.

2. A. Overallocated

Study Tip:	debit balance	=	underallocated overhead
	credit balance	=	overallocated overhead

B. Manufacturing Overhead   12,000
      Cost of Goods Sold   12,000

Study Tip: Because too much overhead was allocated to jobs throughout the year, the cost of goods sold account contains more overhead than was actually incurred. Therefore, it needs to be reduced by the amount of the overallocation.

3.

Factory Building Depreciation	$ 50,000
Factory Equipment Depreciation	21,900
Property Taxes - Manufacturing	42,000
Indirect Materials	2,700
Factory Equipment Repair Expense	6,600
Indirect Labor	12,500
Utilities Expense - Manufacturing	9,100
Total Manufacturing Overhead	$144,800

4.

a. Work in Process Inventory	62,000	
Materials Inventory		62,000
b. Work in Process Inventory	32,600	
Manufacturing Wages		32,600
c. Work in Process Inventory	18,000	
Manufacturing Overhead		18,000
d. Finished Goods Inventory	87,000	
Work in Process Inventory		87,000

5.

Work in Process Inventory

Bal. 12,575	
(a) 62,000	87,000 (d)
(b) 32,600	
(c) 18,000	
Bal 38,175	

VI. Beyond the Numbers

In many respects, the question is unfair because one would need a great deal of additional information before one could determine if direct materials or direct labor are the appropriate cost drivers to use as the manufacturing overhead allocation base. However, as you were given just the two choices, it should be apparent that direct materials is the more appropriate of the two. Why? First, a comparison of the two total amounts reveals the cost of direct materials is over twice the amount of direct labor. Second, the total direct labor charged to the jobs is even less than the indirect labor charged to manufacturing overhead. Therefore, between the two, direct materials would appear to be the more appropriate cost driver.

VII. Demonstration Problems

Demonstration Problem #1 Solved and Explained

Requirements 1, 2 & 3 (T-accounts)

Materials Inventory			Work in Process Inventory			Finished Goods Inventory	
1/1 28,000	38,000 B.		1/1 41,250	73,275 G.		1/1 63,425	116,135 H.
A. 31,500	4,050 C.		B. 38,000			G. 73,275	
Bal. 17,450			D. 8,100			Bal. 19,565	
			F. 11,400				
			Bal. 25,475				

Work in Process Inventory Subsidiary Ledger

Job 420			Job 423			Job 424	
1/1 24,364	30,489 G.		1/1 8,370	13,390 G.		1/1 8,516	12,971 G.
B. 4,000			B. 3,200			B. 2,450	
D. 925			D. 860			D. 1,270	
F. 1,200			F. 960			F. 735	

Job 425			Job 426			Job 427	
B. 7,100	10,250 G.		B. 14,700			B. 4,300	6,175 G.
D. 1,020			D. 3,110			D. 585	
F. 2,130			F. 4,410			F. 1,290	
			Bal. 22,220				

Job 428	
B. 2,250	
D. 330	
F. 675	
Bal. 3,255	

Finished Good Inventory Subsidiary Ledger

Job 419	
1/1 24,215	24,215 H.

Job 420	
1/1 30,489	30,489 H.

Job 421	
1/1 21,910	21,910 H.

Job 422	
1/1 16,300	16,300 H.

Job 423	
G. 13,390	

Job 424	
G. 12,971	12,971 H.

Job 425	
G. 10,250	10,250 H.

Job 427	
G. 6,175	

Requirement 2 (record transactions)

	Accounts and Explanation	PR	Debit	Credit
A.	Material Inventory		31,500	
	Accounts Payable			31,500
B.	Work in Process Inventory		38,000	
	Materials Inventory			38,000
C.	Manufacturing Overhead		4,050	
	Materials Inventory			4,050
D.	Manufacturing Wages		10,125	
	Wages Payable			10,125
	Work in Process Inventory (.80 × $10,125)		8,100	
	Manufacturing Overhead (.20 × $10,125)		2,025	
	Manufacturing Wages			10,125
E.	Manufacturing Overhead		5,365	
	Accumulated Depreciation-Manufacturing Equip.			1,600
	Accounts Payable			3,765
F.	Work in Process Inventory (.30 × $38,000)		11,400	
	Manufacturing Overhead			11,400
G.	Finished Goods Inventory		73,275	
	Work in Process Inventory			73,275
H.	Accounts Receivable		186,000	
	Sales Revenue			186,000

	Cost of Goods Sold		116,135	
	Finished Goods Inventory			116,135
I.	Cost of Goods Sold		40	
	Manufacturing Overhead			40

Points to Remember

In transaction D, it is important to distinguish between direct labor and indirect labor. Direct labor is 80% of the total manufacturing wages of $10,125, or $8,100. The remaining amount is indirect labor.

In transaction F, it is important to note that overhead is allocated based on *direct materials*. The only direct materials in this problem are the $38,000 of direct materials in transaction B.

To prepare the entry for item I, it is necessary to know the balance in the Manufacturing Overhead account:

Manufacturing Overhead

(C) 4,050	
(D) 2,025	
(E) 5,365	(F) 11,400
Bal. 40	(I) 40
Bal. 0	

Since the account has a debit balance, we credit it in order to bring its balance to zero, and transfer the balance to Cost of Goods Sold.

Requirement 3 See T-account for Manufacturing Overhead above.

Requirement 4 (overhead)

A debit balance in the Manufacturing Overhead account indicates that Manufacturing Overhead is underallocated. The T-account in requirement 3 indicates that Manufacturing Overhead had a debit balance of $40 prior to closing the account.

Requirement 5 (cost of goods sold)

Cost of Goods Sold

(H) 116,135	
(I) 40	
Bal. 116,175	

Demonstration Problem #2 Solved and Explained

Pat's Pottery
Schedule of Cost of Goods Manufactured
Month Ended January 31, 20X9

Beginning work in process inventory			$41,250
Direct materials			
Beginning inventory	$28,000		
(A) Purchases of direct materials	27,450		
Materials available for use	55,450		
Less: Ending inventory	17,450		
Direct materials used		$38,000	
Direct labor		8,100	
Manufacturing overhead			
Indirect materials	4,050		
Indirect labor	2,025		
Depreciation - factory equipment	1,600		
Miscellaneous	3,765		
(B) Total manufacturing overhead		11,440	
Total manufacturing costs incurred			57,540
Total manufacturing costs to account for			98,790
Less: Ending work in process inventory			25,475
(C) Cost of goods manufactured			$73,315

A. Because we only include 'direct materials purchased' in this section, the total materials purchased ($31,500) have been reduced by the amount of indirect materials used ($4,050).

B. Total manufacturing overhead includes the actual costs *incurred*, not the actual amount allocated.

C. The cost of goods manufactured shown on the schedule ($73,315) differs from the amount recorded in entry (G) ($73,275) for the following reasons:

$73,275 is the amount which includes the *allocated* manufacturing overhead, not the actual overhead incurred. After entry (I) is recorded and posted, the Cost of Goods sold account is increased because manufacturing overhead was underallocated (i.e. too little was allocated to production).

Study Tip: Remember, Finished Goods Inventory does not appear on this schedule. They are reported on the Income Statement and used to calculate Cost of Goods Sold.

Chapter 22 - Cost-Volume-Profit Analysis

CHAPTER OVERVIEW

In Chapters 20 and 21 you learned about a particular type of management accounting concerned with manufacturing businesses wherein direct materials are converted into finished goods. We now turn our attention to Cost-Volume-Profit (CVP) analysis to more closely examine "costs" and how they change relative to changes in output. The interaction of costs and volume results in changes in profits (or losses). The learning objectives for this chapter are to

1. Identify how changes in volume affect costs.
2. Use CVP analysis to compute breakeven points.
3. Use CVP analysis for profit planning, and graph the cost-volume-profit relations.
4. Use CVP methods to perform sensitivity analyses.
5. Compute income using variable costing and absorption costing

CHAPTER REVIEW

Objective 1 - Identify how changes in volume affect costs.

Cost behavior is the way that costs change as volume changes. A **cost driver** is any factor that affects costs. You were introduced to cost drivers in Chapter 19. The three patterns of cost behavior are:

1. **Total variable costs** change in direct proportion to changes in volume or level of activity. However, on a per unit basis, variable costs are constant. Examples of variable costs include direct materials, sales commissions, and delivery expense. Suppose CDs have a cost of $6 per disk when purchased for resale. If a retailer sells 1,000 CDs, cost of goods sold will be $6,000. However, if 2,000 CDs are sold, cost of goods sold will be $12,000. Thus, the more CDs the retailer sells, the higher the cost of goods sold will be; thus, the cost of goods sold is variable in total, and constant at the $6 variable cost per unit.

2. **Total fixed costs** do not change in total despite wide changes in volume. Examples of fixed costs include expenses such as rent and depreciation. Suppose the rent for a store is $5,000 per month. The storeowner will pay $5,000 per month whether sales increase, decrease, or remain the same. However, on a per unit basis, fixed costs will vary. If the rent is $5,000 per month and the retailer sells 1,000 CDs, then the fixed cost per CD is $5 per unit. If the retailer sells 2,000 CDs, then the fixed cost per unit is $2.50. Notice as the number of CDs sold increases, the fixed cost of $5,000 is spread over more units, thus decreasing the cost per unit. Therefore, we can see that the fixed cost per unit is inversely proportional to volume.

3. **Mixed costs** are costs that have both a variable and fixed component. The monthly telephone bill, for example, is based both on local service and long distance service. The amount for local (unlimited) service is a fixed cost, while the amount for long distance service is a variable cost. Therefore, the total telephone bill is a mixed cost.

Study the graphs in your text that illustrate cost behavior patterns (Exhibits 22-1, 22-2, and 22-3). The variable cost graph begins at the origin (zero volume, zero cost) and increases in a straight line, whose slope equals the variable cost per unit. As the slope of the line gets steeper, the more the variable cost per unit increases. The fixed cost graph is a horizontal line that intersects the cost (vertical) axis at the fixed cost level. The mixed cost graph intersects the cost axis at the level of the fixed cost component, and its slope equals the variable cost per unit.

When budgeting costs, companies use the **relevant range concept**. Relevant range is the band of volume where total fixed costs remain constant and the variable cost per unit remains constant. These relationships will be different in other ranges. See Exhibit 22-4 in your text.

Objective 2 - Use CVP analysis to compute breakeven points.

Cost-volume-profit analysis is often called **breakeven analysis**. The **breakeven point** is the sales level at which operating income is zero. If sales are below the breakeven point, the result is a loss. If sales are above the breakeven point, the result is a profit. Decision-makers use cost-volume-profit analysis to answer questions such as, "How much do we need to sell to breakeven?" or "If our sales are some specific amount, what will our profit be?"

CVP analysis assumes the following:
1. The only factor that affects costs is changes in volume.
2. Managers can classify each cost (or the components of mixed costs) as either variable or fixed.
3. Both costs and revenues are linear throughout the relevant range of volume.
4. Inventory levels will not change.
5. The sales mix of products will not change. **Sales mix** is the combination of products that make up total sales.

There are two approaches used in CVP analysis:

1. **The Income Statement Approach:**

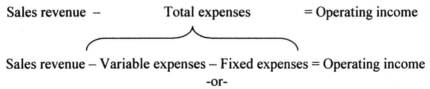

Sales revenue –   Total expenses   = Operating income

Sales revenue – Variable expenses – Fixed expenses = Operating income
-or-
(Sale price per unit × units sold) – (Variable cost per unit × units sold) – Fixed expenses = Operating income

To calculate the breakeven point, operating income in the formula will always be zero. This is because operating income is always zero at breakeven. The equation shows how many units must be sold (and the total dollar amount of the sales) in order to breakeven.

2. The Contribution Margin Approach:

The contribution margin receives its name because it represents the excess of sales revenue over variable costs that contributes to covering fixed expenses and providing operating income.

Breakeven sales in units is computed by dividing fixed expenses plus operating income, where operating income is zero ($0) by the contribution margin per unit:

$$\text{Contribution Margin Per Unit} = \text{Sales Price Per Unit} - \text{Variable Expense Per Unit}$$

$$\text{Breakeven Sales in Units} = \frac{\text{Fixed expenses} + \text{Operating income}}{\text{Contribution Margin Per Unit}}$$

Breakeven sales in dollars is computed by dividing fixed expenses by the contribution margin ratio:

$$\text{Contribution Margin Ratio} = \frac{\text{Contribution margin}}{\text{Sales revenue}}$$

$$\text{Breakeven Sales in Dollars} = \frac{\text{Fixed expenses} + \text{Operating income}}{\text{Contribution Margin Ratio}}$$

Objective 3 - Use CVP analysis for profit planning, and graph the cost-volume-profit relations.

Managers of business are also interested in the sales level needed to earn a target profit. We use the same formula as we did to calculate the breakeven point, except instead of setting operating income to zero, use the target operating income. The profit that a business wishes to earn is called the **target operating income**.

$$\text{Target Sales In Units} = \frac{\text{Fixed Expenses} + \text{Target Operating Income}}{\text{Contribution Margin Per Unit}}$$

$$\text{Target Sales In Dollars} = \frac{\text{Fixed Expenses} + \text{Target Operating Income}}{\text{Contribution Margin Ratio}}$$

Notice that the only difference between computing breakeven sales and target sales is that with target sales, the target operating income amount is added to fixed expenses.

Managers are also interested in knowing the amount of operating income or operating loss to expect at various levels of sales. One convenient way to provide this information is to prepare a **cost-volume-profit graph**.

In order to familiarize yourself with the components of the CVP graph, study these steps and review Exhibit 22-7 in your text:

Step 1: Draw the sales revenue line from the origin through a preselected sales volume.

Step 2: Draw the fixed expense line.

Step 3: Draw the total expense line by computing the variable expenses at your preselected sales volume (Step 1) and then plot them beginning at your fixed expense line.

Step 4: Identify the breakeven point (where sales revenue and total expenses intersect).

Step 5: Identify the operating income and operating loss areas.

Objective 4 - Use CVP methods to perform sensitivity analyses.

Sensitivity analysis is a "what if" technique that managers use to ask what a result will be if a predicted amount is not achieved or if an underlying assumption changes. For example, managers may want to determine answers to the following questions:

- If a special "25% off" sale is held, what is the new breakeven point in units and in sales dollars?
- If a supplier notifies the company of an increase in a key raw material, what will be the new breakeven point?
- If the cost of renting a sales office doubles, how much must our sales increase to cover the new rent expense and not affect operating income?

Each of these scenarios can be analyzed using the breakeven formulas.

The **margin of safety** is the excess of expected or actual sales over breakeven sales. It tells a business how much sales can drop before an operating loss is incurred. The margin of safety may be computed in terms of either dollars or units:

Margin of safety in units = Expected sales in units - Breakeven sales in units
Margin of safety in dollars = margin of safety in units × sale price per unit

Objective 5 – Compute income using variable costing and absorption costing.

GAAP requires that both variable and fixed manufacturing costs be assigned to products. This approach is called **absorption costing** because products "absorb" fixed manufacturing costs as well as variable manufacturing costs. Absorption costing has been used in the financial statements presented throughout this discussion because it conforms to GAAP requirements. However, managers prefer to use an alternative approach called **variable costing** for planning and decision-making. Variable costing assigns variable manufacturing costs to products, but fixed manufacturing costs (property taxes on the factory, depreciation on the building, etc.) are treated as period costs and reported on the income statement when incurred. The argument for the variable costing approach is that fixed manufacturing costs will be incurred regardless of production levels and should therefore be treated as period costs.

Carefully review Exhibit 22-8 in your text. Notice that the only difference between these two approaches is the treatment of fixed manufacturing costs. However, this difference will affect net income, as illustrated in Exhibits 22-9 and 22-10 in your text. Because absorption costing assigns fixed manufacturing costs to inventory, these costs will not appear on the income statement until the units are actually sold, whereas under variable costing all fixed manufacturing costs are included on the income statement when they are incurred. The general rule is that when inventories are increasing, absorption costing income will be higher than variable costing income. The reverse is true when inventories are declining.

TEST YOURSELF

All the self-testing materials in this chapter focus on information and procedures that your instructor is likely to test in quizzes and examinations.

Matching   *Match each numbered term with its lettered definition.*

_____ 1. Cost behavior	_____ 8. Margin of safety
_____ 2. Variable cost	_____ 9. Relevant range
_____ 3. Fixed cost	_____ 10. Variable costing
_____ 4. Mixed cost	_____ 11. Sales mix
_____ 5. Breakeven point	_____ 12. CVP analysis
_____ 6. Contribution margin	_____ 13. Absorption costing
_____ 7. Target operating income	_____ 14. Period costs

A. The amount of unit sales or dollar sales at which revenues equal expenses
B. A costing method that assigns only variable manufacturing costs to products
C. The description of how costs change in response to a shift in the volume of business activity
D. The excess of sales price over variable expenses
E. A band of activity where total fixed costs remain constant and where the variable cost per unit remains constant.
F. A cost that does not change in total as volume changes
G. The excess of expected (or actual) sales over breakeven sales
H. A cost that is part variable and part fixed
I. A cost that changes in total in direct proportion to changes in volume or activity
J. The desired operating income a business wishes to earn
K. Costs reported on the income statement as they are incurred
L. The combination of products that make up total sales
M. A costing method that assigns all manufacturing costs to products
N. A part of the budgeting system that helps managers predict the outcome of their decisions by analyzing relationships among costs, volume, and profit or loss.

II. Multiple Choice   *Circle the best answer.*

Use the following information for Questions 1 through 4:

Movie Mania, Inc. sells DVDs. Last year Movie Mania sold 5,500 cases at $24 per case. The variable cost per case was $14.40 and fixed costs amounted to $28,800.

1. The breakeven point in cases of tapes was:

A. 1,200.   C. 3,000.
B. 2,000.   D. 5,500.

2. The breakeven point in sales dollars was:

A. $66,000.
B. $72,000.

C. $24,000.
D. $14,400.

3. The margin of safety in dollars was:

A. $60,000.
B. $48,000.

C. $51,000.
D. $-0-.

4. If Movie Mania wished to earn an operating income of $34,800, how many cases of tapes would have to be sold?

A. 3,600.
B. 4,400.

C. 5,500.
D. 6,625.

5. Dividing breakeven point in sales dollars by the unit selling price results in the:

A. variable cost per unit.
B. breakeven point in dollars.

C. breakeven point in units.
D. variable cost ratio.

6. Which of the following will decrease the breakeven point?

A. Decreasing fixed costs
B. Increasing fixed costs

C. Increasing variable costs per unit
D. Decreasing selling price

7. Which of the following will increase the breakeven point?

A. Decreasing fixed costs
B. Increasing selling price

C. Decreasing variable cost per unit
D. Decreasing selling price

Use the following graph to answer questions 8 through 10:

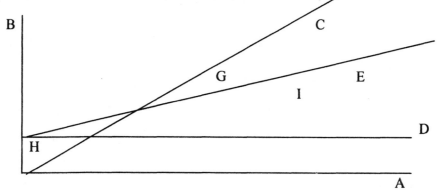

8. Line D must be:

A. the sales line.
B. total expense line.

C. fixed expense line.
D. cannot be determined.

9. If E is the total expense line then I must be:

   A. operating income area.   C. operating loss area.
   B. variable expense area.   D. cannot be determined.

10. If C is the sales line and E is the total expense line then F must be:

    A. breakeven point.   C. total dollars.
    B. total units.   D. cannot be determined.

III. Completion   *Complete each of the following.*

1. The _____ is equal to the sales price per unit minus the variable expenses per unit.

2. A convenient way to determine operating income or loss at various levels of sales is to prepare a _____.

3. _____ and _____ are examples of costs that change proportionately with sales.

4. The_____ is the combination of products that make up total sales.

5. Two approaches used in CVP analysis are the _____ approach and the _____ approach.

6. _____ tells a decision maker how much sales can drop before an operating loss is incurred.

For questions 7 through 10, complete the sentence with **increase, decrease,** or **not affect**.

7. An increase in direct material cost will _____ the contribution margin.

8. An increase in direct labor cost will _____ the breakeven point.

9. A decrease in direct materials costs will _____the breakeven point.

10. An increase in fixed plant insurance will _____the breakeven point.

11. Absorption costing reports all _____ costs as _____ costs on the income statement.

12. Variable costing reports only _____ costs as _____ costs on the income statement.

IV. Daily Exercises

1. Classify each of the following costs as fixed, variable, or mixed. (Assume sales volume is within the relevant range for the current period.)

Cost	Classification
a) Property taxes	Fixed
b) Direct materials	V
c) Depreciation on office equipment	F
d) Advertising expense	F
e) Office salaries expense	F
f) Direct labor	V
g) Manufacturing overhead	Mix
h) Rent expense	F
i) Insurance expense	F
j) Supplies expense	V

2. Bola's Basketry has fixed costs of $420,000. Variable costs are 30% of sales. Assuming each basket sells for $10, what is their breakeven point in unit sales?

$$\$F = CM$$

CM = .70

$$\frac{420,000}{7} = 60,000$$

3. Manuel's Manufacturing sells a product for $8 per unit. If the variable cost is $4.25 per unit, and breakeven is 48,000 units, what are Manuel's fixed costs?

3.75 × 48,000 = $180,000

4. If variable costs are 60% of sales and fixed costs are $230,000 what is the breakeven point in sales dollars?

CMn = .40

$$\frac{230,000}{.40} = 575000$$

V. Exercises

1. A monthly income statement for Bijan's Burritos appears as follows:

Sales		$280,000
Cost of Goods Sold		120,000
Gross Margin		160,000
Operating Expenses:		
Marketing Expense	$35,000	
General Expense	70,000	105,000
Operating Income		$ 55,000

Cost of Goods Sold is a variable expense. Marketing expense is 70% variable and 30% fixed. General Expense is half fixed and half variable. In the space below, present a contribution margin income statement for the month.

2. Review the information in Exercise 1 above, and calculate the following:

   a. Contribution margin ratio

   b. Breakeven point in sales

   c. If the frozen burritos sell for $2 per package, what is the breakeven point in units?

   d. By what amount would operating income decrease if sales dropped by 20%?

3. Using the form below and the information in Exercise 1 above, graph Bijan's Burritos total expense (both fixed and variable) and sales, showing clearly the breakeven point calculated in Exercise 2 above.

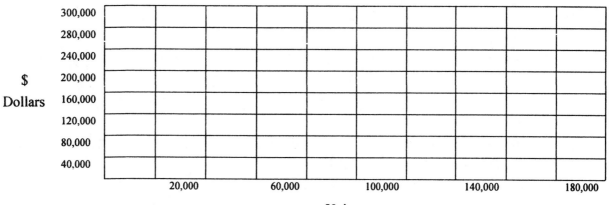

4. A manufacturer of rubber exercise balls provides the following cost information:

Variable cost per ball	$ 9.50
Fixed monthly expenses	$15,000
Selling price per ball	$ 20.00

a. What is the manufacturer's contribution margin per ball and contribution margin ratio?

b. What is the manufacturer's breakeven point in units and dollars?

c. Prove the accuracy of your answers in (b) above by presenting an income statement at breakeven.

d. Assuming the manufacturer's targeted net income is $12,000 per month, and the company is subject to a 40% tax rate, calculate the sales necessary to achieve the targeted net income (after tax).

5. Review the information in Exercise 4 above, assuming the manufacturer achieves the $12,000 targeted net income, after tax. The owner is considering an advertising campaign to increase sales. The cost of the ads would be $5,000 per month. By what amount, expressed in units and dollars, would sales need to increase to justify the advertising expenditure?

VI. Beyond the Numbers

Review Daily Exercise 1. How would your answers change if output remains within the relevant range but the costs listed are classified over a long period?

Cost	Classification
a) Property taxes	_____
b) Direct materials	_____
c) Depreciation on office equipment	_____
d) Advertising expense	_____
e) Office salaries expense	_____
f) Direct labor	_____
g) Manufacturing overhead	_____
h) Rent expense	_____
i) Insurance expense	_____
j) Supplies expense	_____

VII. Demonstration Problems

Demonstration Problem #1

The Gentry Game Corporation is planning to introduce a new table game. The relevant range of output is between 10,000 and 40,000 units. Within this range, fixed expenses are estimated to be $325,000 and variable expenses are estimated at 35% of the $30 selling price.

Required:

1. Using the contribution margin approach, calculate breakeven sales in units and in dollars.

2. If targeted net operating income (pretax) is $120,000, how many games must be sold?

3. Prepare a graph showing operating income and operating loss areas from 0 to 40,000 games, assuming a selling price of $30. Identify the breakeven sales level and the sales level needed to earn operating income of $120,000.

4. If the corporation increases the selling price to $36, how many games must be sold to earn operating income of $60,000? Assume variable costs are 35% of the new selling price.

Requirement 1 (Breakeven sales in units and dollars)

Requirement 2 (Targeted operating income)

Requirement 3 (Graph)

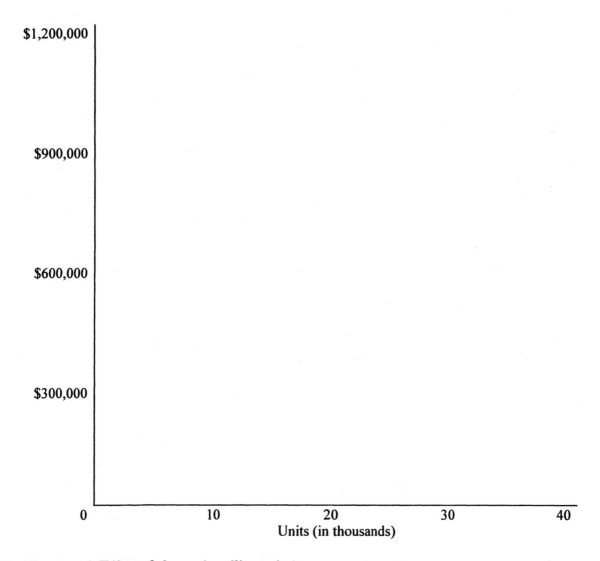

Requirement 4 (Effect of change in selling price)

SOLUTIONS

I. Matching

1. C	3. F	5. A	7. J	9. E	11. L	13. M
2. I	4. H	6. D	8. G	10. B	12. N	14. K

II. Multiple Choice

1. C $28,800 / ($24.00 - $14.40) = 3,000$

2. B $28,800 / [($24.00 - $14.40) / $24.00] = $72,000$

3. A   (5,500 boxes - 3,000 boxes) × $24.00 = $60,000

4. D   ($28,800 + $34,800) / ($24.00 - $14.40) = $63,600 / $9.60 = 6,625

5. C   BE$ = Breakeven sales dollars. BEu = Breakeven in units.
    $Pu = unit selling price.
    BE$ = BEu × $Pu
    BE$ / $Pu = BEu

6. A   BE$ = Breakeven sales dollars. BEu = Breakeven in units.
    $Pu = unit selling price. FC = Fixed Cost
    VCu = Variable cost per unit.

    Recall that BEu = FC /($Pu - VCu)

    Of the answers listed, only A "Decreasing fixed costs" will decrease the breakeven point.

7. D   Refer to 6 above. Note that answer D, "Decreasing selling price," will decrease the contribution margin and increase the breakeven point.

Study tip: If you have difficulty with 5 through 7, consider the formula for the breakeven point in units:

Fixed Expenses / Contribution Margin Per Unit = Breakeven in Units

If the numerator increases, or the denominator decreases, the breakeven point increases. If the numerator decreases, or the denominator increases, the breakeven point decreases.

---

8. C   The sales and total expense line slope upward; only the fixed expense line is flat.

9. B   The variable expense area is the difference between the total expense line and the fixed expense line.

10. A   Total units and total dollars are the A and B axis. F is the breakeven point where sales intersect total expenses.

III. Completion

1. contribution margin per unit
2. cost-volume-profit graph
3. Cost of goods sold, selling commission (other answers may be acceptable)
4. sales mix
5. income statement approach, contribution margin approach
6. The margin of safety
7. decrease (An increase in direct materials is an increase in the variable cost per unit. This decreases the contribution margin.)
8. increase (An increase in direct labor cost is an increase in the variable cost per unit. This decreases the contribution margin. As the contribution margin decreases, the breakeven point increases.)
9. decrease (A decrease in direct materials cost is a decrease in variable cost per unit. This increases the contribution margin. As the contribution margin increases, the breakeven point decreases. Contrast with #8.)
10. increase (An increase in plant insurance is an increase in fixed costs. An increase in fixed costs increases the breakeven point.)
11. manufacturing, product (order important)
12. variable, product (order important)

IV. Daily Exercises

1.

	Cost	Classification
a)	Property taxes	Fixed
b)	Direct materials	Variable
c)	Depreciation on office equipment	Fixed
d)	Advertising expense	Fixed
e)	Office salaries expense	Fixed
f)	Direct labor	Variable
g)	Manufacturing overhead	Mixed (because some are fixed, such as rent, depreciation, etc., whereas others are variable—indirect materials, utilities, for instance)
h)	Rent expense	Fixed
i)	Insurance expense	Fixed
j)	Supplies expense	Variable

2. If VC = 30% of sales, then CM = 70% of sales, or $7 per unit.

$$\frac{\text{Fixed expenses}}{\text{Contribution margin}} = \text{Breakeven point}$$

$$\frac{\$420,000}{\$7} = 60,000 \text{ units}$$

3.

$$\frac{\text{Fixed expenses (FE)}}{\text{Contribution margin}} = \text{Breakeven point}$$

$$\frac{\text{FE}}{\$3.75} = 48,000$$

$$\text{FE} = \$180,000$$

4. If VC = 60% of sales, then CM = 40% of sales.

$$\frac{\text{Fixed expenses}}{\text{Contribution margin ratio}} = \text{Breakeven in sales}$$

$$\frac{\$230,000}{40\%} = \$575,000$$

V. Exercises

1.

Sales		$280,000
Less: Variable Expenses		
Cost of Goods Sold	$120,000	
Marketing Expense	24,500	
General Expense	35,000	179,500
Contribution Margin		100,500
Less: Fixed Expenses		
Marketing Expense	10,500	
General Expense	35,000	45,500
Operating Income		$ 55,000

2.

a. Contribution margin ratio = contribution margin / sales
    = 100,500 / 280,000 = 35.9% (rounded)

b. Breakeven point in sales   = $0 operating income
    = fixed expense / contribution margin ratio
    = $45,500 / 35.9% = $126,741

c. $126,741 / $2 each = 63,371 packages

d.

Sales [($280,000 – 20%($280,000)]		$224,000
Less: Variable Expenses		
Cost of Goods Sold	$96,000	
Marketing Expense	19,600	
General Expense	28,000	143,600
Contribution Margin		80,400
Less: Fixed Expenses		*45,500
Operating Income		$ 34,900

*Fixed expenses remain the same, regardless of sales level (assuming no change in the relevant range). If sales drop 20%, operating income decreases by $20,100 ($55,000-$34,900).

3.

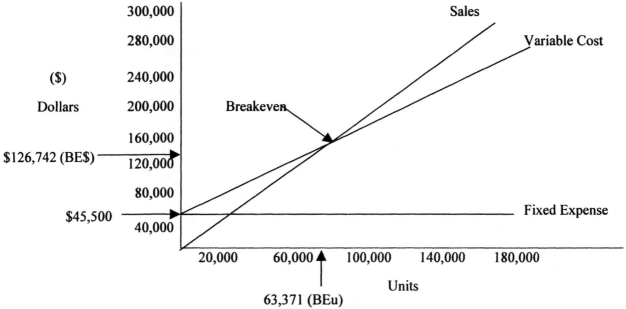

4.

a. Contribution margin   =   sales – variable costs
                          = $20 - $9.50 = $10.50

    Contribution ratio   =   contribution margin / sales
                          = $10.50 / $20.00 = 52.5%

b. Breakeven (units)   =   fixed expenses / contribution margin
                          = $15,000 / $10.50 = 1,428.5714 units

    Breakeven (sales)   =   fixed expenses / contribution margin ratio
                          = $15,000 / 52.5% = $28,571 (rounded)

c.

Sales	$28,571	
Less: Variable Costs (1,428.5714 units × $9.50 ea)	13,571	(rounded)
Contribution Margin	15,000	(rounded)
Less: Fixed Expenses	15,000	
Operating Income	-0-	

d. Since the targeted net income ($12,000) is after-tax, first we have to calculate the pre-tax target income.

pre-tax target income = $12,000 / 60% = $20,000

targeted sales = (fixed expenses + net income) / contribution margin ratio

= ($15,000 + $20,000) / 52.5%

= $35,000 / 52.5% = $66,667 (rounded)

5. The advertising cost is a fixed expense so replace the $15,000 amount with $20,000, then solve as follows:

Target sales (dollars) = ($20,000 + $20,000) / 52.5% = $76,190 (rounded)

Target sales (units) = ($20,000 + $20,000) / $10.50 = 3,810 units

Sales need to increase $9,523 ($76,190 - $66,667) or 476 units (3,810-3,334).

VI. Beyond the Numbers

a) Fixed (while property taxes will probably rise over the long run, they still are a fixed cost)
b) Variable
c) Fixed
d) Mixed (the business will always advertise, but the amount will vary over the long run)
e) Fixed
f) Variable
g) Variable
h) Mixed
i) Possibly mixed (a portion fixed regardless of output with add-ons to reflect changes in output)
j) Variable

VII. Demonstration Problems

Demonstration Problem #1 Solved and Explained

Requirement 1

To compute breakeven in dollars and in units, we need to find the contribution margin per unit and the contribution margin ratio:

$$\begin{array}{lll} \text{Contribution Margin} & = & \text{Sales Price} - \text{Variable Cost} \\ \text{Per Unit} & & \text{Per Unit} \qquad\quad \text{Per Unit} \end{array}$$

$$\begin{array}{ll} \text{Contribution Margin} & = \dfrac{\text{Contribution Margin}}{\text{Sales Price Per Unit}} \\ \text{Percentage or Ratio} & \end{array}$$

Since the variable costs are 35% (0.35) of sales, the contribution margin per unit is:

$$\$30 - (.35 \times 30) = \$30 - \$10.50 = \$19.50$$

The contribution margin ratio is:

$$\$19.50 / 30 = .65$$

The computation of breakeven sales in units is:

$$\begin{array}{ll} \text{Breakeven Sales} & = \dfrac{\text{Fixed Expenses}}{\text{Contribution Margin Per Unit}} \\ \text{in Units} & \end{array}$$

$$\$325,000 / \$19.50 = 16,667 \text{ games}$$

The breakeven point in units is 16,667 games.

The computation of breakeven sales in dollars is:

$$\begin{array}{ll} \text{Breakeven Sales} & = \dfrac{\text{Fixed Expenses}}{\text{Contribution Margin Percentage}} \\ \text{in Dollars} & \end{array}$$

$$\$325,000 / .65 = \$500,000$$

The breakeven point in dollars is $500,000.

Requirement 2

The target operating income is given as $120,000. The number of games that must be sold to earn a target income of $120,000 is:

$$\begin{array}{ll} \text{Target Sales} & = \dfrac{\text{Fixed Expenses} + \text{Target Operating Income}}{\text{Contribution Margin Per Unit}} \\ \text{in Units} & \end{array}$$

$$(\$325,000 + \$120,000) / \$19.50 = 22,821 \text{ games}$$

To achieve the target operating income of $120,000, 22,821 games must be sold.

Requirement 3 (Graph)

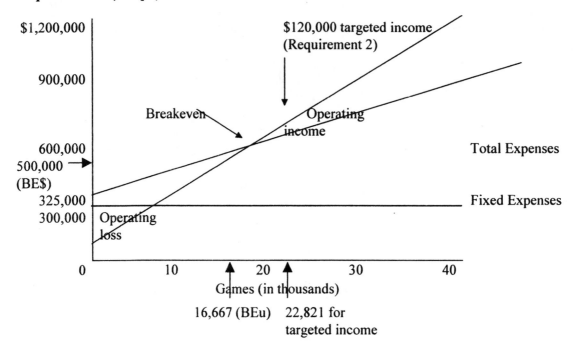

Requirement 4

To find the solution to Requirement 4, you must first determine exactly what item changes. No change in fixed expenses is indicated, and the target operating income of $60,000 remains the same. However, the selling price increases from $30 to $36, an increase of $6. Since variable expenses are 35% of the selling price, the new variable cost is $12.60 (35% × $36). Since the selling price of the game has changed, we must find the new contribution margin per unit in order to use the formula for target sales in Requirement 2. The new contribution margin per unit is:

$$\$36 - \$12.60 = \$23.40$$

Since the contribution margin per unit has increased to $23.40, the new target sales in units will be:

$$(\$325,000 + \$60,000) / \$23.40 = 16,453 \text{ games}$$

Target sales in units has decreased to 16,453 units. This is due to the increase in the selling price and the resulting increase in the contribution margin per unit.

Chapter 23 - The Master Budget and Responsibility Accounting

CHAPTER OVERVIEW

In the last chapter you learned more about costs—specifically how CVP analysis is used to predict outcomes. We now turn our attention to some of the ways managers plan and control their organization's activities using budgets. The learning objectives for this chapter are to

1. Learn why managers use budgets.
2. Prepare an operating budget.
3. Prepare a financial budget.
4. Use sensitivity analysis in budgeting.
5. Prepare performance reports for responsibility centers.

CHAPTER REVIEW

Objective 1 – Learn why managers use budgets.

A **budget** is a quantitative expression of a plan of action that helps managers to coordinate and implement the plan. The benefits of budgeting are:

1. **Planning** - budgets require managers to make plans, set goals, and design strategies for achieving those goals.
2. **Coordination and communication** - since the master budget is an overall company plan, it requires managers to work with other departments to achieve organizational goals and to communicate a consistent set of plans throughout the company.
3. **Benchmarking** - the budget can be used to evaluate performance by comparing actual results with the budgeted ones.

The **performance report** compares actual figures with budgeted figures in order to identify areas that need corrective action. The performance report also serves as a guide for the next period's budget.

The **master budget** is the set of budgeted financial statements and supporting schedules for the entire organization. A master budget has three components:

1) the **operating budget** projects sales revenue, cost of goods sold, and operating expenses leading to the budgeted income statement that projects operating income for the period.
2) the **capital expenditures budget** is the company's plan for the purchase of property, plant, and equipment, and other long-term assets.
3) the **financial budget** projects cash inflows and outflows—the cash budget—the budgeted period-end balance sheet, and the statement of cash flows.

You should study Exhibit 23-5 to understand the flow of information in preparation of the master budget.

Objective 2 - Prepare an operating budget for a company.

The **operating budget** starts with preparation of the sales budget; followed by the inventory, purchases and cost of goods sold budget, and then the operating expenses budget and culminates with the budgeted income statement. The budgeted income statement contains budgeted amounts rather than actual amounts. The steps in preparing the operating budget are as follows:

Step 1. Prepare the **sales budget** (Exhibit 23-7 in your text). Remember that there is no way to accurately plan for inventory purchases or inventory levels without a sales budget. The sales budget will generally schedule sales for each month, and present a total for the entire budget period.

Step 2. Prepare a schedule of the **inventory, purchases, and cost of goods sold, budget** (Exhibit 23-8, in your text). Remember that you need to buy enough inventory to meet both expected sales levels and the desired ending inventory levels. If there is a beginning inventory, it reduces the amount of inventory you need to purchase.

> **Study Tip**: PURCHASES = COST OF GOODS SOLD + ENDING INVENTORY − BEGINNING INVENTORY

Step 3. Calculate **budgeted operating expenses** (Exhibit 23-9 in your text). Remember that some expenses vary with sales, such as sales commissions, while other expenses, such as rent, are fixed amounts from month to month.

The schedules prepared for the operating budget are now used to prepare **the budgeted income statement** (Exhibit 23-10 in your text). Budgeted sales on the income statement were determined by preparation of the sales budget. Budgeted cost of goods sold was determined by the preparation of the inventory, purchases, and cost of goods sold budget. The gross margin is equal to sales minus cost of goods sold. Operating expenses were scheduled on the operating expenses budget. Operating income is equal to the gross margin minus the operating expenses. The one remaining part of the budgeted income statement is interest expense, which is determined from the cash budget. Remember, all of these are budgeted amounts.

Objective 3 - Prepare a financial budget.

Once the operating budget is complete, the second part of the master budget is the **financial budget**. The financial budget includes:

Step 1: Prepare the **cash budget** (also called the **statement of budgeted cash receipts and disbursements**) (see Exhibit 23-14 in your text) details how the business expects to go from the beginning cash balance to the desired ending balance. The cash budget has four major parts:
   1) **Budgeted cash collections from customers** (Exhibit 23-11 in your text) requires that you estimate 1) cash sales and 2) cash collections from credit sales. These amounts should be determined for each period contained in the budget.
   2) **Budgeted cash payments for purchases** (Exhibit 23-12 in your text) uses the inventory, purchases, and cost of goods sold budget from the preparation of the operating budget.
   3) **Budgeted cash payments for operating expenses** (Exhibit 23-13 in your text) uses the operating expenses budget from the preparation of the operating budget.
   4) **Budgeted cash payments for capital expenditures**, if any. The budgeted acquisition of long-term assets appears in the **capital expenditures budget**, which is discussed in more detail in Chapter 26.

Step 2: Prepare the **budgeted balance sheet** (Exhibit 23-15 in your text) to project each asset, liability, and owner's equity account based on the plans outlined in the previous schedules.

Step 3: Prepare the **budgeted statement of cash flows** (Exhibit 23-16 in your text). Information for the cash flow budget is obtained from the previously completed budgets; specifically the cash collections and cash disbursements schedules, the cash budget, and the beginning balance of cash. These amounts are organized into the standard cash flow format: operating, investing, and financing activities.

Objective 4 - Use sensitivity analysis in budgeting.

Remember that the master budget models the company's *planned* activities. What happens if actual results differ from the plan? **Sensitivity analysis** is a "what-if" technique that asks what a result will be if a predicted amount is not achieved or if an underlying assumption changes.

Computer spreadsheets are particularly useful in answering many of the questions that arise when there is a difference in an assumption or an actual result because their speed permits managers to react and adjust more quickly.

Objective 5 - Prepare performance reports for responsibility centers.

Responsibility accounting is a system for evaluating the performance of each responsibility center and its manager. A **responsibility center** can be any part or subunit of an organization whose manager is accountable for specific activities. Responsibility accounting performance reports compare budgets with actual results for each center.

Four common types of responsibility centers are:
1) **Cost centers:** Generate no revenue and managers are accountable only for controlling costs.
2) **Revenue centers:** Exist where managers are primarily accountable for generating revenues, although, they may also have some responsibility for controlling costs.
3) **Profit centers:** Exist where managers are responsible for both revenues and expenses, and therefore, profits.
4) **Investment centers:** Such as a single department store in a chain where managers are responsible for generating sales, controlling expenses, and managing the amount of investment required to earn income.

Management by exception is a strategy in which management investigates important deviations from budgeted amounts. Responsibility and authority are delegated to lower-level employees; management does not become involved unless necessary. Exhibit 23-20 in your text illustrates a **performance report** that stresses variances. The format of a performance report is a matter of personal preference of the users. Basically, the report compares actual and budgeted performance at different levels of the organization.

TEST YOURSELF

All the self-testing materials in this chapter focus on information and procedures that your instructor is likely to test in quizzes and examinations.

I. Matching   *Match each numbered term with its lettered definition.*

_____ 1. Master budget
_____ 2. Responsibility center
_____ 3. Sales budget
_____ 4. Cash budget
_____ 5. Sensitivity analysis
_____ 6. Operating budget

_____ 7. Financial budget
_____ 8. Capital expenditures budget
_____ 9. Responsibility accounting
_____ 10. Management by exception
_____ 11. Cash collections from customers budget

A. A company's plan for purchases of property, plant, equipment, and other long-term assets
B. Details how the business expects to go from the beginning cash balance to the desired ending balance
C. Directs management's attention to important differences between actual and budgeted amounts.
D. A system for evaluating the performance of each responsibility center and its managers
E. Projects cash inflows and outflows, the period ending balance sheet, and budgeted cash flow statement
F. Requires an estimate of 1) cash sales and 2) cash collections from credit sales.
G. Consists of the sales budget, inventory, purchases, and cost of goods sold budget, and operating expenses budget.
H. The cornerstone of the master budget.
I. A part, segment, or subunit of an organization whose manager is accountable for specified activities
J. A "what if" technique that asks what a result will be if a predicted amount is not achieved or if an underlying assumption changes
K. The comprehensive budget that includes the operating budget, the capital expenditures budget, and the financial budget

II. Multiple Choice   *Circle the best answer.*

1. A variance occurs when

   A. actual results exceed budgeted amounts.
   B. actual result is less than budgeted amounts.
   C. actual results differ from budgeted amounts.
   D. none of the above.

2. Which of the following is a cost center?

   A. The men's department in a retail store
   B. The West coast division of a large oil refinery
   C. The administrative division of a corporation
   D. The local branch of a statewide chain store

3. When preparing the master budget, the first step is the

   A. financial budget.
   B. operating budget.
   C. the cash budget.
   D. the capital expenditures budget.

4. When preparing the operating budget, the first step is

    A. the purchase budget.
    B. the sales budget.
    C. the operating expense budget.
    D. the inventory budget.

5. An example of a profit center is:

    A. the housewares department in a department store.
    B. the accounting department in a hardware store.
    C. both of these.
    D. neither of these.

6. An example of an investment center is:

    A. a department store in a chain of stores.
    B. the delivery department of an auto parts store.
    C. the shipping department of a manufacturer.
    D. both B and C.

7. Which factor is important in an effective responsibility accounting system?

    A. Control over operations
    B. Access to information
    C. Both of these
    D. Neither of these

8. Responsibility accounting systems are used for:

    A. finding fault.
    B. placing blame for failure to meet goals.
    C. determining who can explain specific variances.
    D. both finding fault and placing blame for failure to meet goals.

9. Which of the following is a analytical technique that asks what a result will be if a predicted amount is not achieved or if an underlying assumption changes?

    A. Management by exception
    B. Responsibility accounting
    C. Responsibility center
    D. Sensitivity analysis

10. Which of the following compares actual amounts with budgeted amounts in order to identify areas that need corrective action?

    A. The master budget
    B. Performance report
    C. The operating budget
    D. The budgeted statement of cash flows

III. Completion   *Complete each of the following statements.*

1. The benefits of budgeting are 1) _____ 2) _____ and 3) _____ .

2. The budgeted income statement can be prepared after the _____ has been completed.

3. _____ are primarily evaluated by their ability to generate revenues.

4. The three components of the master budget are _____ , _____ , and _____ .

5. To determine what might happen if predicted outcomes are not achieved or underlying assumptions change, managers use _____ .

6. _____ are evaluated on their ability to control costs.

7. Budgeted purchases for long-term assets are included in the_____ budget.

8. The financial budget consists of the _____ , the _____ , and the _____ .

9. A _____ results when actual results differ from projected results.

10. The _____ compares actual results with budgeted figures.

IV. Daily Exercises

1. Assuming Inventory increased by $9,000 during the period and Cost of Goods Sold was $245,000, what were purchases?

$9000

245000
9000
254000

2. If ending Accounts Receivable is 50% greater than beginning Accounts Receivable, cash receipts from customers are $400,000 and credit sales are $500,000, calculate the beginning and ending Accounts Receivable balances.

3. Susana's Shoes has three locations in Anytown, USA. The owner received the following data for the third quarter of the current year:

	Revenues		Expenses	
	Budget	Actual	Budget	Actual
West Store	$220,000	$250,000	$210,000	$198,000
Center Store	187,000	175,000	146,000	150,000
East Store	713,000	874,000	706,000	696,000

Arrange the data in a performance report, showing third quarter results in thousands of dollars.

V. Exercises

1. Kay's Cameras sells disposable, recyclable cameras for use underwater. The units cost $3 each and are sold for $6 a piece. At the end of the first quarter, 200 cameras were on hand. Projected sales for the next four months are 700 units, 900 units, 1,200 units, and 1,000 units, respectively. Kay wants to maintain inventory equal to 40% of the next month's sales.

Prepare a sales budget and the inventory, purchases, and cost of goods sold budget for the next quarter.

Sales Budget - 2nd Quarter

1st month	2nd month	3rd month	Total

Inventory, Purchases, and Cost of Goods Sold Budget

	1st month	2nd month	3rd month	Total
COGS	2100	2700	3600	
+ Ending Inv V	1080	1440	1200	
− Beg Inv	600	1080	1440	
Purchases	2580	3060	3360	

2. Using the following information, present an income statement for the year ended December 31, 20X5.

a) Consulting Fees Earned were $850,000.

b) Salaries: the staff consists of two full-time consultants, one half-time consultant and an office assistant. The consultants are paid a base salary, plus a 30% commission on fees earned. The base for full-time consultants is $40,000 while the half-time consultant receives a base of $20,000. The office assistant's salary is $35,000.

c) Office rent was $5,500/month for 1/1 – 6/30 at which time it was raised to $6,000 for the remainder of the year.

d) Depreciation on office equipment, computed on the straight-line basis, was $15,000 for the year.

e) Office expenses were $20,000 plus 5% of consulting fees.

f) Travel expenses were 4% of consulting fees.

g) Miscellaneous expenses were 1% of consulting fees.

3. Review the information in Exercise 2 above and the following information, and present a budgeted income statement in the space provided. You may want to first compare your answer for Exercise 2 with the solution.

a) Revenues are expected to increase by 25%.
b) The office assistant will receive a 10% salary increase at the beginning of the year.
c) On 7/1 the lease for the office will be renewed. It is expected to increase by 15%/month.
d) Depreciation will remain unchanged for the year.

4. Review the information from Exercise 3 above and present, in the space provided, a performance report for the year, considering the following additional information.

   a) Revenues increased by 40%.
   b) The growth in revenues required an expansion of the staff by one additional full-time consultant, who was hired on April 1. Also on April 1, base salaries for full-time consultants (including the new hire) were increased to $50,000 while the half-time consultant's base was increased to $25,000. The commission rate remained unchanged.
   c) The July 1 rent increase was 25%.
   d) Travel expenses were 6% of revenues.

	Actual	Budgeted	Variance

5. The Jones-Jackson Partnership owns and operates a sporting goods store specializing in trekking equipment. Sales for the first two quarters of the current year are as follows:

January	$343,200
February	386,000
March	408,000
April	440,900
May	501,800
June	527,100

The partnership's sales are 15% cash and 85% credit. Collections from credit customers are 20% the month of sale, 45% the month following sale, 30% two months following sale, and 4% three months after sale. 1% of credit sales become uncollectible and are written off.

Using the following format, prepare a schedule for budgeted cash collections for April, May and June (round to the whole dollar amounts).

	April	May	June
Cash Sales			
Collections from January			
Collections from February			
Collections from March			
Collections from April			
Collections from May			
Collections from June			
Monthly Totals			
Total for the Quarter			

VI. Beyond the Numbers

Refer to Exercises 3 & 4. The budgeted income statement prepared in Exercise 3 was based on the projection that revenues would increase by 25%. At that projection, the company was still budgeted to generate net income of $386,600. Explain how the actual increase in revenues was 40%, yet the net income fell short of the projected amount by $7,150.

VII. Demonstration Problems

Demonstration Problem #1

Tele-data Communication's cash budget for the first three quarters of 20X8 is given below (note that some of the data is missing and must be calculated). The company requires a minimum cash balance of at least $40,000, and owes $4,000 on a note payable from a previous quarter. (Ignore interest.)

Tele-data Communications
Quarterly Cash Budget
For the Quarter Ended March 31, 20X8

	1	2	3
Beginning cash balance	$ 64,000	$ D	$ 52,000
Add collections from customers	A	280,000	268,000
Cash available	$ B	$ E	$320,000
Deduct disbursements			
Inventory purchases	$124,000	$ F	$ 92,000
Operating expenses	100,000	88,000	120,000
Equipment purchases	40,000	44,000	116,000
Dividends	0	24,000	J
Total disbursements	$264,000	$G	$ K
Excess (deficiency) in cash	$ 28,000	$ 68,000	($ 8,000)
Financing			
Add borrowing	$ C	-	$ 48,000
Deduct repayments	-	H	0
Ending cash balance	$ 40,000	$ I	$ 40,000

Required:

Find the missing value represented by each letter. (Hint: it may not be possible to solve this problem in sequence i.e. A. first, B. second, and so on.)

A.

B.

C.

D.

E.

F.

G.

H.

I.

J.

K.

Demonstration Problem #2

The Baguette Bakery has two departments, wholesale and retail. The company's income statement for the year ended December 31, 20X7 appears as follows:

Net Sales		$1,130,000
Cost of Goods Sold		548,000
Gross Margin		582,000
Operating expenses:		
Salaries	$310,000	
Depreciation	45,000	
Advertising	18,000	
Other	30,000	403,000
Operating income		$ 179,000

Cost of goods sold is distributed $226,000 for wholesale and $322,000 for retail. Salaries are allocated to departments based on sales: wholesale, $472,000; retail $658,000. Advertising is evenly allocated to the two departments. Depreciation is allocated based on square footage: wholesale, 4,000 square feet; retail, 6,000 square feet. Other expenses are allocated based on sales.

Prepare a departmental income statement showing revenue, expenses, and operating income for two departments.

The Baguette Bakery			
Departmental Income Statement			
For the Year Ended December 31, 20X7			
		Department	
	Total	Wholesale	Retail
Net sales	$1,130,000		
Cost of goods sold	548,000		
Gross margin	582,000		
Operating expenses:			
Salaries	310,000		
Depreciation	45,000		
Advertising	18,000		
Other	30,000		
Total operating expenses	403,000		
Operating income	$ 179,000	$	$

SOLUTIONS

I. Matching

1. K	3. H	5. J	7. E	9. D	11. F
2. I	4. B	6. G	8. A	10. C	

II. Multiple Choice

1. C A variance does not imply direction, only a difference.

2. C The men's department is a profit center, while choices B and D are investment centers.

3. B The order is operating budget, the capital expenditures budget, and financial budget (which includes the cash budget).

4. B The operating budget always begins with the sales budget - the others are prepared after the sales budget is completed.

5. A The accounting department is a cost center.

6. A Both choices B and C are cost centers.

7. C Both the control over operations and access to information are important factors in an effective responsibility accounting system.

8. C Responsibility accounting systems are not intended to find fault or place blame.

9. D Sensitivity analysis is a "what-if" technique that asks what a result will be if a predicted amount is not achieved or if an underlying assumption changes.

10. B The performance report compares actual figures with budgeted figures in order to identify areas that need corrective action.

III. Completion

1. planning; coordination and communication; benchmarking
2. operating budget
3. Revenue centers
4. operating budget, capital expenditures budget, financial budget
5. sensitivity analysis
6. Cost centers
7. capital expenditures
8. cash budget, budgeted balance sheet, budgeted statement of cash flows
9. variance
10. performance report

IV. Daily Exercises

1. Beginning inventory + Purchases - Ending inventory = Cost of goods sold
   X + Purchases - (X + \$9,000) = \$245,000
   Purchases   = \$254,000

2. Beginning Accounts Receivable = X
   Ending Accounts Receivable = 150%X
   Credit Sales = \$500,000

   Beginning Accounts Receivable + Credit Sales – Receipts from customers =
   Ending Accounts Receivable
   $\quad X \quad$ + \$500,000 - \$400,000 $\quad$ = 150%X
   Beginning Accounts Receivable = \$200,000
   Ending Accounts Receivable = 150% × \$200,000 = \$300,000

3.

Operating income by location	Budgeted Income	Actual Income	Variance Favorable (Unfavorable)
West Store			
(220-210)	10		
(250-198)		52	42
Center Store			
(187-146)	41		
(175-150)		25	(16)
East Store			
(713-706)	7		
(874-696)		178	171
	\$58	\$255	\$197

269

V. Exercises

1.

Sales Budget – 2nd Quarter

1st month	2nd month	3rd month	Total
$4,200	$5,400	$7,200	$16,800

Multiply number of units by unit cost.

Purchases, Cost of Goods Sold, and Inventory Budget

	1st month	2nd month	3rd month	Total
Cost of Goods Sold[1]	$2,100	$2,700	$3,600	$8,400
+ Desired Ending Inventory[2]	1,080	1,440	1,200[5]	1,200
Subtotal	3,180	4,140	4,800	9,600
- Beginning Inventory[3]	600[4]	1,080	1,440	600
= Purchases	$2,580	$3,060	$3,360	$9,000

[1] Cost of Goods Sold is 50% of budgeted sales: $3/$6 = 50%

[2] Desired Ending Inventory is 40% of the following month's Cost of Goods Sold.

[3] Beginning Inventory is 40% of current month's Cost of Goods Sold (or simply last month's Ending Inventory!)

[4] Beginning Inventory is 200 units × $3 ea = $600

[5] The next month's projected Cost of Goods Sold = 1,000 units × $3 ea = $3,000; Ending Inventory = 40% × $3,000 = $1,200

2.

Consulting Fees Earned		$850,000
Less: Operating Expenses		
Salaries and Commissions Expense	$390,000	
Rent Expense	69,000	
Depreciation Expense	15,000	
Office Expense	62,500	
Travel Expense	34,000	
Miscellaneous Expense	8,500	579,000
Net Income		$271,000

Calculations:

Salaries and Commissions	
2 Full-time Consultants	$ 80,000
1 Half-time Consultant	20,000
30% of Consulting Fees	255,000
Office Assistant	35,000
Total	$390,000

Rent Expense = 6 × $5,500 + 6 × $6,000	=	69,000
Office Expense = $20,000 + .05 × $850,000	=	62,500
Travel Expense = .04 × $850,000	=	34,000
Miscellaneous Expense = .01 × $850,000	=	8,500

3.

Budgeted Income Statement

		$1,062,500
Consulting Fees Earned		$1,062,500
Less: Operating Expenses		
Salaries and Commissions Expense	$457,250	
Rent Expense	77,400	
Depreciation Expense	15,000	
Office Expense	73,125	
Travel Expense	42,500	
Miscellaneous Expense	10,625	675,900
Net Income		$ 386,600

Calculations:

Salaries and Commissions	
Consultants Base	$100,000
30 % of Consulting Fee	318,750
Office Assistant	38,500
Total	$457,250

Rent Expense = 6 × $6,000 + 6 × $6,900	=	77,400
Office Expense = $20,000 + .05 × $1,062,500	=	73,125
Travel Expense = .04 × $1,062,500	=	42,500
Miscellaneous Expense = .01 × $1,062,500	=	10,625

4.

Performance Report

	Actual	Budgeted	Variance
Consulting Fees Earned	$1,190,000	$1,062,500	$127,500
Salaries and Commissions	551,750	457,250	(94,500)
Rent Expense	81,000	77,400	(3,600)
Depreciation Expense	15,000	15,000	0
Office Expense	79,500	73,125	(6,375)
Travel Expense	71,400	42,500	(28,900)
Miscellaneous Expense	11,900	10,625	(1,275)
Net Income	$ 379,450	$ 386,600	$ (7,150)

Calculations:
  Salaries and Commissions
    2 Full-time Consultants:

$40,000 \times 2 \times 3/12$	=	$ 20,000
$50,000 \times 2 \times 9/12$	=	75,000

    1 Full-time Consultant:

$50,000 \times 9/12$	=	37,500

    1 Half-time Consultant

$20,000 \times 3/12$	=	5,000
$25,000 \times 9/12$	=	18,750
30% Commission		357,000
Office Assistant		38,500
		$551,750

Rent Expense = $6 \times \$6,000 + 6 \times \$7,500 = 81,000$
Office Expense = $\$20,000 + .05 \times \$1,190,000 = 79,500$
Travel Expense = $.06 \times \$1,190,000 = 71,400$
Miscellaneous Expense = $.01 \times \$1,190,000 = 11,900$

5.

	April	May	June
Cash Sales	$ 66,135	$ 75,270	$ 79,065
Collections from January	11,669		
Collections from February	98,430	13,124	
Collections from March	156,060	104,040	13,872
Collections from April	74,953	168,644	112,430
Collections from May		85,306	191,939
Collections from June			89,607
Monthly Totals	$407247	$446,384	$486,913
Total from Quarter			$1,340,544

VI. Beyond the Numbers

Even though the company had an actual increase of 40% in revenues rather than the projected 25%, total operating expenses had only been expected to increase approximately 16.7% ($675,900/$579,000), when they actually increased 40.0% ($810,550/$579,000). So, while revenues increased 15% over budget, the expenses increased 23.3% over budget, thus resulting in a lower net income for the year.

VII. Demonstration Problems

Demonstration Problem #1 Solved and Explained

The solution is given in the order in which the exercise may be worked.

B. Cash available - Total disbursements = Excess (deficiency)
   B - $264,000 = $28,000
   B = $292,000

A. Beginning cash balance + Cash collections = Cash available
   $64,000 + A = $292,000
   A = $228,000

C. Excess + Borrowing = Ending cash balance
   $28,000 + C = $40,000
   C = $12,000

D. $40,000; the beginning cash balance for any quarter is the ending cash balance from the previous quarter.

E. Beginning cash balance + Cash collections = Cash available
   $40,000 + $280,000 = E
   E = $320,000

I. $52,000; the ending cash balance for any quarter is the beginning cash balance for the next quarter.

H. Excess - Repayments = Ending cash balance
   $68,000 - H = $52,000
   H = $16,000

G. Cash available - Total disbursements = Excess
   $320,000 - G = $ 68,000
   G = $252,000

F. Inventory purchases + Operating expenses + Equipment purchases + Dividends = Total disbursements
   F + $88,000 + $44,000 + $24,000 = $252,000
   F = $96,000

K. Cash available - Total disbursements = (deficiency)
   $320,000 - K = ($8,000)
   $320,000 + $8,000 = K
   K = $328,000

J. Inventory purchases + Operating expenses + Equipment purchases + Dividends = Total disbursements
   $92,000 + $120,000 + $116,000 + J = $328,000
   $328,000 + J = $328,000
   J = $0

273

Demonstration Problem #2 Solved and Explained

<table>
<tr><td colspan="4" align="center">The Baguette Bakery</td></tr>
<tr><td colspan="4" align="center">Departmental Income Statement</td></tr>
<tr><td colspan="4" align="center">For the Year Ended December 31, 20X7</td></tr>
<tr><td></td><td></td><td colspan="2" align="center">Department</td></tr>
<tr><td></td><td>Total</td><td>Wholesale</td><td>Retail</td></tr>
<tr><td>Net sales</td><td>$1,130,000</td><td>$472,000</td><td>$658,000</td></tr>
<tr><td>Cost of goods sold</td><td>548,000</td><td>226,000</td><td>322,000</td></tr>
<tr><td>Gross margin</td><td>582,000</td><td>246,000</td><td>336,000</td></tr>
<tr><td>Operating expenses:</td><td></td><td></td><td></td></tr>
<tr><td>　Salaries</td><td>310,000</td><td>129,487</td><td>180,513</td></tr>
<tr><td>　Depreciation</td><td>45,000</td><td>18,000</td><td>27,000</td></tr>
<tr><td>　Advertising</td><td>18,000</td><td>9,000</td><td>9,000</td></tr>
<tr><td>　Other</td><td>30,000</td><td>12,531</td><td>17,469</td></tr>
<tr><td>　Total operating expenses</td><td>403,000</td><td>169,018</td><td>233,982</td></tr>
<tr><td>Operating income</td><td>$ 179,000</td><td>$ 76,982</td><td>$102,018</td></tr>
</table>

Calculations:

Salaries:
Wholesale $[(\$472,000 \div \$1,130,000)] \times \$310,000 = \$129,487$
Retail $[(\$658,000 \div \$1,130,000)] \times \$310,000 = \$180,513$

Depreciation:
Wholesale $[4,000 \div (4,000 + 6,000)] \times \$45,000 = \$18,000$
Retail $[6,000 \div (4,000 + 6,000)] \times \$45,000 = \$27,000$

Advertising:
Wholesale $\$18,000 \div 2 = \$9,000$
Retail $\$18,000 \div 2 = \$9,000$

Other:
Wholesale $(\$472,000 \div \$1,130,000) \times \$30,000 = \$12,531$
Retail $(\$658,000 \div \$1,130,000) \times \$30,000 = \$17,469$

Chapter 24 - Flexible Budgets and Standard Costs

CHAPTER OVERVIEW

In Chapter 23 you were introduced to the master budget and its components. In addition, you learned how budgeted amounts are compared with actual results as one means of evaluating performance. The topics in the previous chapter provide a foundation for those covered in this chapter—flexible budgets and standard costs. The learning objectives for this chapter are to

1. Prepare a flexible budget for the income statement.
2. Use the flexible budget to show why actual results differ from the static budget.
3. Identify the benefits of standard costs and learn how to set standards.
4. Compute standard cost variances for direct materials and direct labor.
5. Analyze manufacturing overhead in a standard cost system.
6. Record transactions at standard cost and prepare a standard cost income statement.

CHAPTER REVIEW

Objective 1 – Prepare a flexible budget for the income statement.

As you learned in previous chapters, **cost behavior** may be fixed or variable. Mixed costs have both variable and fixed components. Cost behaviors are valid only for a relevant range of activity.

The master budget is a **static budget** that is prepared for only one level of sales volume. Once developed, the static budget does not change. In Chapter 23, you studied the **performance report** that compares actual with budgeted results to show **variances** (differences). A variance is labeled as favorable if it increases operating income and unfavorable if it decreases operating income.

In contrast to the static budget, a **flexible budget** is a summarized budget that managers can easily compute for several different volume levels. Flexible budgets separate variable costs from fixed costs. Generally, the flexible budget is prepared for the actual volume achieved (that is, when actual volume is known). Review Exhibit 24-2 in your text.

To prepare a flexible budget, we use the **flexible budget formula for total cost**:

Flexible budget total cost = (number of output units × variable cost per output unit) + Total fixed cost

Note, it is the variable costs that put the "flex" in the flexible budget, because budgeted total fixed costs remain constant within the relevant range.

Study Exhibit 24-3 in your text to understand the preparation of a flexible budget income statement.

The flexible budget cost line can be graphed for further analysis. The vertical axis of the budget graph shows total expenses and the horizontal axis shows the level of volume. Both budgeted and actual results can be graphed. Remember that the only valid portion of the graph is the area within the relevant range. Refer to Exhibit 24-4 and 24-5 in your text for a graph of a flexible budget and a graph of actual and budgeted total expenses.

Objective 2 – Use the flexible budget to show why actual results differ from the static budget.

Managers must examine why a variance occurred to identify any problems and to take corrective action. To analyze variances, managers begin by using the flexible budget for the number of units actually sold to divide the static budget variance into two broad categories:

- **Sales volume variance**—arises when the number of units actually sold differs from the static budget sales. This equals the difference between a *static* budget amount and a *flexible* budget amount.
- **Flexible budget variance**—arises when the company actually earned more or less revenue, or incurred more or less cost, than expected for the actual level of output. This equals the difference between the *actual* amount and a *flexible* budget amount.

See Exhibit 24-6 in your text.

Objective 3 - Identify the benefits of standard costs and learn how to set standards.

A **standard cost** is a budget for a single unit. When using a standard cost system, each input has both a price standard and a quantity standard.

Price standards are established for direct materials, direct labor, and manufacturing overhead. Accountants work with managers and suppliers to set the price standards for direct materials; with human resource managers to set direct labor cost standards; and with production managers to estimate variable and fixed manufacturing overhead expenses.

Engineers and production managers set quantity standards for direct materials and direct labor.

The benefits to an organization of standard costs are:

1. Providing the unit amounts needed for budgeting
2. Help management control operations by setting target levels of operating performance
3. Motivating employees by setting goals against which performance will be evaluated
4. Providing a unit cost basis for establishing selling prices
5. Reducing clerical costs

See Exhibit 24-8 in your text

Objective 4 - Compute standard cost variances for direct materials and direct labor.

Variances between actual and standard costs are separated into **price variances** and **efficiency variances** for direct materials and direct labor.

Direct Materials:

The total flexible budget variance for direct materials is separated into the price variance and the efficiency variance. The **direct materials price variance** measures the difference between the actual and the standard price of materials for the amount of materials used.

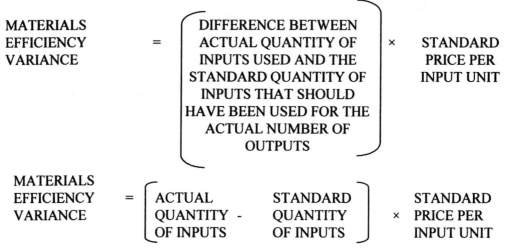

MATERIALS
PRICE VARIANCE = [DIFFERENCE BETWEEN ACTUAL AND STANDARD PRICES PER INPUT UNIT] × ACTUAL QUANTITY OF INPUTS

MATERIALS
PRICE
VARIANCE = [ACTUAL PRICE PER INPUT UNIT – STANDARD PRICE PER INPUT UNIT] × ACTUAL QUANTITY OF INPUTS

If the actual unit price is less than the standard unit price, the variance is favorable. If the actual unit price is greater than the standard unit price, the variance is unfavorable.

The **direct materials efficiency variance** measures whether the quantity of materials actually used to make the actual number of outputs is within the standard allowed for that number of outputs. This is computed as the difference between the actual quantity of inputs used and the standard quantity of inputs allowed for the actual number of outputs multiplied by the standard price per unit of the input.

MATERIALS
EFFICIENCY
VARIANCE = [DIFFERENCE BETWEEN ACTUAL QUANTITY OF INPUTS USED AND THE STANDARD QUANTITY OF INPUTS THAT SHOULD HAVE BEEN USED FOR THE ACTUAL NUMBER OF OUTPUTS] × STANDARD PRICE PER INPUT UNIT

MATERIALS
EFFICIENCY
VARIANCE = [ACTUAL QUANTITY OF INPUTS - STANDARD QUANTITY OF INPUTS] × STANDARD PRICE PER INPUT UNIT

Note that INPUTS THAT SHOULD HAVE BEEN USED FOR ACTUAL OUTPUT is equal to standard input per unit times actual units produced. If inputs actually used are less than the inputs that should have been used, the variance is favorable. If inputs actually used are greater than the inputs that should have been used, the variance is unfavorable.

Exhibit 24-13 in your text summarizes the direct materials variance computations.

Direct Labor:

The **direct labor price variance** measures the difference between the actual rate per labor hour and the STANDARD rate per labor hour.

$$
\begin{array}{c}
\text{LABOR} \\
\text{PRICE VARIANCE}
\end{array}
=
\left[
\begin{array}{c}
\text{DIFFERENCE BETWEEN} \\
\text{ACTUAL AND STANDARD} \\
\text{UNIT PRICES OF INPUTS}
\end{array}
\right]
\times
\begin{array}{c}
\text{ACTUAL QUANTITY OF} \\
\text{INPUTS}
\end{array}
$$

$$
\begin{array}{c}
\text{LABOR} \\
\text{PRICE} \\
\text{VARIANCE}
\end{array}
=
\left[
\begin{array}{c}
\text{ACTUAL PRICE PER} \\
\text{INPUT UNIT}
\end{array}
-
\begin{array}{c}
\text{STANDARD PRICE PER} \\
\text{INPUT UNIT}
\end{array}
\right]
\times
\begin{array}{c}
\text{ACTUAL} \\
\text{QUANTITY OF} \\
\text{INPUTS}
\end{array}
$$

The **direct labor efficiency variance** measures the difference between the hours actually used and hours that should have been used for the output achieved.

$$
\begin{array}{c}
\text{LABOR} \\
\text{EFFICIENCY} \\
\text{VARIANCE}
\end{array}
=
\left[
\begin{array}{c}
\text{ACTUAL} \\
\text{QUANTITY OF} \\
\text{INPUTS}
\end{array}
-
\begin{array}{c}
\text{STANDARD QUANTITY} \\
\text{OF INPUTS}
\end{array}
\right]
\times
\begin{array}{c}
\text{STANDARD PRICE} \\
\text{PER INPUT UNIT}
\end{array}
$$

Note that these equations are identical to the direct materials variance equations. Exhibit 24-14 in your text summarizes direct labor variance computations.

The advantage to the company of calculating these variances is that management can investigate when the variances are significant.

In addition to direct materials and direct labor, variances are also calculated for manufacturing overhead as one means of evaluating performance.

Objective 5 – Analyze manufacturing overhead in a standard cost system.

As you learned in Chapter 20, manufacturing overhead is allocated to production using a predetermined overhead rate. The first step in accounting for manufacturing overhead is to calculate the predetermined overhead rate. This rate is based on the amounts from the static (master) budget, which provides known amounts at the beginning of the year. See Exhibit 24-16. Once the standard predetermined manufacturing overhead rate is calculated, the next step is to identify the standard quantity of the allocation base allowed for the actual number of outputs, and then allocate the manufacturing overhead. To allocate manufacturing overhead (MOH) to production, you use the formula:

$$
\begin{array}{c}
\text{MOH ALLOCATED} \\
\text{TO PRODUCTION}
\end{array}
=
\begin{array}{c}
\text{STANDARD} \\
\text{PREDETERMINED} \\
\text{MOH RATE}
\end{array}
\times
\begin{array}{c}
\text{STANDARD QUANTITY OF THE} \\
\text{ALLOCATION BASE ALLOWED FOR} \\
\text{THE ACTUAL NUMBER OF OUTPUTS}
\end{array}
$$

Overhead variances are computed differently from material and labor variances. The **total manufacturing overhead variance** is the difference between actual overhead cost, which is accumulated as costs are incurred, and the standard manufacturing overhead allocated to production. Manufacturing overhead variances are commonly separated into the:

- **Overhead flexible budget variance**, which is the difference between the actual overhead cost and the flexible budget overhead for the actual number of outputs.
- **Production volume variance**, which is the difference between the manufacturing overhead cost in the flexible budget for actual outputs, and the standard overhead allocated to production. The production volume variance is favorable when actual output exceeds expected output.

Exhibit 24-17 in your text summarizes this two-variance approach.

Objective 6 - Record transactions at standard cost and prepare a standard cost income statement.

To record purchases of direct materials:

Materials Inventory	XX		
Direct Materials Price Variance	X	or	X
Accounts Payable			XX

To record direct materials used:

Work in Process Inventory	XX		
Direct Materials Efficiency Variance	X	or	X
Materials Inventory			XX

To record direct labor costs incurred:

Manufacturing Wages	XX		
Direct Labor Price Variance	X	or	X
Wages Payable			XX

To assign direct labor to production:

Work in Process Inventory	XX		
Direct Labor Efficiency Variance	X	or	X
Manufacturing Wages			XX

To record actual overhead costs incurred:

Manufacturing Overhead	XX	
A/P, Accum. Dep., etc.		XX

To allocated overhead to production:

Work in Process Inventory	XX	
Manufacturing Overhead		XX

To record completion of units:

Finished Goods Inventory	XX	
Work in Process Inventory		XX

To record cost of sales:

Cost of Goods Sold	XX	
Finished Goods Inventory		XX

The overhead variances are recorded when the Manufacturing Overhead account is reduced to zero (closed). See Exhibit 24-18.

In all of these entries, credit variances are favorable, debits are unfavorable. At year-end, all variance accounts are closed with a reconciling net debit (or credit) to Income Summary.

A **standard cost income statement** lists cost of goods sold at standard cost followed by the specific variances for direct materials, direct labor, and manufacturing overhead. Remember, debit variances are unfavorable (and therefore added to the cost of goods sold amount) while credit variances are favorable (and therefore deducted from the cost of goods sold amount). This format shows management what needs to be improved or corrected. See Exhibit 24-19 in your text.

Helpful Hint: Review the Decision Guidelines titled *Standard Costs and Variance Analysis.*

TEST YOURSELF

All the self-testing materials in this chapter focus on information and procedures that your instructor is likely to test in quizzes and examinations.

I. Matching   *Match each numbered term with its lettered definition.*

_____ 1. Price variance
_____ 2. Standard cost
_____ 3. Variance
_____ 4. Efficiency variance
_____ 5. Production volume variance
_____ 6. Bench marking

_____ 7. Sales volume variance
_____ 8. Static budget
_____ 9. Flexible budget
_____ 10. Flexible budget variance
_____ 11. Overhead flexible budget variance

A. A budget prepared for only one level of activity
B. The difference between an actual amount and the corresponding budgeted amount
C. The difference between the actual quantity of input used and the standard quantity of input allowed for actual output, multiplied by the standard unit price of input
D. Difference between an amount in the flexible budget and the actual results
E. Difference between a revenue, expense, or operating income in the flexible budget, and the revenue, expense, or operating income amount in the master budget
F. Difference between total actual overhead (fixed and variable) and the flexible budget overhead amount for actual production volume
G. Difference between the actual unit price of an input (materials and labor) and a standard unit price, multiplied by the actual quantity of inputs used
H. Difference between the flexible budget overhead for actual production and standard overhead applied to production
I. Predetermined cost that management believes the business should incur in producing an item
J. Set of budgets covering a range of volume rather than a single level of volume
K. Using standards based on "best practice" level of performance

II. Multiple Choice   *Circle the best answer.*

1. As volume decreases, which of the following is true?

   A. Total variable costs decrease
   B. Variable cost per unit decreases

   C. Fixed cost per unit decreases
   D. Total fixed costs increase

2. A budget covering a range of activity levels is a:

   A. Flexible budget
   B. Static budget

   C. Conversion budget
   D. Pliable budget

3. Flexible budgets can be used as:

   A. a planning tool.
   B. a control device.

   C. both a planning tool and a control device.
   D. neither a planning tool nor a control device.

281

4. One possible explanation for a favorable sales volume variance and an unfavorable flexible budget variance is:

   A. higher than expected sales and costs.
   B. higher than expected sales and lower than expected costs.
   C. lower than expected sales and higher than expected costs.
   D. lower than expected sales and costs.

5. The term standard cost usually refers to ___ cost. The term budgeted cost usually refers to ___ cost.

   A. unit, unit   C. total, unit
   B. unit, total   D. total, total

6. Price variances relate to:

   A. direct materials only.   C. manufacturing overhead only.
   B. direct labor only.   D. both direct materials and direct labor.

7. A production volume variance relates to:

   A. direct materials only.   C. manufacturing overhead only.
   B. direct labor only.   D. both direct materials and direct labor.

8. In a standard cost income statement, gross margin equals:

   A. Net sales - cost of goods sold at standard cost
   B. Net sales - operating expenses
   C. Net sales - cost of goods sold at standard cost + unfavorable variances - favorable variances
   D. Net sales - cost of goods sold at standard cost - unfavorable variances + favorable variances

9. At the end of the accounting period, variance account balances are:

   A. carried forward to the next accounting period.
   B. closed to cost of goods sold.
   C. closed to Income Summary.
   D. none of the above.

10. The difference between the actual overhead cost and the flexible budget overhead for actual production is the

   A. production volume variance.   C. sales volume variance.
   B. flexible budget variance.   D. overhead flexible budget variance.

III. Completion *Complete each of the following statements.*

1. _____ are resources given up to achieve a specific objective.
2. Total _____ costs change proportionately with changes in volume or activity.
3. Total _____ costs do not change during a given time period over a wide range of volume.
4. A _____ cost has both variable and fixed components.
5. If rent expense is fixed at $1,000 per month and sales increase from 2,500 units to 10,000 units, the rent per unit is _____ percent of the original amount.
6. A(n) _____ variance for materials or labor measures whether the quantity of inputs used to make a product is within the budget.
7. A(n) _____ variance for materials or labor measures how well a business keeps unit prices of materials and labor within standards.
8. A budget prepared for only one level of volume is called a _____ budget.
9. A _____ refers to any group of individual items.
10 A _____ variance increases net income; while a _____ variance decreases net income.

IV. Daily Exercises

1. Nello's Delicatessen produces pasta sauce, which is sold in one-quart containers. The pasta is made in 10 gallon batches. Each 10 gallon batch requires the following:

Ingredients	Cost
90 pounds of tomatoes	25¢/lb
2 head of garlic	90¢ ea.
20 pounds of onions	15¢/lb
2 gallons red wine	$6.50/gallon
2 cups olive oil	20¢/ounce
8 ounces fresh herbs	10¢/ounce

In addition, the one quart container in which the sauce is sold costs the business 9¢. Calculate the standard cost to produce one quart of pasta sauce.

2. To produce a 2-pound loaf of sourdough bread, the San Francisco Bakery's standard material cost is 80¢ per loaf (40¢ per pound). During the first week of March, the San Francisco Bakery purchased 120,000 pounds of ingredients costing $47,400 and paid $1,200 for 60,000 sacks. The week's production was 59,550 loaves of bread. Compute the direct materials price, efficiency, and total materials variances. Assume all ingredients purchased and sacks purchased were used in production.

3. Review the information in Daily Exercise 2 above and journalize entries to record the materials variances.

.		

4. Review the information in Daily Exercise 2 above. San Francisco Bakery's direct labor standard is .020 direct labor hours per unit of output, at a standard cost of $11.75 per hour . For the first week of March, production required 1,200 direct labor hours and the total direct labor cost was $14,700. Compute the direct labor price, efficiency, and total direct labor variances.

5. Review the information in Daily Exercise 4 above and journalize entries to record labor variances.

V. Exercises

1. If variable costs are $5.00 per unit, the relevant range is 6,000 to 15,000 units, and total costs were $60,000 for 8,000 units:

   A. How much were fixed costs?

   B. What is the flexible budget formula for total costs?

   C. At the 10,000 units level, what are total budgeted costs?

2.

Actual production	3,300	units
Actual cost (6,700 feet of direct materials)	$33,701	
Standard price	$ 4.75	per foot
Materials efficiency variance	$ 2,660	F

A. Compute the materials price variance.

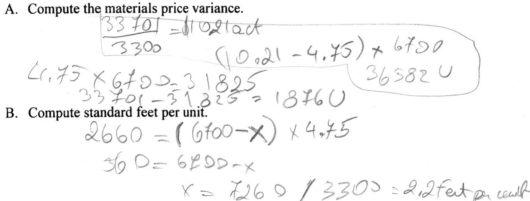

$$\frac{33701}{3300} = \$10.21 \, act$$

$$(10.21 - 4.75) \times 6700$$

$$36582 \, U$$

$$4.75 \times 6700 = 31825$$

$$33701 - 31825 = 1876 \, U$$

B. Compute standard feet per unit.

$$2660 = (6700 - X) \times 4.75$$

$$560 = 6700 - X$$

$$X = 7260 / 3300 = 2.2 \text{ feet per unit}$$

3. Assuming 2,400 hours of direct labor were budgeted for actual output at a standard rate of $12.00 per hour and 2,500 hours were worked at a rate of $11.75 per hour.

A. Compute the labor price variance.

$$(2500 - 2400) \times 12 = \$1200$$

$$(12 - 11.75) \times 2500 = \$625 \, F$$

B. Compute the labor efficiency variance.

$$(2500 - 2400) \times 12 = \$1200 \, U$$

4. The Massimo Manufacturing Company hopes to produce 360,000 units of product during the next calendar year. Monthly production can range between 20,000 and 40,000 units. Per unit variable manufacturing cost have been budgeted as follows: direct materials, $2; direct labor, $2.50; and overhead, $1.25. Prepare a flexible budget for 20,000, 30,000, and 40,000 units of output.

VI. Beyond the Numbers

Refer to the information (and solution) for Exercise 4 above. During June, 30,000 units were manufactured. Costs incurred were as follows: $59,000 for direct materials, $77,250 for direct labor, and $37,300 for overhead. Were the costs controlled?

_____

_____

_____

_____

_____

VII. Demonstration Problems

Demonstration Problem #1

A flexible budget for Miyamoto, Inc., is presented below:

Miyamoto, Inc.
Flexible Budget
For the Year Ended December 31, 20X6

	Budget Formula per unit	Various Levels of Volume		
Units	-	40,000	48,000	56,000
Sales	$4.75	$190,000	$228,000	$266,000
Variable expenses	$2.20	88,000	105,600	123,200
Fixed expenses		56,000	56,000	56,000
Total expenses		144,000	161,600	179,200
Operating income		$ 46,000	$ 66,400	$ 86,800

The static (master) budget is based on a volume of 48,000 units. Actual operating results for 20X6 are as follows:

Sales (49,500 units)	$227,700
Variable expenses	106,920
Fixed expenses	57,570

Required:

1. Prepare an income statement performance report for 20X6.
2. Show that the total variances in operating income account for the net difference between actual operating income and the static (master) budget income.

Requirement 1 (income statement performance report)

Miyamoto, Inc.
Income Statement Performance Report
For the Year Ended December 31, 20X6

	(1) Actual Results at Actual Prices	(2) (1) - (3) Flexible Budget Variances	(3) Flexible Budget for Actual Volume Achieved	(4) (3) - (5) Sales Volume Variances	(5) Static (Master) Budget
Units					
Sales	$	$	$	$	$
Variable expenses					
Fixed expenses					
Total expenses					
Operating income	$	$	$	$	$

Requirement 2 (reconciling variances)

$_____

_____

$=======

$_____

_____

$=======

Demonstration Problem #2

Fun Fabric uses a standard cost system. They produce specially manufactured goods in large batches for catalogue companies featuring unusual decorative household items. They have just received an order for 10,000 units of a decorative wall hanging. Their standard cost for one wall hanging is:

Direct materials - 2.5 feet @ $2/ft	$ 5.00
Direct labor 1.5 hours @ $8/hr	12.00
Overhead 1.5 hours @ $6/hr	9.00
Standard cost/unit	$26.00

The normal capacity for the factory this period is 16,000 direct labor hours. Overhead costs are equally divided between variable and fixed expenses and are applied on the basis of direct labor hours. Janice Walters, the company president, has promised to have the wall hangings ready for shipment by the end of the month. The customer has agreed to pay $40 each.

During the month the following events occurred:

1. Purchased 27,500 feet of raw materials at $1.90/ft.
2. Received and placed into production 27,500 feet of raw materials.
3. Direct manufacturing wages incurred, 14,700 hours at $8.25/hr.
4. Assigned 15,000 direct labor hours to the job.
5. Recorded $91,600 of overhead costs.
6. Applied manufacturing overhead to the job.
7. The wall hangings were completed.
8. Shipped 10,000 units to the customer and billed the customer $400,000.

Requirements:

1. Journalize the transactions.
2. Post your transactions to the appropriate T-accounts.
3. Record the overhead variances.
4. Prepare a standard cost income statement.

Requirement 1 (journal entries)

Explanation	Debit	Credit

Requirement 2 (post to T-accounts)

Materials Inventory	Direct Materials Price Variance	Direct Materials Efficiency Variance

Manufacturing Wages	Direct Labor Price Variance	Direct Labor Efficiency Variance

Manufacturing Overhead

Work in Process Inventory	Finished Goods Inventory	Cost of Goods Sold

Requirement 3 (record overhead variances)

Explanation	Debit	Credit

Requirement 4

Fun Fabric
Standard Cost Income Statement

SOLUTIONS

I. Matching

1. G	3. B	5. H	7. E	9. J	11. F
2. I	4. C	6. K	8. A	10. D	

II. Multiple Choice

1. A   Variable costs on a per unit basis are not affected by changes in volume (B). Fixed cost per unit increases as volume decreases (C). Total fixed costs do not change as a result of volume changes in the relevant range of production (D).

2. A   A static budget is prepared for only one level of activity (B). Answers C and D have no meaning.

3. C   All budgets are used for planning. Since the flexible budget is prepared for the actual level of activity achieved, it provides for precise control.

4. A   The sales volume variance measures differences between the static budget and the flexible budget for actual volume achieved. The flexible budget variance measures differences between actual results and the flexible budget for actual volume achieved. Accordingly, higher than expected sales could be expected to give a favorable sales volume variance, and actual costs above flexible budget costs could be expected to give an unfavorable flexible budget variance.

5. B   A standard cost is a carefully predetermined cost that is usually expressed on a per-unit basis. It is a target cost, a cost that should be attained. Budgeted costs are total costs. Think of a standard variable cost as a budget for a single unit.

6. D   Price variances relate to materials and labor.

7. C   Production volume variances relate to overhead. The variances relating to direct materials and direct labor are the price and efficiency variances.

8. C   Unfavorable variances are added to cost of goods sold and favorable variances are deducted.

9. C   Because the variances relate to only the current period, they are closed out to Income Summary at the end.

10. D   Overhead flexible budget variance, which is the difference between the actual overhead cost and the flexible budget overhead for the actual number of outputs.

III. Completion

1. Costs
2. variable
3. fixed
4. mixed
5. 25 percent (2,500 units / 10,000 units)
6. efficiency
7. price
8. static
9. cost pool
10. favorable; unfavorable

IV. Daily Exercises

1.

Tomatoes	90 lbs × 25¢/lb	=	$22.50
Garlic	2 heads × 90¢ ea.	=	1.80
Onions	20 lbs × 15¢/lb	=	3.00
Wine	2 gallons × $6.50 ea.	=	13.00
Olive Oil	16 oz. × 20¢/oz.	=	3.20
Herbs	8 oz. × 10¢/oz	=	.80
Total			$44.30

$44.30 / 40 quarts	=	$1.1075
Container		.09
Total		$1.1975

2.

Actual cost (120,000 lbs @ $0.395)	$47,400
Less: Budgeted unit cost × actual inputs	
(120,000 lbs × $0.40)	48,000
Materials price variance	$ 600 F

Budgeted costs for actual inputs (see above)	$48,000
Less: Standard cost for actual production	
((59,550 × 2 lbs) × $0.40)	47,640 (rounded)
Materials efficiency variance	$ 360 U

Total flexible budget variance = Materials price variance + Materials efficiency variance
= 600 F + 360 U
= $ 240 F

3.

Materials Inventory (120,000 lbs × $0.40)	48,000	
Direct Materials Price Variance		600
Accounts Payable (120,000 lbs × $0.395)		47,400
Work in Progress Inventory (119,100 lbs × $0.40)	47,640	
Direct Materials Efficiency Variance	360	
Materials Inventory (120,000 lbs × $0.40)		48,000

4.   Actual cost (1,200 hours @ $12.25) $14,700
       Less: Budgeted unit cost × actual usage
            (1,200 × $11.75)   14,100
           Labor price variance $ 600 U

       Budgeted costs for actual hours (see above) $14,100
       Less: Standard cost for actual production
            (1,191 × $11.75)   13,994 (rounded)
           Labor efficiency variance $ 106 U

       Total flexible budget variance = Labor price variance + Labor efficiency variance
                         = 600 U + 106 U
                         =$ 706 U

5.

Manufacturing Wages (1,200 × $11.75)	14,100	
Direct Labor Price Variance	600	
Wages Payable (1,200 × $12.25)		14,700
Work In Process Inventory (1,191 × $11.75)	13,994	
Direct Labor Efficiency Variance	106	
Manufacturing Wages		14,100

V. Exercises

1. A. Total costs = Fixed costs + Variable costs
        $60,000 = X + ($5 × 8,000)
          60,000 = X + $40,000
        $20,000 = X

        Fixed costs were $20,000

    B. Total budgeted costs = ($5 × # of units produced) + $20,000

C. Total budgeted costs = ($5 × 10,000) + $20,000 = $70,000

2. A. Actual cost $33,701

       Less: Budgeted unit cost x actual usage

                ($4.75 x 6,700)   31,825

             Materials price variance $ 1,876 U

    B. $2,660 F = (6,700 feet - X) × $4.75

       X = 7,260 feet = inputs that should have been used

       7,260 feet / 3,300 units = 2.2 standard feet

3. A. Actual cost (2,500 hours @ $11.75) $29,375

       Less: Budgeted unit cost × actual usage

                (2,500 × $12.00)   30,000

             Labor price variance $ 625 F

    B. Budgeted costs for actual hours (see above) $30,000

       Less: Standard cost for actual production

                (2,400 × $12.00)   28,800

             Labor efficiency variance $ 1,200 U

4.

Massimo Manufacturing Company
Monthly Flexible Budget Report

Output	20,000	30,000	40,000
Variable costs			
Direct materials ($2)	$ 40,000	$ 60,000	$ 80,000
Direct labor ($2.50)	50,000	75,000	100,000
Overhead ($1.25)	25,000	37,500	50,000
	$115,000	$172,500	$230,000

VI. Beyond the Numbers

To answer the question we need to compare actual results with the budget.

Massimo Manufacturing Company
Budget Report
For the Month Ended June 30, 20XX

	Actual	Budget	Variance
Units	30,000	30,000	0
Variable costs			
Direct materials	$ 59,000	$ 60,000	$1,000 F
Direct labor	77,250	75,000	2,250 U
Overhead	37,300	37,500	200 F

Totals	$173,550	$172,500	$1,050 U

Overall, costs were controlled. The unfavorable variance for total variable costs was less than 1% of the budgeted amount (1,050 / 172,500). However, this overall result has been adversely affected by a 3% (2,250 / 75,000) unfavorable variance in direct labor costs while both direct materials and overhead show favorable variances.

VII. Demonstration Problems

Demonstration Problem #1 Solved and Explained

Requirement 1 (income statement performance report)

Miyamoto, Inc.
Income Statement Performance Report
For the Year Ended December 31, 20X6

	(1) Actual Results at Actual Prices	(2) (1) - (3) Flexible Budget Variances		(3) Flexible Budget for Actual Volume Achieved	(4) (3) - (5) Sales Volume Variances		(5) Static (Master) Budget
Units	49,500	0		49,500	1,500	F	48,000
Sales	$227,700	$7,425	U	$235,125	$7,125	F	$228,000
Variable expenses	106,920	1,980	F	108,900	3,300	U	105,600
Fixed expenses	57,570	1,570	U	56,000	-		56,000
Total expenses	164,490	410	F	164,900	3,300	U	161,600
Operating income	$ 63,210	$7,015	U	$ 70,225	$3,825	F	$ 66,400

Explanations:

Column 1 contains actual results that were presented in the problem statement.

Column 3

Column 3 contains the flexible budget for the volume actually sold. Actual sales were 49,500 units. Budgeted revenue is $235,125 ($4.75 per unit × 49,500). Budgeted variable expenses are $108,900 ($2.20 per unit × 49,500). Budgeted revenue and budgeted variable expenses may be calculated by multiplying units actually sold by the budget formula amounts in the flexible budget. Note that fixed expenses of $56,000 are constant at all the production levels presented in the flexible budget.

Column 5

The amounts in column 5 are the static, or master budget amounts. The problem notes that the static budget is based on 48,000 units, a volume level also found in the flexible budget.

Column 2

The flexible budget variances are the differences between actual results (column 1) and flexible budget amounts (column 3).

298

For example, the flexible budget variance for sales is $7,425 U (actual sales were less than the flexible budget amount).

For example, the flexible budget variance for variable expenses is $1,980 F (actual variable expenses were less than the flexible budget amount.) It may help to remember that spending less than planned is favorable, while spending more is unfavorable.

<u>Column 4</u>

Sales volume variances are the differences between flexible budget amounts for actual sales and static budget amounts. Note that no sales volume variance exists for fixed expenses, since fixed are constant within the relevant range. The criteria to determine whether the variances are favorable or unfavorable are the same as detailed in the explanation for column 2.

Requirement 2 (reconciling variances)

Static (master) budget operating income $66,400
Actual operating income at actual prices 63,210
    Total difference to account for $ 3,190 U

Sales volume variance $3,825 F
Flexible budget variance   7,015 U
    Total net variance $3,190 U

Since the unfavorable flexible budget variance is greater than the favorable sales volume variance, the overall net variance is unfavorable.

Demonstration Problem #2 Solved and Explained

Requirement 1 (journal entries)

1)	Materials Inventory (27,500 × $2)	55,000	
	Direct Materials Price Variance (27,500 × $.10)		2,750
	Accounts Payable (27,500 × $1.90)		52,250
2)	Work in Process Inventory (25,000 × $2)	50,000	
	Materials Efficiency Variance (2,500 × $2)	5,000	
	Materials Inventory		55,000

299

3)	Manufacturing Wages (14,700 × $8)	117,600	
	Direct Labor Price Variance (14,700 × $.25)	3,675	
	Wages Payable (14,700 × $8.25)		121,275
4)	Work in Process Inventory (15,000 × $8)	120,000	
	Direct Labor Efficiency Variance (300 × $8)		2,400
	Manufacturing Wages		117,600
5)	Manufacturing Overhead	91,600	
	Various accounts		91,600
6)	Work in Process (15,000 × $6)	90,000	
	Manufacturing Overhead		90,000
7)	Finished Goods Inventory (10,000 × $26)	260,000	
	Work in Process		260,000
8)	Cost of Goods Sold	260,000	
	Finished Goods Inventory		260,000
	Accounts Receivable	400,000	
	Sales		400,000

Requirement 2 (post to T-accounts)

Materials Inventory
(1) 55,000 | (2) 55,000

Direct Materials Price Variance
 | (1) 2,750

Direct Materials Efficiency Variance
(2) 5,000 |

Manufacturing Wages
(3) 117,600 | (4) 117,600

Direct Labor Price Variance
(3) 3,675 |

Direct Labor Efficiency Variance
 | (4) 2,400

Manufacturing Overhead
(5) 91,600 | (6) 90,000

Work in Process Inventory		Finished Goods Inventory		Cost of Goods Sold	
(2) 50,000	(7) 260,000	(7) 260,000	(8) 260,000	(8) 260,000	
(4) 120,000					
(6) 90,000					

Requirement 3 (record overhead variances)

Explanation	Debit	Credit
Production Volume Variance (1)	3,000	
Overhead Flexible Budget Variance (2)		1,400
Manufacturing Overhead (3)		1,600

(1) the fixed portion of overhead costs ($3) times the difference between normal capacity and budgeted or, $3 × 1,000 hour = $3,000.

(2) the difference between actual overhead ($91,600) and the sum of the budgeted variable ($3 × 15,000) and normal fixed ($3 × 16,000) or, $45,000 + $48,000 = $93,000 - $91,600 = $1,400

(3) the balance in the manufacturing overhead account

Requirement 4

Fun Fabrics
Standard Cost Income Statement

Sales revenue		$400,000
Cost of goods sold at standard cost	$260,000	
Manufacturing cost variances:		
Direct materials price variance	(2,750)	
Direct materials efficiency variance	5,000	
Direct labor price variance	3,675	
Direct labor efficiency variance	(2,400)	
Overhead flexible budget variance	(1,400)	
Production volume variance	3,000	
Cost of goods sold at actual cost		265,125
Gross margin		$134,875

Study Tips: The standard cost income statement reports cost of goods sold at standard cost, then modifies this amount by the variances for direct materials, direct labor and overhead. Debit variances reflect additions to cost of goods sold while credit variances are deductions. The standard cost income statement is for internal purposes only.

Chapter 25 - Activity-Based Costing and Other Cost Management Tools

CHAPTER OVERVIEW

As businesses attempt to remain competitive in an international environment they strive for competitive advantages. Some of these involve better management of costs, efforts to deliver higher quality products to the customer, and the introduction of systems that allow management to effectively plan for future operations. While we have been investigating a variety of topics concerning "costs" in recent chapters, we now turn our attention to some of the issues at the forefront of cost management. The learning objectives for this chapter are to

1. Develop activity-based costs (ABC).
2. Use activity-based management (ABM) to make business decisions, including achieving target costs.
3. Decide when ABC is most likely to pass the cost-benefit test.
4. Describe how a just-in-time (JIT) production system works and record its manufacturing costs.
5. Contrast the four types of quality costs and use these costs to make decisions.

CHAPTER REVIEW

Objective 1 – Develop activity-based costs (ABC).

Activity-based costing (ABC) is the result of the need by companies for more accurate information concerning product costs thereby allowing managers to make decisions based on accurate information. **ABC** is a system that focuses on activities as the fundamental cost objects. The costs of those activities become the building blocks for compiling the indirect costs of products, services, and customers. Companies that use ABC continue to trace direct costs (direct materials and direct labor) to cost objects in the same way as you learned in Chapter 20. The challenge addressed by ABC costing is to equitably allocate the indirect costs, both manufacturing and non-manufacturing to the products, services, or customers that caused those costs. ABC recognizes that frequently multiple cost drivers exist. When this occurs, applying costs on the basis of a single cost driver results in distorted product costs. Organizing cost information by activity provides detailed information not available using a single application rate. Applying ABC to products requires these seven steps:

1. Identify the activities.
2. Estimate the total indirect cost of each activity.
3. Identify the allocation base for each activity's indirect costs.
4. Estimate the total quantity of each allocation base.
5. Compute the cost allocation rate for each activity:
   Allocation rate = Estimated total indirect costs of activity (Step 2)
   for activity   Estimated total quantity of cost allocation base (Step 4)
6. Obtain the actual quantity of each allocation base used by the cost object
7. Allocate the costs to the cost object:
   Allocated activity cost = Allocation rate for activity (step 5) × Quantity of allocation base used by the cost object (step 6)

Objective 2 - Use activity-based management (ABM) to make business decisions, including achieving target costs.

Activity-based management (ABM) refers to using activity-based cost information to make more accurate decisions that both increase profits while satisfying customer needs. Once the product pricing has been determined, other decisions based on product pricing can be made with accuracy. For instance, deciding whether to produce something or simply purchase it from a supplier can now be more accurately determined. In addition, ABC may highlight issues regarding production levels, product mix and selling price.

Value engineering is used to reevaluate activities to reduce costs while satisfying customer needs. To accomplish this requires companies to use cross-functional teams so representatives from marketing, production, design, and accounting analyze the product to estimate how proposed changes will affect costs.

The traditional way to determine a product's selling price was to accumulate costs from the entire value chain and then add an amount for profit. Target pricing uses a completely different approach. With target pricing, the sales price is determined first, based on the amount that customers are willing to pay for the product or service. This target price is then reduced by the profit with the resulting difference being the target cost for the product. See Exhibit 25-10.

Target sale price – Desired profit = Target cost

With the target cost available, managers are now able to re-examine the results of value engineering and attempt to identify appropriate cost reduction strategies. If there is a larger variance between the re-calculated costs and target cost, then, the need exists for additional value engineering analysis to reduce costs further. If costs cannot be reduced further, then the difference will affect the amount of profit realized by the company. See Exhibit 25-11.

Objective 3 – Decide when ABC costing is most likely to pass the cost-benefit test.

While the concept behind ABC is simple--products cause activities, and activities consume resources--, ABC systems can be extremely complex and therefore costly. To implement ABC successfully, the benefits should exceed the costs. Generally, companies in competitive markets are more likely to benefit from ABC. In addition, companies with high indirect costs, multiple product lines using varying resources, and companies with varying production levels for those product lines are likely to benefit.

Existing cost systems may need revision when management cannot explain changes in profits, when bids are lost (or won) unexpectedly, when competitors under-price the company but remain profitable, when employees "don't believe the numbers," where a single-allocation-based-system exists and when production has been re-engineered but the accounting system has not.

> **Study Tip:** Carefully review the ABC Decision Guidelines in your text so you become familiar with ABC costing.

Objective 4 - Describe how a just-in-time (JIT) production system works and record its manufacturing costs.

In a **traditional production system,** large inventories of raw materials, work in process, and finished goods are maintained. However, maintaining large inventories is a problem since inventory ties up cash that could be used for other purposes. In addition, large amounts of inventory may result in problems caused by inferior quality, obsolescence, and could cause production bottlenecks to be overlooked.

The actual manufacturing processes in a traditional production system can also result in inefficiencies. The actual physical movement of goods in process can be quite long resulting in further inefficiencies. **Throughput time** is a term used to describe the time between the receipt of raw materials and the completion of a finished good. As an equation it is expressed as follows:

Throughput time = Processing time + waiting time + moving time + inspection time + reworking time

Whereas processing time adds value to a product, the other elements in the equation are **non-value-added** activities and considered waste.

Just-in-time (JIT) production systems (introduced in Chapter 19) are designed to eliminate the waste found in a traditional system. Underlying JIT systems are the following four concepts:

1. **Arrange production activities in self-contained cells**- processes are arranged so production is continuous without interruption or work in process inventories.
2. **Short setup times** - JIT minimizes the amount of time required for setup on machines used for more than one product.
3. **Broad employee roles** - in a traditional system, employees are trained to complete one specific task. Under JIT, employees are crossed-trained to do more than operate a single machine. This promotes greater flexibility, boosts morale and lowers costs.
4. **Small batches produced just-in-time** - under JIT businesses schedule production in small batches *just in time* to satisfy needs. Production does not begin until an order is received. This is referred to as a "**demand-pull**" system because the customer's order (the demand) "pulls" the product through the manufacturing process. In turn, the product acts as a "demand" to "pull" raw materials into the manufacturing process.

Review Exhibit 25-13 in your text for a comparison of a traditional system with a JIT system.

Under JIT costing, a backflush costing system is used. Backflush costing is a standard costing system that starts with output completed and works backwards to apply manufacturing costs to units sold and to inventories. Backflush costing takes less time and is less expensive to use than the traditional standard costing.

In a JIT system, no distinction is made between raw materials inventory and work in process. Instead they are combined into one account, Raw and in Process (RIP).

When materials are acquired:

RIP Inventory	XX	
Accounts Payable		XX

Recorded at actual amounts

As conversion costs are incurred:

Conversion Costs	XX	
Various Accounts		XX

Recorded at actual costs

When the number of units of finished product is known:

Finished Goods Inventory	XX
RIP Inventory	XX
Conversion Costs	XX

The amount for each account above is based on standard costs.

When goods are sold:

Cost of Goods Sold	XX	
Finished Goods Inventory		XX

Recorded at standard amounts

Price variances are recorded at the time materials are acquired while efficiency variances are not recorded until goods have been completed. Over/underallocated conversion costs are transferred to Cost of Goods Sold.

Objective 5 - Contrast the four types of quality costs and use these costs to make decisions.

Quality is the conformance of the attributes of a product or service to a specific set of standards.

Four types of **quality costs** are:
- **Prevention costs** are incurred to *avoid* poor quality goods and services.
- **Appraisal costs** are incurred to *detect* poor quality goods and services.
- **Internal failure costs** are incurred when the company detects and corrects poor-quality goods or services *before* delivery to customers.
- **External failure costs** are incurred when the company does not detect poor-quality goods or services until *after* delivery to customers.

See Exhibit 25-15 in your text for examples of quality costs.

TEST YOURSELF

All the self-testing materials in this chapter focus on information and procedures that your instructor is likely to test in quizzes and examinations.

I. Matching   *Match each numbered term with its lettered definition.*

_____ 1. Internal failure costs
_____ 2. Activity-based costing
_____ 3. Prevention costs
_____ 4. Appraisal costs
_____ 5. Activity-based management
_____ 6. External failure costs

_____ 7. Just-in-time costing
_____ 8. Target price
_____ 9. Target cost
_____ 10. Backflush costing
_____ 11. Value-engineering

A. Systematically evaluating activities in an effort to reduce costs while satisfying customer needs
B. A system that focuses on activities as the fundamental cost objects and uses the costs of those activities as building blocks for compiling the costs of products and other cost objects
C. A standard costing system that starts with output completed and works backward to apply manufacturing cots to units sold and to inventories
D. Allowable cost to develop, produce, and deliver the product or service
E. What customers are willing to pay for the product or service
F. Costs incurred in detecting poor quality goods or services
G. Costs incurred to avoid poor quality goods or services
H. Using activity-based cost information to make decisions that increase profits while satisfying customers' needs
I. Another term for just-in-time costing
J. Costs incurred when poor quality goods or services are not detected until after delivery to customers
K. Cost incurred when poor quality goods or services are detected before delivery to customers

II. Multiple Choice   *Circle the best answer.*

1. In manufacturing, all the following are non-value-added activities except:

   A. inspection time.
   B. moving time.

   C. processing time.
   D. reworking time.

2. The first step in an ABC system is:

   A. estimate the total indirect costs.
   B. identify the allocation base.

   C. identify the activities.
   D. estimate the total quantity of each allocation base.

3. Raw Materials Inventory and Work in Process Inventory are combined in

   A. target costing.
   B. value engineering.

   C. activity based costing.
   D. a JIT costing system.

4. All of the following are characteristics of quality costs except:

A. use of benchmarking for evaluation
B. difficult to measure

C. difficult to identify individual components
D. types of financial performance measures

5. Which of the following are likely to use activity-based costing system?

A. Financial institutions
B. Retailer

C. Textile manufacturer
D. All of the above

6. Which of the following is an example of an external failure cost?

A. Reworking time
B. Cost to honor warranties

C. Training program costs
D. Inspection costs

7. All of the following are nonfinancial measures of quality except:

A. amount of machine "down" time.
B. return on sales.

C. unit failure.
D. training hours per employee per month.

8. Value engineering is most closely associated with:

A. just-in-time costing.
B. activity-based management.

C. target costing.
D. none of the above.

9. Backflush costing is most closely associated with:

A. target costing.
B. just-in-time system.

C. value engineering.
D. activity-based costing.

10. Cross-training employees is a feature of which of the following?

A. Target costing
B. Just-in-time costing

C. Activity based costing
D. Value engineering

III. Completion *Complete each of the following.*

1. Four characteristics common to the just-in-time inventory are:
   1. _____
   2. _____
   3. _____
   4. _____
2. Combining raw materials and work in process inventories is a feature of a _____ system.

Identify the following acronyms:

3. ABC _____
4. ABM_____
5. RIP_____
6. JIT_____
7. Quality costs are features of _____.
8. The four types of quality costs are: 1) _____,
   2)_____, 3) _____,
   and 4)_____.
9. Demand-pull refers to a production process where _____ triggers the manufacturing process.
10. Of the four types of quality costs, the one that is potentially the most devastating to a company is
    _____.

IV. Daily Exercises

1. Classify each of the following quality costs as a prevention cost, an internal failure cost, an appraisal cost, or an external failure cost.

   a. Direct materials and direct labor costs incurred to repair defective products returned by customers
   b. A training class for customer service representatives to teach them techniques for completing customer orders quickly, efficiently and correctly
   c. Salary of a technician who randomly selects goods from the warehouse and tests them for conformance to company specifications
   d. Time and materials costs incurred to rework those items determined by the testing technician as below standard
   e. $28,000 balance in Sales Returns for the return of defective products
   f. Fee paid to pick up and dispose of rejected products from production area

   a. _____
   b. _____
   c. _____
   d. _____
   e. _____
   f. _____

2. List the following ABC system steps in correct order (use 1 through 7):

_____ A. Identify the allocation base for each activity's indirect costs.
_____ B. Identify the activities
_____ C. Obtain the actual quantity of each allocation base used by the cost object
_____ D. Estimate the total quantity of each allocation base
_____ E. Estimate total indirect costs of each activity
_____ F. Allocate the costs to the cost object
_____ G. Compute the cost allocation rate for each activity

3. Zollner Tool and Die has collected the following information on overhead costs:

ACTIVITY	AMOUNT	COST DRIVER
Machine setups	$90,000	Number of setups
Machining	325,000	Number of machine hours
Inspecting	42,000	Number of inspections

During the period, Zollner estimates they will have 675 machine setups, 15,000 machine hours and a total of 1,350 inspections. Calculate the overhead rate for machine setups, machining and inspecting.

$$\frac{90000}{675} = \$133.33$$

$$\frac{325000}{15000} = 21.67$$

$$\frac{42000}{1350} = 31.11$$

186.11

4. Totally Tees manufactures specialty T-shirts sold at music festivals and uses a JIT costing system. The standard cost for their basic model is $4.50 for raw materials and $1.10 for conversion costs. For a recently completed order of 12,000 shirts, the following costs were incurred:

Raw material purchases $54,000
Conversion costs   12,480

Prepare journal entries for this order using JIT costing.

V. Exercises

1. Trendy Trunks Manufacturing Co. uses activity-based costing to account for its manufacturing process. The direct materials for each trunk cost $3,700. Each trunk includes 60 parts, and finishing requires 15 hours of direct labor time. Each trunk requires 225 welds. The manufacture of 10 Trendy Trunks requires two machine setups.

Manufacturing Activity	Cost Driver Chosen as Application Base	Conversion Cost per Unit of Application Base
Materials handling	Number of parts	$ 5.00
Machine setup	Number of setups	$800.00
Welding of parts	Number of welds	$ 3.00
Finishing	Direct labor hours	$ 32.00

Compute the cost of each trunk.

Handwritten annotations on the conversion cost column: "× 60", "× .2", "+225", "× 15", then "165 +", "3700", "$5315"

2. Review the information in Daily Exercise #3, and assume the following additional information. Zollner manufactures one standard product (a drill bit used in furniture construction) and two specialty products, a gear and a corkscrew. Machine setups, machining hours, and inspections for the three products were:

Activity	Drill Bits	Gears	Corkscrews
Machine setups	520	90	65
Machine hours	8,900	3,200	2,900
Inspections	820	270	260

Calculate the total overhead costs for each of these three products.

3. Review the information in Daily Exercise #3, but assume Zollner uses a traditional cost allocation system for overhead. The allocation base is number of units produced, and during the current period Zollner's production was as follows:

Drill bits	520,000
Gears	90
Corkscrews	1,300
Total units	521,390

A. Calculate overhead costs assigned to each product based on production.

B. Compare your results with these in Exercise #2. Which method is more realistic, and why?

4. Fab's Fashions Company uses a JIT costing system, with trigger points at the time of direct materials purchase and the transfer of completed goods to finished goods. The company has received an order for 20,000 sweaters at $15 each. The standard direct materials cost is $6.50 per sweater and a standard conversion cost of $5.50 per sweater. Direct materials were purchased for $129,000 and conversion costs totaling $110,400 were incurred. 20,000 sweaters were produced and shipped to the customer.

Prepare journal entries for the above transactions.

Date	Accounts	Debit	Credit

VI. Beyond the Numbers

Clothing manufacturers typically produce 5% more units than called for in a contract. Called "overruns," these excess units are deemed necessary because of anticipated defects in some of the units produced. Usually, these defects are the result of faulty direct materials and/or workmanship. Part of the overrun cannot be reworked and is scrapped. Other parts can be reworked but are not needed to fill the order. A third part is simply excess. Many times, the excess that is not scrapped is sold to a factor that then resells the merchandise to an outlet store where it is sold as "seconds."

Analyze a typical 5% overrun with respect to quality costs—prevention, appraisal, internal failure, and external failure.

_____
_____
_____
_____
_____
_____
_____
_____
_____
_____
_____
_____
_____

VII. Demonstration Problems

Demonstration Problem #1

Conor Cup Company manufactures environmentally friendly cups in two sizes for coffee bars offering carryout service. The company uses a traditional system for allocating manufacturing overhead costs. Last year, the following results were reported:

	8 oz. cups	12 oz. cups	Total
Direct materials	$1,350,000	$1,800,000	$ 3,150,000
Direct Labor	400,000	600,000	1,000,000
Overhead	2,400,000	3,600,000	6,000,000
Total	$4,150,000	$6,000,000	$10,150,000

Overhead costs were allocated on the basis of direct labor costs. Last year 510,000 cases of 8 oz. cups were manufactured (each case contains 500 cups) and 800,000 cases (each containing 300 cups) of 12 oz. cups were manufactured.

Requirement:

Calculate the cost per cup and the cost per case for each size.

Demonstration Problem #2

Refer to the information in Demonstration Problem #1.

You have been asked by the company controller to analyze the allocation of overhead costs to the two products using an activity-based costing system. You begin by analyzing the specific components of the $6,000,000 in overhead costs assigned last year. Your investigation determines the following:

Components	Cost
Indirect materials	$ 300,000
Supervisors' salaries	450,000
Equipment depreciation	3,150,000
Equipment conversion costs	1,500,000
Miscellaneous overhead	600,000
Total	$6,000,000

In consultation with the controller, the following decisions are made regarding costs and cost drivers:

Cost	Cost Driver
Indirect materials	Direct materials
Supervisors' salaries	Direct labor cost
Equipment depreciation	Hours of equipment use
Equipment conversion costs	Number of conversions
Miscellaneous overhead	Cases of output

Further investigation disclosed the following:

The equipment was used 70% for the 12 oz. cups and 30% for the 8 oz. cups. The equipment was converted a total of 120 times during the year, 90 times for the 12 oz. cups and 30 times for the 8 oz. cups.

Requirements:

1. Apply activity-based costing using the results of your investigation to allocate overhead to each size of cup.
2. Calculate the per-cup cost for each size of cup given your results in requirement 1.

Requirement 1

Requirement 2

SOLUTIONS

I. Matching

1. K	3. G	5. A	7. C	9. D	11. H
2. B	4. F	6. J	8. E	10. I	

II. Multiple Choice

1.   C   Non-value-added activities are those that do not add value to the product. Inspecting, moving, and reworking are examples of non-value added activities. Processing costs are value-added activities.

2.   C
   1. Identify the activities.
   2. Estimate the total indirect cost of each activity.
   3. Identify the allocation base for each activity's indirect costs.
   4. Estimate the total quantity of each allocation base.
   5. Compute the cost allocation rate for each activity:

   $$\text{Allocation rate for activity} = \frac{\textbf{Estimated total indirect costs of activity (Step 2)}}{\textbf{Estimated total quantity of cost allocation base (Step 4)}}$$

   6. Obtain the actual quantity of each allocation base used by the cost object
   6. Allocate the costs to the cost object:

   $$\text{Allocated activity cost} = \text{Allocation rate for activity (step 5)} \times \text{Quantity of allocation base used by the cost object (step 6)}$$

3.   D   RIP (Raw and In Process) is a feature of just-in-time costing.

4.   D   Quality costs are nonfinancial performance items.

5.   D   Activity-based costing is a concept of accumulating costs using multiple cost drivers and is not specific to particular businesses or industries - it can be used by any organization.

6.   B   External failures are those that occur after the customer has received the product or service. Of the four options, the only one that would involve a customer is the cost of warranties.

7.   B   Return on sales is the only choice listed that can be expressed in financial terms.

8.   C   Value engineering refers to techniques used to reduce the cost of a product while maintaining its satisfaction to the customer. Value engineering is one way to achieve target costing.

9.   B   Target costing, value engineering and activity-based costing all relate to either cost measurement (ABC) or cost reduction (target costing and VE). Backflush costing is synonymous with just-in-time costing.

10.   B   Cross training is a prominent feature of just-in-time costing.

III. Completion

1. arrange production activities in self-contained cells, short setup times, broad employee roles, small batches produced just-in-time (order not important)
2. JIT costing
3. ABC = activity-based costing;
4. ABM = activity-based management
5. RIP = Raw and In Process
6. JIT = just-in-time
7. total quality management
8. prevention costs, appraisal costs, internal failure costs, external failure costs
9. the receipt of a customer order
10. external failure costs

IV. Daily Exercises

1. a. external failure cost
    b. prevention cost
    c. appraisal cost
    d. internal failure cost
    e. external failure cost
    f. internal failure cost

2.

3	A.
1	B.
6	C.
4	D.
2	E.
7	F.
5	G.

3. Machine setups = \$90,000/675 = \$133.33/setup
    Machining = \$325,000/15,000 hrs = \$21.67/hour
    Inspecting = \$42,000/1,350 = \$31.11/inspection

4.

RIP Inventory	54,000	
Accounts Payable		54,000
Conversion Costs	12,480	
Accounts Payable		12,480
Finished Goods Inventory	67,200	
RIP Inventory		54,000
Conversion Costs		13,200
Cost of Goods Sold	67,200	

Finished Goods Inventory		67,200

Conversion Costs	720	
Cost of Goods Sold		720

V. Exercises

1.

Direct materials	$3,700
Materials handling (60 parts @ $5.00)	300
Machine setup ($800 x 2 / 10)	160
Welding (225 x $3.00)	675
Finishing (15 x $32.00)	480
Total cost	$5,315

2.

Drill Bits

Activity	Number	Cost
Machine setups ($133.33)	520	$ 69,333 (rounded)
Machine hours ($21.67)	8900	192,833 (rounded)
Inspections ($31.11)	820	25,511 (rounded)
Total		$287,677

Gears

Activity	Number	Cost
Machine setups ($133.33)	90	$12,000
Machine hours ($21.67)	3200	69,333
Inspections ($31.11)	270	8,400
Total		$89,733

Corkscrews

Activity	Number	Cost
Machine setups ($133.33)	65	$ 8,667
Machine hours ($21.67)	2900	62,833
Inspections ($31.11)	260	8,089
Total		$79,589

3.

A. Total overhead costs =	$ 90,000	
	325,000	
	42,000	
	$457,000	

Drill bits = 520,000 / 521,390 × $457,000 = $455,782
Gears = 90 / 521,390 × $457,000 = $78.88
Corkscrews = 1,300 / 521,390 × $457,000 = $1,139

B. It is obvious a traditional costing system based on production drastically distorts the allocation of overhead. It would also be distorted if only one of the activities (setups, hours, or inspections) were the allocation base. Granted, this is an extreme example but it does serve to illustrate the point that activity-based costing can result in a more realistic application of overhead.

> **Study Tip:** Remember, ABC relates only to overhead, not direct materials or direct labor.

4.

RIP Inventory	130,000	
Direct materials price variance		1,000
Accounts Payable		129,000
Conversion costs	110,400	
Various accounts		110,400
Finished Goods Inventory	240,000	
RIP Inventory		130,000
Conversion costs		110,000
[($6.50 + $5.50) × 20,000)]		
Cost of goods sold	240,000	
Finished Goods Inventory		240,000
Accounts Receivable	300,000	
Sales		300,000
Cost of goods sold	400	
Conversion costs		400
(To transfer underapplied overhead)		

VI. Beyond the Numbers

Ideally, a manufacturer should strive for zero defects. However, this is not always possible. To obtain defect-free material, the manufacturer needs to work closely with the supplier(s). This is a prevention cost. During the manufacturing process, appraisal costs are involved as a result of inspection costs. In addition, internal failure costs are incurred to both rework (when possible) and to dispose of units that can neither be reworked nor sold as seconds. If you analyze the situation carefully you will see that there are no external failure costs. The clothing manufacturer ships only goods that conform to the order. Any excess goods that can be sold are factored to an outlet store. As long as the costs associated with the excess are considered when they are sold, no external failure costs are involved. As stated above, zero defects is the ideal and something companies should strive to achieve. However, given the 5% excess, clothing manufacturers seem to have adjusted well enough to cover the costs incurred with the excess (one of the fastest growing segments in retailing are the "outlets").

VII. Demonstration Problems

Demonstration Problem #1 Solved and Explained

8 oz. cups:

Total cost	$4,150,000
Total cups (510,000 cases × 500 ea)	255,000,000
Cost per cup ($4,150,000 / 255,000,000)	$0.01627
Cost per case ($4,150,000 / 510,000)	$8.14

12 oz. cups:

Total cost	$6,000,000
Total cups (800,000 cases × $500 ea)	240,000,000
Cost per cup ($6,000,000 / 240,000,000)	$0.025
Cost per case ($6,000,000 / 800,000)	$7.50

Demonstration Problem #2 Solved and Explained

Requirement 1

Component	Cost	8 oz.	Calculations	12 oz.	Calculations
Indirect material	$300,000	$128,571	$\frac{\$1,350,000}{\$3,150,000} \times \$300,000$	$ 171,429	$\frac{\$1,800,000}{\$3,150,000} \times \$300,000$
Supervisor's salary	450,000	180,000	$\frac{\$400,000}{\$1,000,000} \times \$450,000$	270,000	$\frac{\$600,000}{\$1,000,000} \times \$450,000$
Equipment depreciation	3,150,000	945,000	30% × $3,150,000	2,205,000	70% × $3,150,000
Conversion costs	1,500,000	375,000	30/120 × $1,500,000	1,125,000	90/120 × $1,500,000
Miscellaneous	600,000	233,588	$\frac{\$510,000}{\$1,310,000} \times \$600,000$	366,412	$\frac{\$800,000}{\$1,310,000} \times \$600,000$
Total		$1,862,159		$4,137,841	

Requirement 2

8 oz. cups

	$1,350,000	(Direct materials)
	400,000	(Direct labor)
	1,862,159	(Overhead - from Requirement 2)
Total cost	$3,612,159	

or $3,612,159 / 255,000,000   = $0.0142 per cup

<u>12 oz. cups</u>

	$1,800,000	(Direct materials)
	600,000	(Direct labor)
	4,137,841	(Overhead - from Requirement 2)
Total cost	$6,537,841	

or $6,537,841 / 240,000,000 = $0.027 per cup

Chapter 26 - Special Business Decisions and Capital Budgeting

CHAPTER OVERVIEW

In recent chapters you have learned about a variety of issues all related to the topic of "costs." Most of these issues looked at costs (and behavior) in the short run. When costs are correctly recorded and carefully analyzed, a business is in a better position to plan for future operations. We now turn our attention to some special decisions businesses frequently must make and to issues concerning the acquisition of long-term (capital) assets. The learning objectives for this chapter are to

1. Identify the relevant information for a special business decision.
2. Make five types of short-term special business decisions.
3. Use payback and accounting rate of return models to make longer-term capital budgeting decisions.
4. Use discounted cash flow models to make longer-term capital budgeting decisions.
5. Compare and contrast the four capital budgeting methods.

CHAPTER REVIEW

Objective 1 – Identify the relevant information for a special business decision.

To achieve business goals, managers must develop strategies by choosing among alternative courses of action. Managers make decisions by:

- Defining business goals
- Identifying alternative courses of action
- Gathering and analyzing relevant information to compare alternatives
- Choosing the best alternative to achieve goals.

The key in choosing the best alternative is focusing on information that is *relevant*. Relevant information is expected future data that differs among alternatives. Information that does not differ is irrelevant and will not change a business decision. See Exhibit 26-1 and 26-2 in your text.

Objective 2 – Make five types of short-term special business decisions.

One approach to short-term decision-making is called the **relevant information approach** (also called the incremental analysis approach). This approach focuses on two factors for making short-term special decisions:

1. Focus on *relevant* revenues, costs, and profits
2. Use a *contribution margin approach* that separates variable costs from fixed costs

Now, let's take a look at five types of short-term decisions. Each of these short-term decisions is evaluated by comparing the expected increase in revenues to the expected increase in expenses. If there is no change in fixed expenses, then they are not relevant to the decision-making process and are ignored. Thus, the decision will be based on comparing the expected increase in revenues to the expected increase in *variable* expenses. Review Exhibits 26-4 and 26-5.

Correctly analyzing a business decision requires you to ignore **irrelevant costs**. A cost that is the same for all decision alternatives is NOT relevant and must be ignored. You should consider only those costs and revenues that change between alternatives.

1. **Special sales order.** The example in your text that analyzes whether to accept the special sales order of oil filters is an excellent example of a special sales order. Using the conventional income statement as the basis for the decision is not the correct approach because of the nature of fixed costs. However, when the question is analyzed using the contribution margin format, the irrelevant costs (fixed expenses) are ignored and a better decision results.

2. **Dropping products, departments, and territories**. When considering when to drop products, departments, or territories, with *no change* in fixed costs, the only relevant information is the expected decreases in revenues and variable costs, which together show the contribution margin and change in operating income. Study Exhibit 26-7 in your text. When considering when to drop products, departments, or territories with *a change* in fixed costs, the analysis must include the change in fixed costs as well as changes in variable costs and revenues. Refer to Exhibit 26-8 for an example. The key to deciding whether to drop products, departments or territories is to compare the lost revenue against the costs that can be saved from dropping them. If the lost revenues from dropping a product, department or territory exceed the cost savings from dropping them, then do not drop them. If the cost savings exceed the lost revenues from dropping a product, department, or territory, then drop them.

3. **Product mix.** When deciding which product to emphasize, it is necessary to determine whether a constraint or limiting factor exists. A **constraint** is a factor that restricts production or sales of a product. Constraints may be stated in terms of labor hours, machine hours, materials, or storage space. To maximize profits, the decision rule to follow when deciding which product to emphasize is to emphasize the product with the highest contribution margin per unit of the constraint. Exhibit 26-9 in your text presents an example of how to maximize the contribution margin per machine hour.

4. **Outsourcing (make or buy)**. The outsourcing decision is one where managers decide whether to buy a component product or service or to produce it in-house. The heart of these decisions is *how best to use available facilities*. The relevant information for the make analysis includes: 1) direct materials, 2) direct labor, 3) variable overhead, and 4) fixed overhead. The relevant information for the buy analysis is: 1) the fixed overhead that will continue whether the part is made or bought and 2) the purchase price to buy the part. The decision rule to follow when deciding whether to outsource is if the incremental costs of making exceed the incremental costs of outsourcing, then outsource; if the incremental costs of making are less than the incremental costs of outsourcing, then do not outsource. This analysis shows whether it is cheaper to make the part or to buy the part. Review Exhibit 26-10 in your text. The analysis in Exhibit 26-10 assumes there is no other use for the facilities freed up. Sometimes facilities can be used to make other products if the product currently produced is purchased from an outside supplier. In the make or buy decision, the alternatives become: 1) make, 2) buy and leave the facilities idle, and

3) buy and use the facilities for other products. When the facilities could be used for some other purpose, then the opportunity cost of the alternative not chosen must be considered. An **opportunity cost** is the benefit foregone by not choosing an alternative course of action. An opportunity cost is not a business transaction and is therefore not recorded in the accounting records. It is only used as a consideration in making a decision between alternatives. As indicated in Exhibit 26-11 the alternative with the lowest net cost is the *best use of the facilities.*

5. **Selling as is or processing further.** The sell as is or process further decision rule to follow is if extra revenue (from processing further) exceeds the extra cost of processing further, then process further. If the extra revenue (from processing further) is less than the extra cost of processing further, then do not process further. Exhibit 26-13 illustrates the sell as is or process further decision. Note that past historical costs of inventory are **sunk costs**—they cannot make a difference to the decision; the sunk costs are irrelevant because they are present under both alternatives.

Study Tip: Review the Decision Guidelines title *Short-Term Special Business Decisions* in your text.

Objective 3 – Use payback and accounting rate of return models to make longer-term capital budgeting decisions.

Capital budgeting refers to budgeting for the acquisition of capital assets—assets used for a long period of time. There are four popular capital budgeting decision models presented in this chapter. They help managers evaluate and choose among alternatives. Whether the acquisition of a capital asset is desirable depends on its ability to generate net cash inflows—that is inflows in excess of outflows—over the asset's useful life.

1) **Payback** is the length of time it takes to recover, in net cash inflows, the dollars invested in a capital outlay. The payback model measures how quickly managers expect to recover their investment dollars.

    If annual net cash inflows are equal each year, then:

    PAYBACK PERIOD $=$ $\dfrac{\text{AMOUNT INVESTED}}{\text{EXPECTED ANNUAL NET CASH INFLOWS}}$

The decision rule is to invest only if payback period is shorter than the asset's useful life. Investments with shorter payback periods are more desirable, *only if all other factors are the same.* However, investment decisions should not be made based on payback period alone because the payback period only highlights the length of time required to recover an investment, and does not consider profitability. See Exhibit 26-14 for an illustration of the payback model where net cash inflows are equal each year.

2) The **accounting rate of return** measures the operating income an asset generates.

    ACCOUNTING RATE OF RETURN $=$ $\dfrac{\text{AVERAGE ANNUAL OPERATING INCOME}}{\text{AVERAGE AMOUNT INVESTED IN THE ASSET}}$

| AVERAGE ANNUAL OPERATING INCOME FROM ASSET | = | AVERAGE ANNUAL NET CASH INFLOW FROM ASSET | - | ANNUAL DEPRECIATION ON ASSET |

$$\text{AVERAGE AMOUNT INVESTED} = \frac{\text{AMOUNT INVESTED} + \text{RESIDUAL VALUE}}{2}$$

See Exhibit 26-15 for an example of this calculation. Companies that use the accounting rate of return model set a minimum required rate of return. The decision rule is if the expected accounting rate of return exceeds the required rate of return, then invest; if it does not, then do not invest.

Although the accounting rate of return measures profitability, it ignores the time value of money, a topic you were introduced to in Chapter 15.

Objective 4. – Use discounted cash flow models to make longer-term capital budgeting decisions.

The following two models consider the timing of the cash outlay for the investment and the timing of the net cash inflows that result. These models are the most commonly used in capital budgeting.

3) **Net present value** is a decision model that brings cash inflows and outflows back to a common time period by discounting these expected future cash flows to their present value, using a minimum desired rate of return. The **minimum desired rate of return** used to calculate present value is called the **discount rate** (also called the hurdle rate, required rate of return, cost of capital, and target rate). Exhibit 26-17 in your text illustrates present value analysis in which the annual cash inflows are equal (an annuity) and Exhibit 26-19 illustrates the same analysis in which the annual cash inflows are different. Note that when the annual cash inflows are equal, you use Exhibit 26-16, Present Value of an Annuity of $1, to find the present value factor. When the cash inflows are not equal, you use Exhibit 26-18, Present Value of $1, to find the present value factor for each year you have cash inflows.

The steps to determine the net present value of a project are:

1. Find the present value of annual cash inflows.
2. Find the present value of the residual, if any.
3. Add (1) and (2) to obtain the present value of the net cash inflows.
4. Subtract the investment (which is already in present value terms) from the present value of the net cash inflows (3) to obtain the net present value of the project.

The net present value method is based on cash flows and considers both profitability and the time value of money. The decision rule is to only invest in capital assets if the net present value is positive.

4) **Internal rate of return** is another discounted cash flow model. The internal rate of return (IRR) is the rate of return that a company can expect to earn by investing in the project; the higher the IRR, the more desirable the project. The IRR is the discount rate that makes the net present value of an investment project equal to zero. There are three steps in calculating the internal rate of return:

1. Identify the expected net cash inflows.

2. Find the discount rate that makes the present value of the total cash inflows equal to the present value of the cash outflows. Work backwards to find the discount rate that makes the present value of the annuity of cash inflows equal to the amount of the investment by solving the following equation for the annuity present value (PV) factor:

Investment = Expected annual net cash inflow × Annuity PV factor

$$\text{Annuity PV factor} = \frac{\text{Investment}}{\text{Expected annual net cash inflow}}$$

3. Turn to the Present Value of an annuity of $1 (Exhibit 26-17) and scan the row corresponding to the project's expected life and choose the column with the number closest to the annuity PV factor that was calculated in Step 2. to find the interest rate that reflects the IRR.

4. Compare the IRR determined in Step 3 with the minimum desired rate of return. The decision rule is to invest in capital assets if the IRR exceeds the required rate of return. See Exhibit 26-20 in your text.

Objective 5. – Compare and contrast the four capital budgeting methods.

Exhibit 26-21 summarizes some of the strengths and weaknesses of the four capital budgeting models described above. The two discounted cash flow models (net present value and internal rate of return) are favored because they consider both profitability and the time value of money whereas the payback model ignores both while the accounting rate of return considers only profitability.

Study Tip: Review the Decision Guidelines titled *Capital Budgeting* at the end of the chapter.

TEST YOURSELF

All the self-testing materials in this chapter focus on information and procedures that your instructor is likely to test in quizzes and examinations.

I. Matching   *Match each numbered term with its lettered definition.*

_____1. Accounting rate of return
_____2. Capital budgeting
_____3. Decision model
_____4. Time value of money
_____5. Opportunity cost
_____6. Relevant information
_____7. Annuity

_____8. Constraint
_____9. Discount rate
_____10. Net present value
_____11. Payback period
_____12. Sunk cost
_____13. Internal rate of return

A. A method or technique for evaluating and choosing among alternative courses of action
B. Actual outlay incurred in the past and present under all alternative courses of action; irrelevant because it makes no difference to a current decision
C. Expected future data that differs between alternative courses of action
D. Formal means of making long-range decisions for investments such as plant locations, equipment purchases, additions of product lines, and territorial expansions
E. Item that restricts production or sales
F. Calculated as average annual net cash inflow from asset minus annual depreciation on asset, divided by average amount invested
G. Length of time it will take to recover, in net cash inflows from operations, the dollars of a capital outlay
H. Management's minimum desired rate of return on an investment, used in a present value computation
I. The benefit that can be obtained from the next best course of action in a decision
J. Method of computing the expected net monetary gain or loss from a project by discounting all expected cash flows to their present value and deducting the cost of the investment, using a desired rate of return
K. Stream of equal periodic amounts
L. The fact that one can earn income by investing money for a period of time
M. The rate of return on a project that makes the net present value equal to zero

II. Multiple Choice   *Circle the best answer.*

1. Relevant information:

   A. is expected future data.
   B. differs among alternative courses of action.
   C. does not include sunk costs.
   D. all of the above.

2. The standard income statement categorizes expenses:

   A. into cost of goods sold and selling and administrative expenses.
   B. into variable expenses and fixed expenses.
   C. both A and B.
   D. neither A nor B .

3. The contribution margin income statement categorizes expenses:

   A. into cost of goods sold and selling and administrative expenses.
   B. into variable expenses and fixed expenses.
   C. both A and B.
   D. neither A nor B .

4. Select the correct statement concerning the payback period.

   A. The longer the payback period, the less attractive the asset.
   B. The shorter the payback period, the less attractive the asset.
   C. The longer the payback period, the more attractive the asset.
   D. Both B and C are correct.

5. The accounting rate of return considers:

   A. the timing of cash flows.   C. profitability.
   B. the time value of money.   D. all of these.

6. The net present value method of capital budgeting considers:

   A. only cash flows.
   B. only the time value of money.
   C. both cash flows and the time value of money.
   D. the length of time to recoup the initial investment.

7. If a potential investment has a negative net present value:

   A. it should be accepted in all situations
   B. it should be rejected in all situations
   C. it should be accepted if payback is less than five years
   D. it should be rejected if the accounting rate of return is less than 16%

8. The internal rate of return (IRR) method, while similar to the net present value (NPV) method, differs from it in the following respect(s):

   A. IRR identifies expected future cash flows.
   B. IRR identifies the excess of the project's present value over its investment cost.
   C. IRR identifies a specific rate of return for the investment.
   D. all of the above

9. Which of the following capital budgeting decision models is based on profitability?

   A. Payback   C. Net present value
   B. Accounting rate of return   D. Internal rate of return

10. In deciding whether to take a year off from college and work full-time or continue in school and work part-time, the opportunity cost is:

    A. the amount of money already invested in your education.
    B. the amount saved from college expenses by working full-time.
    C. the amount of earnings foregone by selecting one option over the other.
    D. the difference between the projected total income of the two options.

III. Completion   *Complete each of the following.*

1. A(n) _____ income statement is more useful for special decision analysis than the standard income statement.
2. The item that restricts production or sales is called a _____ .
3. Fixed costs are only relevant to a special decision if _____ _____ .
4. A(n) _____ is the cost of the foregone next best alternative, or profit given up, by selecting one alternative over another one.
5. _____ costs are not formally recorded in the accounting records.
6. The major weakness of the payback is that it _____ _____ .
7. An investment should be rejected if its net present value is _____ .
8. A project's internal rate of return (IRR) is that rate of interest that makes the present value of the project's cash inflows and cash outflows _____ .
9. The _____ refers to earning income by investing money for a period of time.
10. Generally accepted accounting principles are based on accrual accounting whereas capital budgeting is based on _____ .

IV. Daily Exercises

1. Place the following in correct sequence (1 through 4):

    _____a. Define business goals
    _____b. Gather and analyze relevant information to compare alternatives
    _____c. Identify alternative courses of action
    _____d. Choose the best alternative to achieve the goals

2. Compute the payback period given the following information:

Cost of new machinery	$450,000
Useful life	9 years
Annual depreciation	$50,000
Annual net cash inflow attributed to new machinery	$18,000

3. Continental Manufacturing produces a component that sells for $62. The manufacturing cost per component is $38. Variable manufacturing costs are $29 and fixed manufacturing costs are $9 per unit. Continental has received an offer for 8,000 components; however, the components will have to be slightly modified to conform to metric measurements. Modifying each component will cost 50¢. The buyer is willing to pay $33 for each component. Assuming Continental has excess capacity, identify the relevant and irrelevant factors in deciding to accept the offer.

4. Using the information in Daily Exercise #3 above, decide whether Continental should accept the offer.

5. Molinari, Inc., is planning to construct a new facility at a total cost of $25,000,000. The project will have a 20-year life at the end of which it will be abandoned. It is expected to generate net income of $3,750,000. Calculate the accounting rate of return of the new facility.

6. Review the information in Daily Exercise #5 above and consider the following additional information. Net cash inflows from the new facility are expected to be $5,000,000 annually for 20 years. Calculate the cash payback period.

7. Review the information in Daily Exercises #5 and #6 above and consider the following additional information. Molinari has a 12% minimum rate of return on investment. Calculate the net present value of the investment, using the discounted cash flows. (Hint: you'll need the present value tables in your text.)

V. Exercises

1. A clothing wholesaler has offered to pay $20 per unit for 2,500 hats. This offer would put idle manufacturing capacity in use and not affect regular sales. Total fixed costs will not change. There will be only half the normal variable selling and administrative costs on this special order.

Normal selling price per hat	$25.00
Variable costs per hat:	
Manufacturing	14.00
Selling and Administrative	3.00
Fixed costs per hat:	
Manufacturing	2.00
Selling and Administrative	2.50

A. What is the relevant information associated with this special order?

B. What difference would accepting this special order have on company profits?

2. Braden, a bright young CPA, has provided you with the following information:

Salary at current position	$40,000
Revenues expected by opening his own office	125,000
Expenses expected for the new office	100,000

A. What is the opportunity cost associated with working at his current position?

B. What is the opportunity cost associated with starting his own business?

C. From purely a quantitative standpoint, what should he do?

3. Eric's Nursery is concerned that operating income is low, and is considering dropping its garden implements department. The following information is available:

	Total	Plants & Fertilizers	Garden Implements
Sales	$425,000	$225,000	$200,000
Variable expenses	239,500	91,500	148,000
Contribution margin	185,500	133,500	52,000
Fixed expenses	153,000	81,000	72,000
Operating income (loss)	$ 32,500	$ 52,500	($ 20,000)

Eric can avoid $48,000 of his nursery's fixed expenses by dropping the Garden Implements division.

Determine whether Eric should drop the Garden Implements department.

VI. Beyond the Numbers

Review the information in Exercise #2 and list additional considerations (both quantitative and qualitative) that might influence Braden's decision.

_____

_____

_____

_____

_____

VII. Demonstration Problems

Demonstration Problem #1

A. S&L Inc., produces two products, S and L, with the following per unit data:

	Product	
	S	**L**
Selling price	$50	$24
Variable expenses	30	15
Units that can be produced each hour	4	8

The company has 8,000 hours of capacity available. Which product should the company emphasize?

B. Body Works, Inc., has the following manufacturing costs for 4,000 of its natural bath sponges:

Direct materials	$ 6,000
Direct labor	3,000
Variable overhead	2,000
Fixed overhead	5,000
Total	$16,000

Another manufacturer has offered to sell Body Works similar sponges for $3.25 each. By purchasing the sponges outside, Body Works can save $2,000 of fixed overhead cost. The released facilities can be devoted to the manufacture of other products that will contribute $2,000 to profits. What is Body Works' best decision?

	Alternatives		
	Make	**Buy and leave facilities idle**	**Buy and use facilities for other products**

Decision:

Demonstration Problem #2

The data for a piece of equipment follows:

Cost	$40,000
Estimated annual net cash inflows:	
Year 1	12,000
Year 2	12,000
Year 3	12,000
Year 4	12,000
Residual value	8,000
Estimated useful life	4 years
Annual rate of return required	12%

The present value of an amount of $1 at 12% is:

Year	1	2	3	4
Interest factor	0.893	0.797	0.712	0.636

The present value of an annuity of $1 at 12% is:

Year	1	2	3	4
Interest factor	0.893	1.690	2.402	3.037

Required:

1. What is the payback period for the equipment?
2. What is the accounting rate of return for the equipment?
3. What is the net present value of the equipment?
4. Indicate whether each decision model leads to purchase or rejection of this investment. Would you decide to buy the equipment? Give your reason.

Requirement 1 (payback period)

Requirement 2 (accounting rate of return)

Requirement 3 (net present value analysis)

Requirement 4 (decision)

337

SOLUTIONS

I. Matching

1. F	3. A	5. I	7. K	9. H	11. G	13. M
2. D	4. L	6. C	8. E	10. J	12. B	

II. Multiple Choice

1. **D** Relevant information is the expected future data that differ between alternative courses of action. A sunk cost is an actual outlay that has been incurred in the past and is present under all alternatives. Sunk costs are irrelevant.

2. **A** Answer B describes the contribution margin format income statement.

3. **B** Answer A describes the "standard" income statement format.

4. **A** Payback is the length of time it will take to recover, in net cash flow from operations, the dollars of a capital outlay. The shorter the payback the better. The longer it is, the less attractive.

5. **C** The accounting rate of return is calculated by:
   Average Annual Operating Income ÷ Average amount invested.
   By looking at the numerator, answer C can be seen to be the best.

6. **C** The net present value method computes the present value of expected future net cash flows and compares that present value to the initial investment. Answer C covers this approach.

7. **B** The initial investment is subtracted from the present value of the investment's expected future cash flows. If negative, the investment does not recover its cost. If positive, the investment generates a return above the minimum required. Only projects with zero or positive net present value should be considered.

8. **C** Both the NPV and IRR methods make use of expected future cash flows (answer A). Answer B is not correct because it describes only NPV. Only the IRR method (and not NPV) generates a specific rate of return for the project.

9. **B** The accounting rate of return model is based on profitability; the other three models are based on net cash flows.

10. **C** The opportunity cost is the benefit obtained from the next best course of action, so if the decision is to remain in school, the opportunity cost is the full-time wages not earned, whereas if the decision is to work full-time, the opportunity cost is the foregone part-time income.

III. Completion

1. contribution margin (The contribution margin format highlights how costs and income are affected by decisions.)
2. limiting factor, constraint (Such things as the size of the factory labor force, available storage space, availability of raw materials, available machine time, or market share can act as constraints.)
3. fixed cost differs among alternatives (Recall: a cost is relevant only if it differs between alternatives. A cost can differ between alternatives and still be fixed for each alternative.)
4. opportunity cost (It is not the usual outlay (cash disbursement) cost. If you quit your job to start your own business, the salary from the job you gave up is the opportunity cost of starting your own business.)
5. Opportunity (Since these costs do not involve giving up an asset or incurring a liability, they are not recorded.)
6. ignores profitability and the time value of money (Because of these shortcomings, the payback period can lead to unwise decisions.)
7. negative (If negative, the investment does not recover its cost. If positive, the investment generates an acceptable rate of return. Only projects with zero or positive net present value should be considered.)
8. equal
9. time value of money
10. cash flows

IV. Daily Exercises

1.

1	A.
3	B.
2	C.
4	D.

2. $450,000 / $18,000 = 25 years

3.

Relevant
Variable manufacturing costs ($29)
Additional 50¢ cost/component
Continental has excess capacity
The $33 selling price

Irrelevant
The $62 selling price
$9.00 fixed costs

4. If the offer is accepted

Sales (8,000 × $33)	$264,000
Less: Variable Costs (8,000 × $29)	232,000
Additional Variable Costs (8,000 × 50¢)	4,000
Increase in Net Income	$28,000

5.

$$\text{Accounting rate of return} \ = \ \frac{\text{Average annual operating income}}{\text{Average amount of investment in asset}}$$

$$= \ \frac{\$3,750,000}{(\$25,000,000/2)}$$

$$= \ 30\%$$

6.

$$\text{Cash payback period} \ = \ \frac{\text{Amount invested}}{\text{Net cash inflows}}$$

$$= \ \frac{\$25,000,000}{\$5,000,000}$$

$$= \ 5 \text{ years}$$

7.

	Present Value at 12%	Net Cash Inflow	Total Present Value
Present value of equal annual net cash inflows for 20 years	7.469	$5,000,000	37,345,000
Investment			25,000,000
Net present value of new facility			$12, 345,000

V. Exercises

1. A. The relevant information is the special order price of $20 per unit, the variable manufacturing cost of $14 per unit, and one-half the normal variable selling and administrative expenses which amount to $1.50 per unit ($3 × 1/2).

    B. Additional revenues from special order (2,500 × $20) $50,000
        Less: Variable manufacturing cost (2,500 × $14)   (35,000)
        Less: Variable selling and admin. cost (2,500 × $1.50)   (3,750)
        Increase in profits $11,250

2. A. The opportunity cost is the net revenue given up by keeping the existing position: $125,000 revenue - $100,000 expense = $25,000.

    B. The opportunity cost is the cost of giving up the existing position: $40,000.

    C. The current position pays $40,000. Going into business will net $25,000. Keeping the present position makes Braden $15,000 better off.

3. The relevant information is the contribution margin that would be lost if the garden implements department is eliminated and the fixed costs that would be eliminated. The nursery would lose the $52,000 contribution margin if the department is closed and would reduce fixed costs by $48,000. The lost contribution margin is $4,000 greater than the reduction in fixed costs ($52,000 contribution margin lost - $48,000 fixed costs eliminated), so the department should not be closed. The nursery is $4,000 better off by keeping it.

VI. Beyond the Numbers

Probably the most significant quantitative consideration is the potential increase in salary compared with the potential increase in income from the business. For instance, if salary increases are likely to average 10% over the foreseeable future while the business growth potential is 20% annually, in a few years the income from the business will surpass the salary. An important qualitative consideration is being an employee versus your own boss. Frequently, it is the intangible costs and benefits that cloud the issue and make decision-making so complex.

VII. Demonstration Problems

Demonstration Problem #1 Solved and Explained

A. Product to Emphasize

	Product	
	S	**L**
(1) Units that can be produced each hour	4	8
(2) Contribution margin per unit*	$20	$9
(3) Contribution margin per hour (1) × (2)	80	72
Capacity: Number of hours	× 8,000	× 8,000
Total contribution margin for capacity	$640,000	$576,000

* Contribution margins: S: $50 - $30 = $20; L: $24 - $15 = $9

Decision: The Company should emphasize Product S because its contribution margin at capacity is greater by $64,000.

Explanation:

When a constraint exists, such as the number of hours available, we must conduct our profit analysis in terms of the constraint. Since only 8,000 hours are available, our profit will be greatest if we produce the products that offer the highest contribution margin per hour. To compute the contribution margin per hour for each product, multiply the contribution margin per unit of each product times the number of units of each product that can be produced per hour.

Study Tip: The product with the highest contribution margin per hour will provide the highest profit.

B. Make or Buy

	Alternatives		
	Make	Buy and leave facilities idle	Buy and use facilities for other products
Direct materials	$ 6,000	-	
Direct labor	3,000	-	
Variable overhead	2,000	-	
Fixed overhead	5,000	$ 3,000	$ 3,000
Purchase price from outsider	-	13,000	13,000
Total cost of obtaining sponges	16,000	16,000	16,000
Profit contribution from other products	-	-	(2,000)
Net cost of obtaining 4,000 sponges	$16,000	$16,000	$14,000

Decision: The Company should buy the sponges and use the facilities for other products.

Explanation

Continuing to make the sponges will cost the same $16,000 that it currently costs. The current cost to produce is relevant because it will change if the sponges are purchased. If the sponges are purchased, the relevant information is the purchase price and the amount of fixed overhead that *will continue.* The problem tells us that $2,000 of fixed overhead will be saved. Since total fixed overhead is $5,000, $3,000 ($5,000 - $2,000) of fixed overhead will continue, and the sponges will cost $16,000. If the facilities are used to earned an additional $2,000 profit, the net cost of the sponges is $14,000 ($16,000 - $2,000). For this alternative, the additional relevant information is the profit from the other product that could be produced.

Study Tip: Relevant information differs among alternative courses of action.

Demonstration Problem #2 Solved and Explained

Requirement 1 (payback period)

When the annual net cash flows are constant, the payback period is equal to the amount of the investment divided by the annual net cash flows.

$40,000 ÷ $12,000 = 3.3 years

Requirement 2 (accounting rate of return)

The accounting rate of return is average annual operating income from the investment divided by the average amount invested. Average annual operating income is equal to net cash inflows from operations (0) minus annual depreciation (D). Average amount invested is the sum of the investment (I) plus residual value (RV) divided by 2.

R = (O - D) ÷ [(I + RV) ÷ 2] = ($12,000 - $8,000*) ÷ [($40,000 + $8,000) ÷ 2] = 0.167 = 16.7%
* D = ($40,000 - $8,000) ÷ 4 years = $8,000

Requirement 3 (net present value analysis)

The steps to determine the net present value of a project are:

Present value of net equal annual cash inflows ($12,000 × 3.037)	$ 36,444
Present value of residual value ($8,000 × 0.636)	5,088
Present value of the equipment	41,532
Investment	40,000
Net present value	$ 1,532

Explanations:

Since the annual cash flow is the same amount, $12,000, it is an annuity. Multiply the annual amount, $12,000, by the present value of an annuity for 4 years. The present value of the cash inflows is $12,000 × 3.037, or $36,444.

The residual value of $8,000 is discounted to its present value ($8,000 × 0.636 = $5,088).

The present value of the equipment is $41,532 ($36,444 + $5,088).

The investment is $40,000.

The net present value of the investment is the present value of the equipment minus the investment.

$$NPV \text{ of Equipment} = \$41,532 - \$40,000 = \$1,532$$

Requirement 4 (decision)

The payback period is less than the useful life of the equipment. The accounting rate of return is higher than the 12% required return. Both methods indicate that the equipment should be purchased. The net present value is positive, which indicates that the rate of return exceeds the 12% required return. This decision model also indicates that the equipment should be purchased. Since the net present value considers both profitability and the time value of money (and the preferred decision model), and is positive in this instance, the equipment should be purchased.